THE KNIGHTS OF THE SCOTTISH WARS OF INDEPENDENCE

CHRIS BROWN has a PhD from St Andrews University. His other books include *William Wallace*, *The Second Scottish Wars of Independence*, *Robert the Bruce: A Life Chronicled*, *The Battle for Aberdeen 1644* and *Scottish Battlefields: 500 Battles that Shaped Scottish History*, all published by Tempus. He is currently writing a new history of the Battle of Bannockburn, forthcoming from Tempus. He lives in Fife in Scotland.

The Second Scottish Wars of Independence

'Fills a yawning void in the Scottish popular historical market... lucid and highly readable'
History Scotland

'Awesomely well-illustrated... a lucidly written account of another
troubled period in Scottish history which is bound to appeal to the general reader'
The Scots Magazine

Robert the Bruce: A Life Chronicled

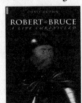

'An excellent anthology' *The Scotsman*
'Indispensable' *The Daily Mail*
'A masterpiece of research... truly a book to treasure' *The Scots Magazine*

The Battle for Aberdeen 1644   William Wallace

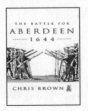   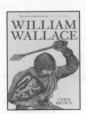

'Readable and balanced'   'The truth about braveheart'
The Scots Magazine   **The Daily Mail**

THE KNIGHTS OF THE SCOTTISH WARS OF INDEPENDENCE

CHRIS BROWN

TEMPUS

Cover illustrations: Stone grave effigy of a soldier from the west of Scotland wearing a bacinet helmet (Tempus Archive TA CD19 4). A particularly ornate example of a stone grave effigy (Tempus Archive TA CD19 5). A bearded Scottish soldier (Tempus Archive TA CD 17 5). A Scottish man-at-arms of the thirteenth/fourteenth century (Tempus Archive TA CD 19 2).

First published 2008

Tempus Publishing
Cirencester Road, Chalford
Stroud, Gloucestershire, GL6 8PE
www.tempus-publishing.com

Tempus Publishing is an imprint of The History Press

British Library Cataloguing in Publication Data.
A catalogue record for this book is available from the British Library.

ISBN 978 0 7524 4393 5

Typesetting and origination by The History Press
Printed and bound in Great Britain

CONTENTS

INTRODUCTION

It could be argued that no other period 'made' Scotland the way it is so much as the Wars of Independence. Many other countries experienced wars of similar or greater duration that were equally devastating[1] but the political consciousness of many Scots is still shaped or influenced by their perceptions of the conflict, particularly of the period 1296–1314.[2] The legacy is as much a matter of romance as of record; the frequent near-extinction of the 'patriotic' party, the adversities and triumphs of William Wallace and Robert I, the fickle nature of the Scottish nobility and the eventual success of the 'nationalist' cause at Bannockburn in 1314. Despite the conflation, exaggeration and, doubtless, pure invention of chroniclers and poets in relation to the *gestes* of Wallace and Bruce, there can be no doubt that both men were genuinely heroic figures to a large body of opinion within their own lifetimes, as well, of course, as being genuinely wicked terrorists to a great deal of the rest of the population. The perception that the wars were 'won' by Bruce at Bannockburn can be dismissed by even the most cursory study of Scotland in the ensuing decade, let alone in the 1330s to 1350s.

What of the 'fickle' nature of the nobility? The regularity with which the great lords of Scotland, Robert Bruce, Earl of Carrick for example, deserted one party for another gives some substance to the argument that the Scots nobility were less than consistent in their support of the 'patriotic' cause. For a variety of reasons discussed elsewhere in this book, it would have been extremely difficult for fourteenth-century

Scots to define an ethically 'proper' standpoint on the thorny question of allegiance. The immediate import of such a question was, as might be expected, severely compromised by the economic, legal, social and political realities of life. The value of being ideologically 'correct' may not have seemed high if it brought the threat of disinheritance, poverty, imprisonment or even death, either on the battlefield or on the gallows.

Historians have worked on the war period in different genres: general political histories, biographies, family and military histories. Inevitably these categories overlap in any period but the history of Scotland in the first half of the fourteenth century is positively saturated with war to the degree that it dominates virtually every aspect of society. In his outstanding work *Scotland: The Later Middle Ages*[3] Ranald Nicholson devoted over 100 pages to the Wars of Independence, a period of sixty years or less, but less than fifty pages to the agriculture, commerce, culture and society of Scotland from the close of the thirteenth century until the middle of the fifteenth. Similarly, Alexander Grant devotes more than fifty pages of his *Independence and Nationhood*[4] to Scotland's fourteenth-century wars, but only twenty-seven to her economy and society over a rather longer period. War is a central theme of the history of Scotland in the later Middle Ages simply because there was so much of it. The pressures of war affected the economy through war damage, militarised the political community in the sense that service was rather more 'active' than it had been before 1296, politicised the clerical community and bred a tradition of Anglo-Scottish antipathy that coloured the relations between the two countries for centuries.[5]

There have been several political studies of the Wars of Independence; E. M. Barron's *Scottish War of Independence*,[6] Colm MacNamee's *The Wars of the Bruces*[7] Michael Penman's *Scottish Civil War*,[8] Michael Brown's *Wars of Scotland*[9] and several excellent articles and essays including Barrow's 'Lothian in the War of Independence'[10] and 'Aftermath of War'[11] and Duncan's 'War of the Scots'.[12] Barron, Penman, MacNamee and Duncan naturally deal with the war from a 'national' perspective. They are concerned with 'national' issues and 'national' outcomes, rather than the course of the war as it affected particular localities. Neither MacNamee nor Brown nor Penman addresses the issues of Lothian to any great extent. MacNamee concentrated on the recovery of the Bruce cause after 1307, the attacks on northern England and the invasion of Ireland, as did Penman. Each region of Scotland will have had a different experience of the war years. In Lothian there was very little in the way of fighting between the Strathord agreement in 1304 and the battle of Bannockburn in 1314 or, despite Edward II's invasions, between 1314 and 1335, but a great deal between 1335 and 1341. In the north-east there was a great deal of action between 1307 and 1309, but little, if any, between 1309 and 1334 and, despite the operations of Edward III, virtually none after the defeat of Sir David Strathbogie at Culblean.

The single military event that has attracted most attention from students of medieval Scotland and the one that is most prominent in the consciousness of the general public is of course the Battle of Bannockburn.[13] Although unquestionably of great significance, the relevance of Bannockburn to the general military experience of medieval Scots has surely been greatly exaggerated. Large open-field engagements were sufficiently rare as to be almost an anomaly. Even when a large army was raised specifically to seek out battle – Edward I in 1301–2 and 1306, Edward II in 1310 and 1319 and Edward III repeatedly[14] – it more often than not disbanded without making any major contact with the enemy.

Despite the wide extent of military service among the political community particularly, it would seem that very few men participated in more than one or two major battles save for a very small group of professional soldiers – men who made a career out of soldiering as opposed to men who discharged their service obligations. The outcome of battle might have significant effects, but the structures and practices of field armies and the tactical application of the constituent elements of such forces are not a good guide to the nature of the war at a more mundane level. It is clear from both record and chronicle accounts that the general practice of active campaigning in fourteenth-century Scotland was almost exclusively conducted by parties of men-at-arms seldom, if ever, greater than a few hundred strong.[15] Though small, these forces were obviously of great significance. The success or otherwise of royal administrations depended on their support and the careers of successful war leaders were built on their ability to draw such men to their service. The lives of those men and women form the subject of this study. Like their counterparts elsewhere, they were subject to the course of events at a national level, but they were also bound by local ties and political considerations.

As the location of the most significant town in the land (certainly after the destruction of Berwick in 1296) and a relatively high concentration of urban development and castles, the three constabularies of Lothian,

Edinburgh, Haddington and Linlithgow constitute one of the most intensively recorded areas of medieval Scotland. Bounded by the Firth of Forth to the north, the River Avon to the west and the Dunglass burn to the east, Lothian was (and continues to be) an administrative unit.[16] It was (and is) also an area of high agricultural productivity and therefore valuable, but vulnerable to attack since there were no significant geographical barriers to be considered. The combination of the political and military significance of Lothian, the relatively wide range of material relating to the military service of the political community of the sheriffdom and the considerable disparity between the perception of Lothian as a warzone and the reality of military conditions as revealed by record sources make it a good choice for the focus of an investigation into the operational and political lives of the men who fought. However, it is important to bear in mind that Lothian is merely a convenient example; the same conditions applied throughout most of Scotland from Inverness to Dumfries. Only the north-west and the Isles differed significantly in military practice. The gentry of Wigtonshire shared the values, privileges and duties of the gentry of Kincardineshire.

The minor gentry who carried the lion's share of the day-on-day operational burdens in these wars were not simply soldiers. They were landholders with estates to run, they had judicial obligations to discharge and they had family responsibilities and political relationships with the crown, with magnates and with one another. These are considered in Chapter 2, 'Rights and Responsibilities' and Chapter 3, 'Landholding in Fourteenth-Century Lothian'. Naturally, for most Lothian men the war had a Lothian focus, and the most obvious aspect of the war would have been the local garrisons. Several Lothian men served in Plantagenet garrisons both in 1296–1314 and 1333–41 as paid soldiers, chiefly as men-at-arms. Many more would have given the customary military service attached to their landholdings to avoid forfeiture.

As sources of employment, centres of administration or as a visible enemy, garrisons were a feature in the life of the community and are examined in Chapter 4. Chapter 5, 'Service and Allegiance' considers the extent and the practicalities of military obligations on Lothian landholders. Most of the individuals appear elsewhere in published compilations of medieval record material including Bain's *Calendar of Documents Relating to Scotland, Regesta Regum Scottorum, Rotuli Scotia, Registrum Magni Sigilli Regum Scotorum, The Exchequer Rolls of Scotland*

and, Stevenson's *Documents Illustrative of the History of Scotland*,[17] the published collections of religious houses, and of Scottish historical societies, the calendars of Chancery, Post Mortem and Miscellaneous Inquisitions, Close Rolls and of course in contemporary narrative accounts such as the *Scalacronica* of Sir Thomas Grey and Bower's *Scotichronicon*.

The careers of several of the major figures of the early fourteenth century have been appraised in some detail, notably in Geoffrey Barrow's *Robert the Bruce and the Community of the Realm of Scotland*,[18] which is of course rather more than a royal biography, Michael Prestwich's *Edward I*[19] and Michael Penman's *David II*.[20] As the definitive source of authority in medieval societies, the study of kingship is crucial to any understanding of the nature of the society and the functioning of government. To achieve effective government, it was necessary for kings to devolve power to earls and other great lords with traditional support, thus providing a source of authority that was both locally credible and sympathetic to the crown. Temporal magnate status need not have been inherited, though generally of course it was. It could be achieved through successful service to the crown. In *The Black Douglases*[21] Michael Brown has made a detailed study of the rapid rise of the Douglas family from minor barons to magnate status through the military abilities of the 'good' Sir James and his descendants. As the Douglas estates grew they naturally acquired existing tenants, thus increasing their military resources, but successful leadership in war could attract the support of men other than their military tenants and other men over whom they had rights of lordship. The men and women who appear in this study are very much the sort of people whose support was actively sought by Sir James and other ambitious lords; the people who could provide them with military and political support in exchange for protection, patronage and political leadership. Alan Young's *The Comyns, Robert the Bruce's Rivals*,[22] examines the rise of a magnate family through consistent crown service over several generations. The power and influence of families like the Douglases and the Comyns was both exerted through, and underpinned by, the lesser nobility, the rank of men and women who were registered on the Ragman Roll[23] of 1296 as being 'of the county of ...' Fife or Lanark or Edinburgh.

In Lothian there was no recent tradition of an intermediate source of authority between the king and the 'county' homagers (the term 'homagers' was used by Bain, and here, to denote those whose status demanded a personal declaration of loyalty to the crown) who formed the local politi-cal and military community. This does not mean that there was no magnate influence in Lothian, but it does mean that the majority of the political community were more likely to be led by local considerations and the trends of local opinion than might be the case in an area dominated by a magnate with wider responsibilities. The existence of a magnate class tends to obscure the lives of their immediate subtenants. Not only are the mag-nates themselves better recorded as individuals due to their relative social and political prominence, but they directed, at least in theory, the activities of their tenants to the extent that often such people did not always need to be named in official documents of restoration or homage and fealty. The allegiance of the superior could be deemed to have included his or her tenants and other dependants. The majority of Lothian landholders were the possessors of relatively small estates and did not have the sort of rela-tionship with great lords that has generally been seen as a vital element in the pyramidal structure that is traditionally, if erroneously, associated with medieval societies. The most significant source of authority in their lives was the king, or at least his appointed officer, the sheriff.[24]

The origins of the high incidence of 'in capite' tenancies in Lothian cannot be definitively demonstrated, though it would seem likely that the large number of relatively small properties and baronies throughout the sheriffdom were conversions from ministerial landholdings[25] in the early twelfth century (if not before) as part of a royal policy aimed at providing the crown with a 'modern' heavy cavalry element of knights and men-at-arms.[26] The status of 'king's tenants', as they are described in the Ragman Roll, is less clear, though they were obviously men (and unlike the 'county' homagers they were all men) of some standing in the community. They may not have enjoyed quite the same status as the 'county' homagers, but the members of both groups had a direct and personal relationship with the crown. Their obligations, military, judicial or financial, were those of individuals, not of a class. This may have been the product of the scale of landholding. The relatively small size of Lothian estates meant that there were few men with the obligation to serve with a retinue of men-at-arms, though such service was extensively owed, and discharged, by the political community. There is, therefore, a high incidence of named individuals in garrison muster rolls and horse valuations. Only a very tiny proportion of the men on station appear as unnamed 'scutifers' or 'socii' in the company of a more prominent individual.

Although the information relating to each individual is slight, the sum of their experiences as a group is very extensive. This does not mean that a synthetic 'typical' model of the Lothian free tenant in the fourteenth century can be constructed. The most consistent factor in the lives of the political community could reasonably be said to be inconsistency. As Alexander Grant writes in *Independence and Nationhood*, '… their actions could only be determined by personal considerations and were bound to be inconsistent.'[27]

Inconsistent or otherwise, the sound administration of Lothian was heavily dependent on the co-operation of the political community. The willingness of the community to accept a particular source of lordship was obviously dependent on what that lordship could do for the community. In the early fourteenth century the party most able to exclude war from Lothian would surely have enjoyed more popular support than its rival. Edward I was able to make his rule in Lothian reasonably secure having won it through battle in 1296. Edward II lost Lothian through battle in 1314, though his influence there must have already been on the wane following the loss of Linlithgow peel and Edinburgh Castle. Both, but obviously Edinburgh particularly, were important indicators of the power of the administration. Edward III won Lothian through battle in 1333 but could not provide the good lordship necessary to secure the allegiance of the community. Robert I gained Lothian through battle as well, though ability to coerce the community into paying for truces indicates that his influence, though not the acceptance of his kingship, was increasingly significant before Bannockburn. Robert I does seem to have been able to make his lordship acceptable to a large portion of the political community of Lothian between 1314 and 1329 given the extensive support there for the Bruce party during Edward III's administration of the sheriffdom. Most of the activity against Edward III's Lothian administration would come from Lothian itself. There is little doubt that Scottish troops from other areas saw service in Lothian during that period, but the daily practice of the war was the work of local men under local leaders, in particular Sir Alexander Ramsay and Sir William Douglas of Lothian.[28] Neither of these men was born into magnate status. They derived their power through developing reputations for consistent success in the field at the head of small forces drawn from minor lairds, burgesses and free tenants, men with specific personal responsibilities in local judicial and military administration.

Throughout the rest of southern and eastern Scotland the range and burden of obligations on the minor gentry would have been much the same as in Lothian, but this does not mean that Lothian was absolutely 'typical' of Scottish, or even 'Lowland' sheriffdoms. It would be reasonable to assume that for practical purposes the legal and military responsibilities of landholders in Dumfriesshire or Aberdeenshire were not radically different to those of their Lothian equivalents, but it should not be assumed that they were identical. Also, for a variety of reasons, the war would not have had an identical impact in each locality.[29] Distance from major concentrations of Plantagenet, Balliol or Bruce sympathy, the influence of local magnates, the ease or otherwise with which the differing factions could exert military or political pressure in a given area and, naturally, the course of the war as a whole at a particular juncture, would all affect the political complexion of each area in different ways.[30]

In 1934 E.M. Barron made the case that not only had Gaelic Scotland borne the brunt of King John's and King Robert's wars between 1296 and 1314, it was, he claimed, a struggle in which Lothian had 'played no part.'[31] Professor Barrow's essay 'Lothian during the First War of Independence'[32] made a very convincing rebuttal of Barron's view, but concentrated on the relatively small numbers of men who turned out for the Bruce cause in 1306. None of these men were lords of the first order, though within the Lothian community they were all quite significant individuals.

Barron hoped to redress what he saw as the marginalisation of the contribution of 'Gaelic' Scotland to the struggle for independence. His conflation of several geographical, cultural and linguistic terms which are themselves misleading (Celtic/ Highland/ Gaelic/ northern versus Anglian/ Lowland/ Teutonic/ southern) compromised the general validity of his position. Victorian scholarship had indeed tended to concentrate on events, and therefore individuals, in the central and southern parts of the country. To a considerable extent this was inevitable; most military activity throughout most of the period did take place south of the Tay. Barron's argument was essentially based more on undermining the contribution of southern Scots than on highlighting the efforts of their northern compatriots. His study was limited to the period 1296–1314. In King Robert's early operations in the west and north-east the importance of recruits from the Isles and west Highlands is unquestioned and Highland men continued to serve in Bruce armies, but clearly Robert's later campaigns were conducted by forces which included a significant quantity of men-at-arms and these could not be raised in large numbers from Highland areas. In King David's reign the pattern of the war was rather different.

It is apparent from chronicle sources that men-at-arms, the overwhelming majority of whom were supplied by the lesser nobility, performed the bulk of the fighting other than at sieges and in the very rare general engagements. These men appear in record as esquires, valets, scutifers and 'homines ad arma' (men-at-arms) with no apparent distinction. Several of them were knights, but most were not. They do not seem to have had the same formalised burdens of responsibilities of English 'knights of the shire', but, like them, were probably indispensable to the administration of government. As sheriff court jurors, and in some cases as barons with jurisdictional responsibilities of their own, and as men with defined military obligations, they were crucial to the administration of civil and criminal justice and to the general conduct of war. In England the activity of the political community of the county can, to a limited extent, be observed in elections for the Commons and in the records of sheriff court proceedings.[33] In Scotland the only political activity that is extensively recorded in surviving documents over lengthy periods is military service, and a great deal of that material relates to service in English garrisons and field armies. Even in that sphere the material hardly constitutes a systematic body of information, but the volume and nature of such record as has survived clearly indicates the significance of the barons, minor lairds and the more prominent burgesses of Lothian to the stability of government in the sheriffdom in the administration as jurors and soldiers.

A very large proportion of these people (or their immediate forbears) appended their seals to the Ragman Roll in the late summer of 1296, acknowledging the kingship of Edward I. Though probably incomplete, the Roll lists the Lothian men and women who were considered, by Edward I's administration, to comprise the political community. The criteria for inclusion are by no means certain, but there can be no doubt that the Ragman Roll lists the people whose acceptance of the new government in 1296 was considered worth acquiring. Their support was sought, and sometimes extorted, by both English and Scottish kings, because it was desirable – sufficiently so that defectors would seem to have been welcomed quite easily when they moved from one party to another. To accept a former enemy into the king's peace rather than forfeit them and grant their property to someone else was preferable for a number of reasons. The recipient of a new grant would very likely have to spend some time there to make his lordship a reality, thus temporarily depriving the king of that person's services. Someone accepted into the king's peace would be more likely to have established his authority on his estates already and be ready to render the due services immediately. They would also be likely to have some useful experience of local affairs and customs and would, hopefully, be a presence in the community that was favourable to the crown.

From the perspective of kings, the minor landholding class was what made the Lothian community 'tick' as an administrative and military entity. In order to understand the pressures that formed their allegiance, it is useful to examine the demands made upon these people, the effect of the war on their lives, their relationship with government, the services demanded and performed and the results of failing to give those services.

There were of course personal factors that cannot be identified at this distance. When landholders were forfeited they obviously had to make some provision for their families. No doubt many found shelter with friends or relations, but that would be no substitute for home, and in the wave of forfeitures made by Edward III in 1335–37 it would not be impossible that all of a person's friends and relatives had been forfeited as well, or that those who had not been forfeited either would not or could not take in more mouths to feed. Equally, in the mid to late 1330s, Lothian men who might have been willing or eager to accept Plantagenet lordship lived in a community where a very large proportion of their neighbours were strongly enough in favour of Bruce lordship to have been forfeited. With the Scots increasingly in the ascendant militarily after the battle of Culblean,[34] Edward apparently less interested in the retention of Lothian after the abandonment of the siege of Dunbar in June 1338, the granting of a truce until 1339[35] and the defeats of English forces at the Crags of Craigie, Blaksollings and Crichtondene,[36] there was little to discourage Lothian men from defection to the Bruce party as long as they could reach an accommodation that would preserve their heritage and their status in the community.

Those who would not or could not make their peace with the Bruce party faced a rather bleak future by the later 1330s. Clearly the Edwardian administration was under increasing pressure from the Scots after 1335 if not before. If Scots in the Plantagenet party were obliged to evacuate their families, even if they could be confident of secure financial support from the English crown, they might well come under family pressure to defect to the Bruce party in order to recover the family home. Financial support from English kings might not, in any case, be a very dependable source of income. In the event of a financial crisis[37] or of a settlement between the Plantagenets and the Bruces, Scots in English peace might easily find themselves abandoned in the interests of a general peace. Domestic issues such as family pressures on men like Alexander Seton, who defected to Edward II sometime after 1308, or the dismal insecurity of an existence on a crown pension for the more fortunate Plantagenet supporters after the 1330s[38] cannot be measured, but are likely to have been uppermost in most people's minds. This is something to be borne in mind amid consideration of the more accessible issues of service, leadership and allegiance. The retention of the family property was of the utmost importance and that was dependent on accepting the lordship of whoever had practical control of the area. In 1296–1314, despite Wallace's march on Haddington, the Balliol party victory at Roslin in 1303 and Robert I's ability to force the community to pay for truces in the three or four years preceding Bannockburn, control lay with the Plantagenets. Between 1314 and 1333, despite Edward II's invasion of 1322 and Edward Balliol's short-lived kingship after Dupplin Muir, it would be the Bruces.

The Lothian administration of Edward III from 1333 to 1341 may not have enjoyed the same apparent degree of acceptance as had that of his father and grandfather. Initially he installed tiny garrisons that may have been of a similar order to traditional 'peacetime' levels in complement and made no immediate effort to repair Edinburgh Castle, slighted by Robert I in 1314. By 1335 he had been forced to commence restoration at Edinburgh and to install a substantial garrison,[39] but when the castle came under siege in 1338, according to John of Fordun[40] and Walter Bower,[41] the community of Lothian accepted the authority of the newly-appointed Bruce party sheriff, Laurence of Preston although the castle had not yet fallen. From the mid 1330s, unlike the period between 1296 and 1314, Lothian was consistently a theatre of operations, and the extent to which Plantagenet government was accepted or effective is very questionable. Not only had there been a great many forfeitures made by 1335–36, itself a sign that the administration had only limited acceptance, but many properties made returns to the sheriff of little or nothing, either because they were 'destroyed' or just 'on account of the war'. The latter term is possibly a tacit admission that that property was no longer under the control of the administration.[42]

The activity of the burghal communities of Lothian is less well-recorded than that of the rural minor gentry. Most of their personal records would have been commercial and of only very transitory significance. The bulk of such burghal record as has survived tends to focus on property rights and, by the later fourteenth century, court cases. The burghal community may have accepted changes in kingship relatively easily. In a sense, they were much more vulnerable than landholders. Lands forfeited could be restored, farms, manors and castles could be repaired, but it would be extremely difficult to restore a business if the capital and stock were lost. It might be a challenge for a restored land-holder to re-establish himself after a long absence, but farm produce is almost always saleable and agricultural land can almost always be rented out. The situation for a burgess returning to business after forfeiture and restoration would have been more difficult; the customers on whom he or she relied in the past would have established relations with other tradespeople or merchants, and the suppliers on whom they relied for stock in the past would have found new clients and might not be in a position to service a new demand.

In Edinburgh and Linlithgow under Edward I and II, and at Edinburgh after 1335 under Edward III there would also be the garrison to consider. Obviously, a force of men-at-arms housed in a strong castle or peel gave the sheriff the power to enforce his rule in the town, but the garrison also became a part of the economy of the town in that it offered opportunities for paid military service and provided customers. The burghs, of course, were bound the crown by their charters.[43] Since the burghal communities had a long tradition of relating to crown officers,[44] it is not surprising that, in the light of all these factors, the inhabitants of Lothian towns seem to have accepted Plantagenet lordship without much apparent rancour.

It was perhaps more difficult for women of the political community, whether burghal or rural, to retain their positions. They may not have been called on to fight or, so far as we know, give court service in person, but they were still obliged to give fealty and homage.[45] They were still obliged to keep on the right side of the de facto government or face forfeiture and therefore obliged to make political decisions. That they did so is clear from the number of women forfeited or described as being 'rebels' and the numbers seeking reconciliation and restoration.[46] Presumably the refusal to perform military service, or performing service for the enemy would be adequate grounds for forfeiture among men, but what form the 'rebellion' of women took is never made clear.

There is no sign that Plantagenet governments ever attempted to call on 'common army' service in Lothian. In part this must be due to the availability of troops from England for large offensives, but the administration may have had doubts about the wisdom of arming large numbers of Scots. In England there were mechanisms in place to ensure that counties and towns bore the expense of arming, and to some extent, provisioning, the men selected for duty, and for paying their wages for the journey from the counties to the muster points. It may have been considered that making such provisions in Scotland would not generate enough men to make the exercise worthwhile. More importantly perhaps, the demand for such service would have been very limited: common army service would not provide the men-at-arms that provided the striking arm element of the garrisons. The failure to demand 'common army' could of course be seen as an indication that the administration did not feel confident that the call would be obeyed in respectable quantity, and that that in itself would undermine the prestige and credibility of the government.

Most of the members of the Lothian political community were simply not so significant on the national stage as to merit much attention in the narrative and chronicle accounts, and this, more than questions about the reliability or bias of the writers, is the most important factor in limiting the usefulness of these sources for a local study. This is not to say that Lothian landholders were not influenced by the wider picture. The growing success and confidence of the Bruce party in the years before Bannockburn and after Culblean must have had an influence on them, as must the surrender of the Balliol party at Strathord in 1304, or the defeats of the Bruce party at Dupplin Muir in 1332 or Halidon Hill in 1333. Nor is it the case that Lothian landholders were free from magnate influence simply because there was no Lothian-based magnate. The Earls of March and Fife both had interests there, and their choices of allegiance would inevitably have carried some weight among the Lothian gentry, if only because they might be perceived as having better access to information on which to base their actions; however neither of them was as commanding a figure in terms of Lothian politics as Sir Alexander Seton or Sir William Douglas of Lothian. Seton and Douglas were barons, and therefore persons of some significance, but there were at least thirty other barons and some hundreds of 'in capite', king's or bishop's tenants and burghal landholders so the influence of the two earls may not have been terribly significant in Lothian like those of other counties in Scotland.

In practice, whether they accepted or welcomed the lordship of Balliol, Bruce or Plantagenet kings, the landholders of Lothian must have been chiefly motivated by personal and commercial concerns. Whose head the crown rested on may have been a matter of some significance, but the quality of the lordship offered was of prime importance. Was it better to have the lordship of Edward II, arguably the rightful superior of Scotland, who could not provide protection or to accept the lordship of Robert I – turncoat, sacrilegious murderer and, in the eyes of some, usurper – who could? However attractive a certain political choice might be, personal and family security must surely have been uppermost in most men's minds, most of the time.

THE SOURCES

The Regesta volumes covering the reigns of Robert I and David II, the Register of the Great Seal of Scotland, the Exchequer and Chamberlain's rolls constitute the entirety of Scottish government records surviving from the period. Naturally, only a very small portion of the information in these volumes applies directly to Lothian, and that which does is of limited value. The sheriff's returns to the crown represent the outcome of his duties, not the performance of them. They tell us only balance due to the crown, not the income and expenditure that produced that balance. Further, we cannot assume that, for example, a practice followed in Dundee or Aberdeen was necessarily identical to that followed in Edinburgh. The actual practice of both military and legal obligation might well be affected by local practice, economy and geography. We should not, for instance, be surprised that Lothian was a better source of cavalry service than Kintyre or that birlinns[47] were more readily available in Argyle than in Lanark. In addition to the records of central government there is an extensive body of material from baronial and ecclesiastical sources. These include *The Morton Registrum*,[48] *The*

Laing Charters,[49] *Liber Cartorum Prioratus Sancti Andree,*[50] *The Chartulary of Coldstream,*[51] *The Chartulary of Neubotle*[52] and *The Charters of Holyrood,*[53] though a very large proportion of the information contained in these volumes relates to periods and topics outwith this study.

English records for Lothian between 1296 and 1314 and again between 1333 and 1341 afford much more information about the political community with references to military service, juror service, homage, forfeitures and restorations. Significant collections of this material are to be found in Stevenson's *Documents Illustrative of the History of* Scotland,[54] *The Chamberlain Roll,*[55] *The Exchequer Rolls of Scotland,*[56] Bain's *Calendar of Documents Relating to Scotland*[57] and McPherson's *Rotuli Scotiae.*[58] Little relating specifically to Lothian during the war years appears in other collections such as the *Calendar of the Close Rolls,*[59] or the *Calendar of Post Mortem Inquisitions.*[60]

The narrative sources tend to be concerned with the fate of the nation, and, inevitably, with the affairs of king and great lords. The focus of the narrative might move to Lothian due to a given event, but soon moves to developments elsewhere. From an operational viewpoint, the most significant chronicle account for the purposes of this study is the *Scalacronica*[61] of Sir Thomas Grey. Unlike the Scottish chroniclers, Fordun, Wyntoun, Barbour and Bower, Grey had no particular agenda within the Scottish political sphere. Beyond his support for Edward Balliol, rather than David Bruce, as King of Scotland, he had no interest in inflating the reputation of one person at the expense of another. More importantly, he had personal experience of the war he describes. Unlike the *Lanercost* compiler, he was socially and professionally familiar with the Scots, and considerably less antagonistic toward them. Most importantly, other chroniclers wrote of the men-at-arms of the period, but Sir Thomas served as one.

Most of the families discussed in this book were of fairly minor significance even within the confines of the Lothian political community and have left no charter chest collection, just a trail of references in official documents – as charter witnesses for example. Unfortunately witness lists have proved to be a much less revealing source of evidence than one might have hoped.[62] Few documents have a complete list of named witnesses,[63] other than crown charters which name only a handful of very prominent men.[64] Many documents, regal, ecclesiastical and lay, make no reference whatsoever to witnesses,[65] have only a very small number of witnesses[66] or name only a selection.[67] These are generally the most prominent persons present and perhaps a family member, the rest of the witnesses appearing merely as 'et aliis', 'et multis aliis' or 'ac multis aliis'.[68] It seems likely that these 'aliis' would have comprised the friends, neighbours and relatives of the parties to the document.[69] It is quite possible that some of the witnesses – named or not – had no formal or legal obligation to take part in the process, but were simply men of substance from the neighbourhood whose acknowledgement of a document was considered desirable. Broadly speaking the unnamed witnesses were the sort of people who held land, formed local juries and owed military service; exactly the sort of people on whom this study is focussed. Were these people named individually it would perhaps give us some valuable insight into the patterns of local leadership, but the presence of a specific individual is not proof positive that that person was an adherent of the granter or the grantee.

The same applies to sigillography. A considerable proportion of sealed documents have lost their seals, but of those that have not, very few bear more than the seal of the granter and the grantee and several would seem never to have had either slits or tongues for the application of seals in the first place.[70] Additionally, the presence of a particular seal does not necessarily prove the presence of the seal's owner. When William Blair resigned the chaplaincy of Heriot in November 1309 he used the seal of the abbot of Dunfermline because 'his [own] seal was unknown to the majority.'[71] It should not be taken for granted that witnesses to a land charter necessarily had any particular personal concern with the subject. George Abernethy witnessed a charter of David de Penicuik in 1373.[72] He may have had local interests; he may simply have been a friend of David who happened to be present.

The political and military history of Scotland in the early fourteenth century has, understandably been the focus of much attention by historians. Like the chroniclers, they too have mostly concentrated on the fate of the country as a whole. The men, and occasionally women, who figure in political histories are almost inevitably people of substance and, perhaps more importantly, status. Because Lothian was not generally an active theatre of war other than between 1334–35 and 1341, and because the great lords and earls hailed from other areas relatively little has been written about local conditions, despite the nature of the conflict.

I

MILITARY ACTIVITY
IN LOTHIAN

PART 1:1296–1304

In 1296 Edward I conquered and deposed his vassal John Balliol in a
matter of five months. The fall of Berwick in March, the apparently brief
cavalry action at Dunbar in April[1] and the subsequent, almost immediate,
surrender of Dunbar castle seems, superficially, to be small reason for the
military and political collapse of the Scottish effort against Edward I in
the spring and summer of 1296. Although King John did not surrender
and abdicate until July it would seem that he made no effort to continue
the fight after March 1296 himself and that nobody else had the capacity
or inclination to continue the fight on his behalf. John's withdrawal and
Edward's pursuit may not, of course, be the whole story. Thirteenth-
century records can hardly be described as all-encompassing, but we can
be confident that Edward's armies were not seriously opposed in any of
the areas they traversed, or at least not sufficiently so to delay seriously,
let alone prevent, their intended operations.[2]

The fall of Dunbar and then Edinburgh castles in 1296 and the ease
with which Edward I was able to install an administration might be construed as evidence to support the contention that Lothian, and the other
counties of the south-east, were particularly amenable to annexation by
the Plantagenets.[3] Other evidence could be construed in a similar light.
We know that Scots served as jurors under Edward I's administration as
early as August 1296[4] and that men from the south-east and south-west

were performing military service in his armies and garrisons.[5] Lothian men sought justice in Edward's courts[6] and the overwhelming majority (so far as we can tell) of the political community became Edward's homagers,[7] all within the first year of the Plantagenet administration.

There are strengths to the 'Anglophile Lothian' point of view adopted by E.M. Barron,[8] but, as Professor Barrow has demonstrated,[9] there are also major weaknesses. The Battle of Dunbar and the fall of the castle would not seem to have resulted in heavy casualties.[10] The proposition that one formation of King Edward's cavalry, alone and unaided, killed Scots in their thousands, simply beggars belief. Nonetheless, the political and moral aspects were enormous. Armies are of little value without leaders and cohesion. Both were lost at Dunbar.

A considerable number of men from all over Scotland were held as prisoners of war, including at least thirty who hailed from or had extensive interests in Lothian, such as Herbert de Morham, David Graham and Edmund de Ramsay, each of whom would defect to and from the Plantagenet cause on a number of occasions. Superficially it would seem unlikely that the absence of so small a number from a political community that consisted of at least 300 men and women[11] would severely restrict the potential for that community to offer armed resistance to an invader, however, there are a number of factors to be considered. The Lothian men who served in the 1296 campaign may not have represented the whole strength of the community in arms, but they must surely be assumed to include a substantial proportion of men with military experience or ambition and also the men with the most extensive military responsibilities, the sheriffs and those with baronial status who had the 'leadership' of men in a given vicinity. The men captured at Dunbar might only be a very small portion of the political community of Lothian, but their absence would have been much more significant in terms of military capacity and organisation than their numbers would suggest. Even if, as a group, the prisoners of war did not represent a disproportionate share of the militarily obliged part of the community, the very fact that they had been in the field inevitably means that they were among the more fit and able members of that group. Some members of the group must, at any time, have been sufficiently youthful, elderly or physically unsuited to war to have been ineligible for service. Some of them would almost certainly have been female or clerics, though these persons presumably provided substitutes or perhaps paid cash in lieu of service.[12]

We can be reasonably confident, then, that the prisoners were men of the right age and capacity – competency is a different matter – to discharge military service. Their absence would have been a hindrance to continuation of the fight, in terms both of personal service as men-at-arms and of local leadership. The number of prisoners held after Dunbar was quite small and we cannot be sure that absolutely all of the 200 or so Scottish prisoners mentioned in record were in fact prisoners of war at all, let alone men captured either in the battle or the subsequent surrender of Dunbar Castle. Nor can we be sure that all those taken at either location are identified in surviving record. Given that over 100 men-at-arms were stationed in Dunbar castle at the time of the battle[13] and that we can safely assume that the armigerous cavalry arm of the Scottish army was rather larger than the balance of 100 men taken during or after the battle, it is clear that the majority of the Scottish men-at-arms serving in King John's army did not fall captive in 1296. They either escaped from the battle and returned home or they were captured or surrendered, had their parole accepted, and were allowed to depart. If this were the case then the number of men who might be expected to give service to the Balliol cause after Dunbar would be further reduced. Regardless of the political rights or wrongs of the situation generally, men who had given their parole could hardly be expected to break it.

Defeat in one battle was not the only factor to weaken the position of King John. From the outbreak of the war he had not enjoyed the support of all the important sources of leadership and manpower in his kingdom. A number of important figures in the political community of Scotland chose to serve in Edward I's army. The Earl of Carrick chose to support Edward, possibly in the hope of being chosen as the successor to King John. His choice of alignment would probably have had little direct effect on the military and political community of Lothian since he had little or nothing in the way of estates there, but the Annandale and Carrick tenants who held property from the Bruce family must surely have been influenced by the earl's decision, thus reducing the number of men-at-arms available to turn out in the Balliol cause. More significantly Patrick, Earl of Dunbar served in the Plantagenet army despite the fact that his countess, Marjorie Comyn[14] (daughter of the late Alexander, Earl of Buchan) held his chief castle, Dunbar, in the Balliol interest. It would be unreasonable to assume that all of the earl's tenants sided against him in the campaign of 1296. Some proportion of the men-at-arms who served under the countess were certainly Lothian men such as Alexander Sinclair, John Currie, Malcolm de Haddington, Brice le Tailleur, Herbert de Morham and Thomas Byset, who all appear in a document dated 16 May 1296 as prisoners of war[15] among more than 100 other Scottish knights and esquires (and one clerk) taken at Dunbar Castle.

It is open to question whether there was any strong support in Lothian for continuing the fight at all. The King of Scotland had been defeated by the King of England. It may have been some time since this had last occurred, but it had happened before. The centre of Lothian administration, Edinburgh Castle, had been occupied by an English garrison on numerous occasions in the past, all of which had proved to be of limited duration. The political community of Lothian may have assumed that Edward's administration would be a temporary institution pending the making of a new King of Scots. No doubt the new king would be very much under the sway of Edward I, but it is difficult to assess whether or not that would have been a real issue to the minor landholders who comprised the bulk of the political community. They did not, after all, have much say in matters of kingship. When Margaret of Norway was acknowledged as heir to Alexander III[16] or when John Balliol was acknowledged as King of Scots[17] the opinion of the freeholders and burgesses of local political communities would not have been a matter of great concern to the spiritual and temporal magnates who formed what we might regard as the 'national' political community. When Edward I took custody of Scottish royal castles in 1291–92[18] it is a virtual certainty that the minor nobles of Lothian were not consulted and that there was no noticeable degree of resistance to Edward's officials. In 1296 not only was there an absence of active resistance in the field, but Edinburgh Castle, a major strength, surrendered after a brief siege. Edward deployed three 'engines' to cast stones into the castle 'day and night' and the garrison sought terms after five days, but the shooting apparently continued for another three days thereafter, though Edward himself had moved on to Linlithgow.[19] Perhaps the garrison had asked better terms than Edward was prepared to concede, but the possibility that Edward was prepared to offer no terms other than unconditional surrender cannot be discounted.

In addition to the shock of defeat and the absence of the prisoners of war, the lack of a generally acknowledged source of lordship to coordinate resistance in the immediate aftermath of Dunbar and Edward's march to Elgin, would have made overt activity in Lothian worthless militarily and dangerous personally. In addition to the obvious risks of combat a man who took up arms against the Edwardian government could be forfeited of his lands. If opposition to Edward were eventually to prove successful he would expect to have his property restored, but what if it failed? He might be restored as part of a general political settlement if the Scots were sufficiently successful in their war with the English to force Edward to negotiate rather than conquer. If Edward was completely successful, and that must have looked like a very real possibility by the winter of 1296, he might never regain his property.

In addition to national political issues, there was a local problem. Although John had been king of Scotland he did not have the benefit of strong personal traditional leadership bonds in Lothian. The Balliol family, though extensive landholders elsewhere in the country, had little if anything in the way of Lothian interests and several men who did have local interests were either prisoners of war, like Herbert de Morham, William Curry, Edmund de Ramsay, William and Henry de Sinclair or were aligned with the Plantagenet cause, like the Earl of March. Also, a great many Lothian men had accepted Edward's kingship by appending their seals to the Ragman Roll. The lack of a major active local political presence with a strong commitment to the Balliol cause, then, may have made it easier for Edward's administration to take up the reins of power in Lothian in 1296. This may have been a lesson learned for those who would gain or attempt to gain Lothian over the next fifty years. As we shall see, there is evidence to suggest that Edward II (if not Edward I), Robert I, Edward III and David II would all elevate men they felt they could rely on to positions of local prominence, presumably in an effort to establish a local habit or tradition of allegiance to the party in question. That traditional local sympathies could be a significant factor in European medieval political life cannot be seriously questioned and we should not expect Scotland to have been radically out of step. Almost forty years after the deposition of his father Edward Balliol was still able to call on traditional loyalty to his family in the south-west.[20]

Mounting resistance to a powerful regime is, under any circumstances, a difficult and dangerous course of action. Even in situations where there is a clearly popular 'national' cause, with an active political force fighting for that cause with the help of sympathetic agencies and even where the occupation's general policies are very brutal, it can take years before resistance becomes a serious issue for the occupying power, let alone start to threaten its stability.[21] In 1296 the defeat of the king's army, the fall of Dunbar and other castles, the passage of Edward I's troops, the fall of Edinburgh Castle, the absence of Lothian military men as prisoners of war or perhaps as fugitives would all have been factors in reducing further the likelihood of local resistance. Furthermore, if it was the case that men who surrendered or were captured gave their parole we should not assume that they all returned home with charger, arms and armour. The surrender of an army might well include safeguards for personal equipment, but by tradition both mount and armament of a man killed or captured were the prizes of his vanquisher and would have a significant cash value.[22] Even if the individual was free to fight, they might not have the means of doing so, or at least not as a man-at-arms.

Despite the disruption of traditional authority and the installation of new officials there was some level of resistance in Lothian within a short time of Edward's conquest. On 23 July 1297 Edward I's treasurer for Scotland, Hugh de Cressingham, wrote to his king that the Scots had appointed baillies and officials in some counties and that no county was properly held '… save for Berwick and Roxburgh, and they only lately.'[23] If anyone was in a position to judge the effective extent of Edward's Scottish government it would have been Cressingham, so it would appear either that Lothian had yet to be secured for Plantagenet rule a year and more after Edward's initial conquest, or that counties which had been effectively secured in 1296 had been recovered by the Scots, or at least lost to the English, by the summer of 1297. Naturally, the defeat of a major English field army at Stirling Bridge in September 1297 did nothing to improve the situation of Edward's administration. In the autumn Wallace was able to lead a force to Haddington, where, on 11 October, he issued an invitation to the merchants of Cologne and Hamburg to resume their Scottish trading operations.[24] His ability to lead a force into the heart of Lothian is perhaps less indicative of the military situation than his ability to extract that force without recorded interference by the garrison forces in the sheriffdom. Additionally, three castles, including the major stronghold of Dirleton, must have been gained by the Scots at some juncture since Edward was obliged to detach a force under Bishop Bek to recapture them.[25] Some consideration must be given to Wallace's motives for mounting his expedition. Militarily and politically, marching a force through Lothian was a matter of some significance. To the Plantagenet administration it was a declaration Balliol supporters were intent on ensuring that even if John's writ did not run in Lothian, Edward's could not be guaranteed. If Wallace could seize Haddington, even if only for a day or two, Edward's government could hardly be said to have control of the land. If Haddington was within Wallace's reach, then so was virtually any other place in Lowland Scotland that did not boast a castle or at least lay within range of a large and active garrison.

In addition to these military and political issues, we should bear in mind that a very large part of the community would have had quite enough disruption and instability in their lives. The tensions between the Bruce and Balliol parties before 1292, the Dunbar campaign and the subsequent occupation would undoubtedly have persuaded some at least that the risks involved in carrying on the war were not warranted by any gain likely to be made even if the aims of the war – and it would be difficult to be clear about what exactly such war aims would be – were completely achieved, a condition that would have seemed unlikely at the time.

Men and women with responsibilities – nobles, free tenant landholders, burgesses – seem to have had nothing to fear from the Edwardian administration so long as they fulfilled their obligations and accepted his rule. As long as that administration was visibly in power they could be reasonably secure in their positions. Although the Balliol administration could not prevent acceptance of Plantagenet lordship by direct military action, they could hardly afford to allow that acceptance to grow into a tradition of allegiance, and therefore of service, unopposed. Wallace may have gone to Haddington to undermine the Plantagenet administration, but he was surely making a point to the local political community as well. Those who were active on behalf of the English administration or considering activity (joining a garrison for example) could not fail to have been concerned at the arrival of a pro-Balliol force deep in Plantagenet-held territory. No doubt Wallace was waving the flag as well as rattling a sabre, but from the point of view of the political community of Lothian the whole exercise may have looked rather more like threatening behaviour than patriotic encouragement. Men like Matthew de Hawthornden and William de Fenton, restored to their properties in the autumn of 1296,[26] had obviously entered the peace of Edward I. In the event of a Balliol restoration they might well find it difficult to justify their actions. Similarly, men who took part in the 'normal' business of the sheriff court, such as the inquisitions in several sheriffdoms into the estate of Elena de la Zouche,[27] could hardly avoid accusations of collaboration with the enemy. The findings of those inquisitions have survived and the jurors who reported to the sheriff of Edinburgh, Hugh Louther, were very clearly Lothian men: Henry de Ormiston, Nicholas de Preston, William son of Geoffrey de Bolton, Henry Ferrur of Tranent, Waldone de North Berwick, David de Pencaitland, Gilbert de Drem, Thomas de Straiton and Jordan de Aldhamston all bore names derived from Lothian landholdings. The others, William de Sydeserf and John Scot, were both Ragman Roll homagers for Lothian. There can be no doubt that these men were discharging their normal judicial obligations, but under the authority of Edward I rather than of King John.

Although there was not a complete absence of armed resistance to the Edwardian government in Lothian in the period between Falkirk in 1297 and the fight at Roslin in 1303 there certainly was not a general state of war throughout the county.[28] Equally we cannot be sure that there was not widespread sporadic violence, only that there was not sufficient activity for it to be regularly cited in Edwardian administration records as an argument for increasing the military establishment. Fluctuation in the size of garrisons is, in any case, a very poor guide to the tactical situation. The enlargement or reduction of any particular garrison or group of garrisons could occur for any number of reasons not immediately related to the progress of the war generally. The availability of men, money and materials, the greater political significance of some locations compared with others, the preference of men to serve in particular areas and their unwillingness to serve in others, would all be issues which, although of some importance to the military administrators of the day, cannot be clearly identified now. Further, having the people, the money and the munitions to provide a garrison does not guarantee the capacity to put that garrison in place, let alone provide for its needs once established. Perhaps most importantly, the level of resource applied to solving any military problem, in this case judging the military force required to achieve local dominance and perhaps additional objectives of which we are unaware, is not simply a product of the availability of the means, but of the subject's estimate of the situation; in this instance the perceived threat constituted by the Scots at a given moment.

That there was a military administration in place by October 1296 is apparent from the appointment of Sir Walter Huntercombe[29] as its commander and various documents[30] relating to the supply of the garrison at Edinburgh. Unfortunately there seems to be no indication of the number of men under command there until 1298. On 25 November Sir John de Kingestone was appointed to relieve Huntercombe as commander in Lothian.[31] On the same day King Edward issued an instruction to Sir Simon Fraser to support Sir John with twenty men-at-arms on barbed (armoured, or at least protected) horses as required due to the fact that the 'constable... has not sufficient force of his own.'[32] Evidently there was a military presence at Edinburgh, and one that contained a heavy cavalry element, albeit one considered inadequate for offensive operations without additional support. The presence of Sir Simon's men may have been more a matter of political significance; a means of ensuring Scottish participation for propaganda purposes. The scale of an operation calling for 200 men-at-arms ordered from Berwick at this time[33] suggests that twenty men-at-arms, though hardly insignificant, was not a vital contribution the force. Sir Walter Huntercombe, now in command at Berwick, was ordered to make a 'foray' against the Scots in the company of Sir Simon 'and others' with 200 men-at-arms. It is quite possible that the phrase 'and others' refers to Scots, perhaps specifically those men from Berwickshire who were in the peace of Edward I. Part of the 'price' of being in Edward's peace and of enjoying one's heritage must surely have been the acceptance of the usual range of responsibilities owed by landlords to their superior or sovereign, including military service obligations.

It would appear that Sir Simon's contribution was of some material significance since he would be providing 10 per cent of the manpower. The intended target for the 'foray' of November 1298 is not mentioned in the sources, either as a security measure or because the intended target was so obvious that it did not need to be stated. It would seem most likely that the intention was to conduct operations in the south-east of Scotland. This is a strong indication that the administration had not established complete control of that part of the country that was most accessible to intervention, but also that the administration could successfully call upon the military service obligations of some proportion of the political community.

The first full description of Sir John de Kingestone's garrison dates from 28 May 1300[34] though, as Dr. Fiona Watson has demonstrated,[35] there were arrangements in place for the logistical support of what was effectively 'a small standing army' from 1298, part of which was stationed at Edinburgh.[36] Although there was a total of sixty-seven men-at-arms in the complement a shortage of chargers reduced the number available for operations to sixty, but Sir John would have been taking a consider-able risk if he committed them all to action away from Edinburgh Castle. There is no doubt that there was a garrison before this date. On 9 August 1298[37] Sir John had informed King Edward that the Scots under the Earl of Buchan and the Bishop of St. Andrews had crossed the Forth and marched on Glasgow, from where they intended to move to the borders with the intention of joining forces with Balliol supporters in the forest of Selkirk. Sir John had received intelligence that Sir Simon Fraser had already met with the leaders of the Scots and that he was intending to defect, if he had not in fact already done so. It would seem that the Scots had already been active in the Edinburgh area since Sir John referred to a day when they 'came suddenly before our castle, and on which Sir Thomas D'Arderne was taken'.[38]

The same letter informs the King of difficulties with the local popu-lace as well as the major initiatives of the Scots. Margaret de Penicuik was reported as having received her son, Hugh, and his men (presumably Sir John assumed that these were men from the Penicuik estate) despite the fact that Hugh was a rebel. Sir John felt obliged to take action and made a descent on the 'ville' of Penicuik and impounded all the cat-tle there.[39] Some local men then demanded the return of their cattle, claiming that they were at peace with the Edwardian administration, and had taken no part in the raid. Sir John returned the cattle to the 'poor people to whom they belonged' and retained the rest, presumably on the assumption that they were the property of Margaret or Hugh de Penicuik or of the 'other ill-doers' that he had reported as being 'har-boured and received by them'. This episode reveals a real operational difficulty for Sir John and his various successors as local commanders in Edward I's Scottish government. How could one adequately and reliably identify the enemy? The 'poor people' of Penicuik might be entirely honest in their claim to be 'at peace'; if so, the confiscation of their cattle would not help them to see the Edwardian government as a source of 'good lordship'.

The sheriff had felt obliged to report the activity of Hugh de Penicuik and take action against him,[40] but that would seem to have been a rela-tively rare instance of active service for the Edinburgh garrison; indeed, the fact that Hugh de Penicuik was able to approach Edinburgh at all could be construed as evidence that at that particular juncture, the garrison was not fit to carry out its duties properly. Although he had obviously been a problem to the administration, Hugh, like the overwhelming majority of Scots seeking to defect, was accepted into Edward's peace without apparent difficulty. Although there is no official instrument recording the restoration of Hugh's property in Scotland, there is a document instructing the Sheriff of Northumberland to restore to him various properties there.[41] It may have been a standard practice of the time that Scots forfeited of property in England had to have individual writs in order to be restored to that property once they were no longer in a state of rebellion, whereas their Scottish properties could be restored as part of a general settlement.

The Scots may not have been able to make noticeable progress within Lothian after the battle of Falkirk, but they were active in its vicinity, notably sending a force under Sir John Comyn of Badenoch and Sir Simon Fraser from Biggar to Roslin in February 1303.[42] The battle that ensued was not particularly large, but was of considerable importance. The ability of the Scots to intercept, engage and defeat a force less than a day's ride from Edinburgh was hardly a sign that the Plantagenet cause was winning the war, or even that it was capable of protecting the inhabitants of Lothian from raiding parties. On the other hand, if Sir Thomas Grey is correct in his assertion that Comyn and Fraser had lifted their siege of Linlithgow,[43] presumably to move against the English force under Manton, Dunbar and Segrave, that may be an indication that the Scots did not have the necessary strength to prevent the siege being lifted by an English expeditionary force on even a relatively modest scale, though it would also suggest that the English garrisons were unable to prevent a siege being imposed in the first place, hence the necessity for a relief column.

According to Thomas Grey the Scottish force had been in action at the new peel at Linlithgow, over thirty miles away, until 20 February when they lifted their investment and moved south.[44] Given the difficulties of communication Segrave may have been under the impression that the Scots were still engaged there, and felt that he could raise the siege and perhaps bring the Scots to battle. Certainly Reimund Walrund and Robert Seueldedy were paid the substantial sum of thirty shillings for making a night reconnaissance to Linlithgow in search of the Scottish army.[45] Alternatively, the Scots may have had wind of his intention to move on Linlithgow and decided to intercept him once they were sure of his line of approach. Either way, it is clear that both the Scots and the English were prepared to offer or accept battle.

The initial attack occurred at the village of Roslin, where Sir John Segrave and Patrick, Earl of Dunbar, currently in Plantagenet allegiance,[46] had halted for the night. Superficially it might seem that the Plantagenet commanders were not expecting an attack at all, let alone a night attack, since they chose not to 'close up' their formation, but left the advance guard at 'a league distant at a hamlet' or even divided into three formations 'two leagues apart.'[47] There are a number of possible explanations for the division of the English force. Since the action took place in February we can be confident that the weather conditions would be far too cold for men and horses to be lying out through the night. Unless the force was very small indeed it would almost inevitably be too large to be accommodated in a modest Lothian village and a further billeting area would be required whether an attack was expected or not, so division of force was probably forced on Sir John and the Earl, regardless of tactical preference.

The failure of the English command to perceive, and take steps to neutralise, the threat posed by Comyn's force is clearly demonstrated by the resulting engagement; however Comyn's force was not necessarily a reflection of an extensive sympathy with the Balliol cause among Lothian landholders merely because the fight took place in their neighbourhood. The location of a battle is the product of a wide range of factors; if the English force had chosen a different route there might have been no engagement at all, and since the engagement was very much a function of war at what we might reasonably see as a 'national' level, it would not be inevitable, or even particularly significant, that any Lothian men were involved. Sir John Comyn's force was, in all probability, an ad hoc formation, assembled from immediately available manpower to respond to a threat or take advantage of an opportunity. Unquestionably there were Lothian men in the Balliol camp generally, but their presence at, or absence from, any particular action should not be seen as a determining factor in the location of that action since they might already be committed elsewhere. Similarly, that neither of the leaders of the Scots were Lothian men and that the Earl of Dunbar was in the Plantagenet force is not indicative of the political leanings of the Lothian community.

With the exception of Wallace, the leadership of the Balliol cause was generally vested in senior nobles. The nearest thing to a Lothian magnate would have been Earl Patrick, who, with English garrisons surrounding his Earldom, could hardly be expected to do anything other than accept Plantagenet government throughout the period 1296–1314.

Although a battlefield success, Roslin illustrates the weakness of the Balliol cause. A battle could be forced in Plantagenet-held territory, and a successful outcome gained, but the Balliol party was not in a position to exert lordship in Lothian any more than Wallace had been in 1297. The restoration of King John may have seemed like a realistic possibility once he had been released into the custody of the Pope[48] and then to that of Philip IV,[49] but the peace agreed between Philip and Edward in 1303,[50] endorsed in advance by John, destroyed any likelihood of that and in February 1304 the Balliol party came to Edward's peace, mostly under quite generous conditions.[51] The light nature of the penalties imposed on the Balliol party activists can be interpreted in two ways. Edward may have sought to bring Scots to his allegiance through demonstrating a degree of magnanimity in the hope that these men would become his agents in the future administration of Scotland, a possibility supported by the fact that a number of these men served the Plantagenet government for years to come; men like Sir William Oliphaunt who held Stirling Castle against Edward I in 1304, was a prisoner of war in England until 1308, but was an officer in Edward II's government, commanding the Perth garrison until it fell to Robert I in January 1313, at which point (or shortly thereafter) he joined the Bruce party. Alternatively he may have decided that the war could not be brought to a satisfactory conclusion through force of arms. Edward must have been aware that he was unlikely to live for very much longer. The generosity of his terms perhaps indicates a degree of desperation to achieve a political settlement.

Several factors discouraged Lothian men from supporting the Balliol party in 1296–1304. Obviously the power of the Plantagenet administration was a major consideration, as was the inability of the Guardians to counter that power. Wallace's seizure of Haddington probably made some impression on the local political community, but not enough to bring large numbers of recruits to the Balliol cause. There is no evidence to suggest that the community of Lothian was hostile to the Balliol party, but equally there is nothing to suggest that they were very well-disposed to it either. The absence of significant local leaders with a strong commitment to King John was therefore a significant issue in itself. Men whose position in society relied on the patronage of King John might be expected to take up arms on his behalf since they might be compromised by his deposition, but the political community of Lothian in 1296–1304 were, in the main, men whose local prominence pre-dated John's reign. The Balliol party really had very little to offer as an incentive for Lothian men to resist the Plantagenet government other than the prospect of political independence from England. Many of them had, in any case, given their allegiance to Edward I in 1296. They may not have had much choice and medieval jurists certainly understood the nature of duress, but in practical terms, opposing Edward I's government was unlikely to result in anything better than forfeiture and possibly death.

Despite the victory at Roslin, the Balliol party had run its course by early 1304. The French had abandoned the cause of King John (as had John himself) and made peace with England. The country was exhausted by the effort of fighting, the magnates had accepted Edward's rule through the Strathord agreement and by August 1305 the sole active representative of the Balliol cause was Sir William Wallace. Wallace was no longer the figure he had been in 1297. His defeat at Falkirk in 1298 had undermined his authority completely. He still enjoyed some sympathy, but he was unable to revitalise the Balliol cause as a serious proposition for ejecting the English. Indeed, by 1305 he may have been seen as something of an embarrassment, an obstacle to a political settlement and therefore more part of the problem than the solution. At the close of hostilities in 1304 there was no longer any effective 'patriotic' leadership. The Balliol cause had been identified with the 'patriotic' cause for obvious reasons, but with John himself rejecting any prospect of restoration, what would the Scots have been fighting for?

PART 2: 1304-1314

It is unlikely that the Strathord armistice, or Robert the Bruce's seizure of the crown, had much immediate impact on the lives of Lothian people. War broke out again in 1306, but then there had been war almost continually for the better part of a decade, largely conducted well away from Lothian. The resumption of hostilities undoubtedly forced Edward I to maintain a rather greater level of military commitment in Scotland than he would have liked, though there would seem to be no evidence of extraordinary garrison expenditure in Lothian in the first few years of the Bruce war.

The Bruce cause did enjoy some measure of support among the Lothian gentry; a number of men were forfeited by Edward[52] for their adherence to Robert I in 1306. A handful more, some of whom had in fact been active in the Bruce cause for two or three years, were forfeited by Edward II in 1312.[53] The majority of the Lothian political community remained in Edwardian allegiance until 1314. As mentioned above, and more fully explored in Chapter 5, the Bruces had no established 'constituency' of support in Lothian, but even if they had, the presence of an extensive network of Plantagenet garrisons would have limited their activity. Had such sympathy existed and had it expressed itself in armed activity throughout Lothian (the latter would not have been an inevitable result of the former) the defeat of King Robert at Methven would surely have brought it to an end, at least temporarily.

Several men, (though hardly a major, or even particularly significant segment of the political community as a whole) with extensive interests in Lothian did support Robert I. Michael Wemyss, William de Somerville, Alexander Fraser and Alexander de Lindsay turned out for Robert at the time of, or immediately after, his enthronement as did the tenants of Sir Henry de Pinkney, an English knight who had inherited land at Ballencrieff and at Luffness castle near Aberlady.[54] Wemyss, Somerville, Fraser and Lindsay were all men of some standing, probably quite prominent among the political community of Lothian, but with extensive interests elsewhere – Lindsay and Somerville in Lanark and Wemyss in Fife. They were hardly magnates, but they were fairly prominent people. Ballencreiff was a property of some significance which was held 'in capite' from the king for the service of one knight. In 1296 the most significant tenants of the estate had been Alexander Lindsay (presumably the same Alexander Lindsay forfeited in 1306 for supporting Robert I, John de Bickerton), Thomas de Colville and Henry Pinkney, the brother and heir of the late Robert. It is reasonable to assume that Henry sought the forfeiture of Lindsay, Bickerton and Colville rather than the unnamed and unnumbered cottars mentioned in the Post Mortem Inquisition[55] which had confirmed Henry as the legitimate heir.

For the first eight years of King Robert's reign, the bulk of recorded military service performed by Lothian men was in Edwardian garrisons, either for pay or to fulfil land tenure obligations. The paid men can be traced through muster rolls and horse valuations. Tenure service would not seem to have been recorded on a named basis, but was presumably administered by an official of the sheriff. The significance of the contribution that Lothian men made to the support of Edward II's government cannot be adequately defined in either an administrative or operational context, but it is fair to assume that the political significance to Edward of retaining that support (and preferably extending it) was considerable if he was to maintain his rule. It is not clear that these garrisons were challenged to any significant degree until the autumn of 1310. This can be partially attributed to the fact that King Robert was preoccupied with fighting the Comyn and MacDougal interests in the north and west, and, perhaps to a limited degree, the nature of the forces available to him. The bulk of his troops would seem to have been recruited in the south-west, the west Highlands and the Isles, areas from which he could not expect to raise much in the way of the mounted men-at-arms that he would need to conduct extensive operations in the south and east.

By 1310 he must have been able to extend his rule into areas where he could call on the service of men-at-arms. Not enough perhaps to confront Edward II's expedition of 1310, but enough to harass his retreat and then make a descent on Lothian. A series of truces from November 1309 to the summer of 1310 had allowed Robert to pursue his enemies in the west of Scotland while preventing any expansion by the Plantagenet administration. The end of the truces and the withdrawal of Edward's army gave Robert the opportunity to descend on Lothian in sufficient strength to prevent serious intervention by the garrisons at Edinburgh and Linlithgow, but not, apparently, enough strength seriously to threaten the security of the towns or castles. The Lanercost chronicler tells us '... Robert and his people invaded Lothian and inflicted much damage on those who were in the king's peace',[56] an indication that not everyone resident in Lothian could be considered to be 'in the peace' of King Edward. By November 1312 Edward II was obliged to instruct the commanders of his garrisons in Lothian, Roxburghshire and Berwickshire to prevent their men from infringing truces that the communities of those counties had been obliged to purchase from King Robert.[57]

The absence of reports of actions between the English garrisons and King Robert's troops could be seen as evidence that the garrisons largely had the upper hand. The Scots were unable to force the surrender of castles or, so far as we can tell, deny territory to the administration until some time after 20 August 1313 when the last recorded requisition of stores for Linlithgow from Berwick was authorised.[58] The fall of Linlithgow must surely have had a disheartening affect on Edward's supporters in Lothian, but there were problems within the administration itself. By 1313 the commanders of the garrisons at Edinburgh and Berwick had either lost control of their men or connived at their activities as robbers and kidnappers. The failure to prosecute the guilty parties brought the administration into disrepute, and complaints from the Earl of Dunbar and Sir Adam Gordon failed to move Edward II to take effective action.[59] Edward was not unaware of the difficulties facing his Scottish supporters generally, not just in Lothian. As King Robert extended and consolidated his rule it must have become increasingly clear to the men in Edward's peace that the situation was unlikely to improve without a major intervention by an English army. Edward did make an attempt to mount an offensive in 1310 but could not bring the Scots to battle and failed to make any impression on the situation.[60] Neither troops nor provisions, though demanded in considerable quantities, were forthcoming in adequate quantity and in July 1310, having spent the better part of a year in the north of England and southern Scotland for no discernible gain, he left Berwick for London, giving the Scots a tremendous propaganda victory since they could claim to have repelled the invader without coming to blows. Even so, the fact that the Edwardian administration in Lothian, and throughout the south-east generally, survived at all over the following three years is a testament to its general effectiveness and the extent of its acceptance in the community.

By the close of 1312 Robert I had shown that he could mount operations virtually anywhere in Scotland by making a surprise attack on Berwick which apparently was compromised by a dog barking at the approach of the Scots.[61] The town was held, but the commanders (and complements) of garrisons must have become more aware of their vulnerability. By November 1313 Edward was thanking Lothian landholders for their steadfast support and promising them positive action in the form of a major expedition.[62] His letter lists only seven men as recipients of such letters: Adam de Gordon, Edward de Letham, Robert de Coleville, John Laundells, Alexander Stewart, William de Soulis and Thomas de Somerville. Whilst accepting that these men may have been identified as leaders of their local communities, or even perhaps that they were men who had been entrusted with leadership roles in the Plantagenet administration, their small number needs some consideration. They were not all primarily Lothian men, and probably all had interests in other parts of the country, thus they can hardly be considered a sample of the Lothian political community specifically just because they were all southern nobles. The long-term reliability of even this small group of men must have been open to question. Thomas Somerville had been one of the men who had joined the Bruce party in 1306[63] and John Laundells – described as 'dominus' (lord) – managed to make his peace with King Robert sometime before 1316, when he was a witness to a royal confirmation.[64]

Presumably Edward's declared intention of seeking out the Scots in difficult terrain was not far from the truth; Edward can hardly have expected that Robert would even accept or offer battle, let alone force it. Whatever Edward's general campaign policy in 1314 – if he really had one – his goals were surely more ambitious than the recovery and retention of Lothian. The appearance of a major field force would be an encouragement to the community and discourage defection to the Scots. On the basis of past experience it would be reasonable for Lothian men to assume that King Robert would refuse combat and withdraw across the Forth, allowing Edward to reinstate his administration in areas recently lost, regaining strongholds like the peel at Linlithgow and its satellite establishment at Livingston. More importantly, if Stirling Castle was relieved and the Scots refused battle and retired, Edinburgh Castle, which had fallen to Randolph in March through a coup-de-main operation,[65] would probably be regained as well. If Lothian men thought that Edward's expedition of 1314 was likely to restore his administration they would have been very rash indeed to have declared for Bruce in time to serve in his army at Bannockburn, though at least one, Sir Alexander Seton, whose interests lay primarily in Lothian and Berwickshire, appears to have seen which way the wind was blowing and defected on the eve of the main battle.[66]

PART 3: 1314–1329

The attitude of the Lothian political community to both Bruce and Plantagenet governments seems to have been broadly similar; whichever party could provide the better quality of 'lordship' could reasonably expect to enjoy extensive acceptance and a considerable level of material support. Edward had been able to recruit men-at-arms in significant numbers for paid service;[67] presumably his administrators had been able to collect military service or there would surely be evidence of fines, if not forfeitures for defect of service. Equally, the lack of recorded opposition to Robert I after 1314 and the incidence of Lothian men serving in his armies until the peace of 1328 and at Halidon Hill indicate an acceptance of the Bruce party as the de facto government. This is not to say that the Bruce party enjoyed the wholehearted support of the minor lords of Lothian, only that they apparently fulfilled their obligations to the crown, at least sufficiently not to lose their properties for defect of service. In some measure, the ease with which Lothian free tenants seem to have changed allegiance (and we should bear in mind that that 'ease' may not have been very apparent to the men and women in question) may have been the product of their traditional relationship with the crown. The absence of a magnate whose interests lay primarily in Lothian meant that the primary source of lordship and patronage in the sheriffdom was the king's government.

Robert I may not have been able to impose his rule in Lothian before June 1314, but he was certainly able to impose it thereafter, and, to a great extent, was able to keep the war out of the sheriffdom, largely by mounting operations in Ireland and the North of England.[68] In 1322 Edward II made a serious attempt to restore his administration through force of arms. Although he could raise an army and take it into Lothian,[69] he could not force the Scots to accept battle. King Robert stripped Lothian of provisions and retired across the Forth, keeping his army at Culross until the failure of Edward's fleet to deliver provisions forced him to withdraw.[70] The Scots pursued the English into Yorkshire, winning a striking victory at Byland, from which Edward himself was fortunate to escape.

Robert's ability to carry out a scorched earth policy is clear evidence that he could enforce his will in Lothian.[71] It might be expected that the damage inflicted on his subjects there might cause resentment, but if the community identified the destruction of their property with the aggression of Edward II rather than the policies of Robert I, the popularity of the Bruce cause might actually be enhanced, particularly if Robert made arrangements for the sustenance of those who suffered losses.

Additionally, his willingness to destroy the sheriffdom would have been an indication to the English that he was prepared to ruin it to deny it to them, and to the men of Lothian he would not tolerate resistance to his rule or acquiescence to the enemy. Army service for Lothian men after 1314 was not simply a matter of serving the Bruce cause within the confines of the sheriffdom. King Robert's devastating incursions into the north of England became something of a regular fixture, culminating in the Weardale campaign of 1327 which forced recognition of his kingship from Edward III – or at least from his mother, Isabella, and her partner, Roger Mortimer.[72] The participation of Lothian men in the campaigns of King Robert after 1314 is not of itself a sure indication of the political preferences of the community as a whole, only of the ability of the Bruce party to successfully demand service from that community. It would not be unreasonable to assume that a considerable proportion of the men and women with military obligations would have been happy to avoid making any overt political commitment at all, let alone take up arms in support of Robert I. Nonetheless it would seem that the greater part of the political community of Lothian were prepared to accept his kingship and that they were prepared to discharge the various obligations attached to landholding. Had there been widespread refusal to accept Bruce lordship – and the military commitments that would be required – there would surely have been a spate of forfeitures. It could be argued that the instruments of such forfeitures might not have survived since there would have been no great value in preserving them, but the expectation would have been that the king would have granted such properties to his adherents. Robert I certainly did grant lands and privileges to Lothian men but there is little to indicate that the fall of the English administration in Lothian gave him extensive assets in the sheriffdom with which he could reward supporters. Interestingly, the man who benefited most from the King's patronage was probably Sir Alexander Seton, who, though he declared for Robert I in 1306, returned to Plantagenet allegiance shortly thereafter and remained in that allegiance until the Battle of Bannockburn in 1314. Robert was doubtless pleased to accept Sir Alexander's homage and fealty, but his rewards were probably more a product of his role in the Bruce administration after 1314 and the need to build a structure of Bruce supporters in the south and east than of his timely defection on the battlefield.

PART 4: 1328-1341

If the Bruce party achieved acceptance in Lothian[73] after Bannockburn without serious opposition due to the propensity of the political community to accept the 'government of the day', was that situation, or rather the reverse of it, prevalent in the periods following Dupplin Muir and Halidon Hill? There seems to be no evidence to suggest that Edward Balliol was able to establish his authority effectively in Lothian in the autumn of 1332 and there seems to be no record of a concerted resistance to Edward III in Lothian sufficient to have merited any discussion in surviving record of 1334–35. This might be construed as evidence that the political community of Lothian was, initially at least, prepared to accept a change of kingship. The cession to Edward III of the southern counties by Edward Balliol may have been accepted in 1334–35, though there is little evidence to support or refute that acceptance. Certainly by 1335–36 about one hundred Lothian men and women had been forfeited.[74] Some of these – Godfrey Broun and William de Fresselay – had certainly been in the Bruce party before 1314, and others had benefited from Bruce patronage at the expense of Plantagenet supporters – for example Walter de Bickerton who had apparently become the owner of the Luffness property that had once belonged to the de Pinkney family – but it would surely be unlikely that all of the hundred or more people forfeited during (or perhaps 'by') 1335–36 had been active Bruce supporters or that they had benefited from Bruce patronage if they were not active in his cause. Perhaps we should regard these persons as people who were not so much in the Bruce party as opposed to the Plantagenets. The absence of a document comparable to the Ragman Roll exercise of 1296 does not mean that the new administration did not seek the homage of these individuals. Given the absence of English, let alone Scottish shrieval registers for Lothian in 1334–35 this is hardly a surprise. The freeholders forfeited in 1335–36 would not have constituted anything like a majority of the political community, but they would have been a significant portion of the whole. There is no readily apparent pattern to their rejection of Plantagenet government. There was a greater incidence of forfeiture in the constabulary of Linlithgow than in Haddington, but not enormously so, and the lower incidence of forfeiture in 1334–35 may have been a product of the Earl of Dunbar's allegiance to Edward III. In 1335–36, when the Earl had defected to the Bruce party the incidence of forfeiture rose noticeably in Haddington, but only by a very small margin in Linlithgow. Curiously, Edward does not seem to have considered the reconstruction of Linlithgow to be a worthwhile project, assuming perhaps that it was redundant as long as he held Stirling, nor did he seek to restore Edinburgh Castle until his administration had been in place for some time.

That as many as 100 freeholders and significant tenants should feel sufficiently confident of an eventual Bruce victory to risk life and property suggests that the position of Edward III was less than secure and/or that all of these individuals had made themselves unacceptable to the Plantagenet government through military activity. It is unlikely that they were forfeited simply for accepting Bruce lordship after 1314 or the incidence of forfeiture would be very much greater since presumably all of the free tenants of Lothian had accepted that lordship. Only about one in five was prosecuted.

It is possible that the high number of forfeitures that had been made by 1335–36 was a product of the battle at Culblean in October 1335, where several hundred men from south of the Forth served. However the compotus of 1335–36 may be a reflection of the number of men who were not willing to accept Edward's lordship in 1334–35. The capture of Gilbert Talbot and other English knights near Linlithgow, the first recorded opposition to the Plantagenet–Balliol administration in Lothian,[75] certainly indicates that the occupation was not entirely secure, but the defection of the Earl of Dunbar was almost bound to influence local opinion. Presumably his submission to Edward III after Halidon Hill had encouraged some at least to accept Edward III as their king in 1333. However if March was prepared to declare for the Bruce party at a time when there were English garrisons all around his chief property (Berwick, Roxburgh, Edinburgh once it had been refortified and possibly Dirleton and Yester[76] as well) he must have decided that the risks of rejecting Bruce lordship were greater than the risks of rejecting that of Edward III. Naturally the Earl of Dunbar would have had to have taken a rather wider view of events than the average Lothian free tenant, but he would also have to take the views of his tenants and the local political community in general into account. He may have come to the conclusion that the conquest, or rather the retention, of even the south-east of Scotland was beyond the power of the Plantagenet administration, a conclusion perhaps reinforced in December 1334 by the fact that Edward III failed to lift the siege of Dundarg, leading to the surrender of Henry

Beaumont,[77] a crucial supporter of the Balliol cause in the north-east.[78] Equally he, and indeed men like Sir William Douglas of Lothian and Sir Alexander Ramsay, may have felt that the weight of local opinion favoured the Bruce cause (or at least rejected the Plantagenet one) and that if they wanted to have credibility and influence in the region they had best adopt a 'patriotic' position in politics.

If the Bruce party could secure northern Scotland in the 1330s as they had two decades before, there was every chance that they could regain Lowland Scotland thereafter; not perhaps through a general engagement as at Bannockburn, but through a steady campaign, regaining territories through local superiority. The high incidence of forfeitures, even if they were the product of political activity – which by the nature of the situation must surely have meant military activity for the majority of those forfeited – need not be seen as evidence of outright Bruce support so much as of a rejection of Plantagenet lordship. The garrisons of Edward I and Edward II maintained control of Lothian quite effectively for nearly two decades but they were not necessarily popular. The acceptance of Bruce lordship during the siege of 1338 should not be taken as proof of a general antipathy, but a foreign garrison is seldom popular anywhere. Further, if the townspeople saw the fall of the castle and of the Edwardian administration as inevitable – not an unreasonable conclusion in early 1314 or by the summer of 1338 – they might have been well-advised to nail their colours to the Bruce mast as quickly as they could. Lothian men who saw an eventual Bruce triumph or at least a Plantagenet defeat as being inevitable might adhere to the Bruce party for the same reasons. Some may have genuinely believed that in the long term the Bruces could offer better lordship, but we should not discount patriotic or nationalist motivation as a possibility. In the early 1300s and again in the 1330s some men described themselves primarily as Scots rather than Bruce, Balliol or Plantagenet partisans by declaring that their allegiance was to 'the lion', the heraldic device of the king of Scotland.[79] Fourteenth-century men and women certainly knew their nationality;[80] there are far too many examples of a clear division in the minds of contemporary writers to think otherwise and there may have been a substantial element in the political community that did not so much favour the Bruce cause as reject the Plantagenet–Balliol alternative.

The extensive war damage recorded in the English accounts for Lothian (and the picture is much the same for other southern and eastern counties) demonstrates that the administration of Edward III could not exert the same level of control or provide the same level of protection that had been afforded to the community under either the first Edwardian government or under that of Robert I. There would seem to be no particular pattern to the damage; indeed, it is not clear to what extent the damage in any one instance was the product of Scots or English activity. The Scots had an interest in compelling allegiance: raiding the lands of those who would not accept Bruce lordship as a warning to others would have been a very conventional approach. Equally, burning out the property of defectors as an object lesson to waverers would probably have seemed a useful policy to the English. In all likelihood troops on both sides were less than concerned about whose property was attacked than they were about exerting control over communities and denying resources to the enemy. King Robert was able to make communities buy local truces on terms that were very advantageous. If he had not built a reputation for being able to restrain his men to a worthwhile extent his truces would not have been worth buying. Of course, as long as the community was willing to pay for truces King Robert had no need to take his men into Lothian other than to pass through into Roxburghshire. Robert's men had little opportunity to cause damage, whereas the garrison troops were a continual presence which, as we have already seen, was a source of local friction through failure of discipline.[81]

The striking arm of Edwardian garrisons in Lothian invariably comprised bodies of men-at-arms (see Chapter 4). The advantage of a highly mobile, heavily armed and experienced force is obvious; what is significant is that forces of that nature were clearly unable to achieve local dominance in 1313–14. In order to counter such a force at all, King Robert must have had a force of men-at-arms large enough to be able to neutralise the garrison forces. In 1303 Sir John Comyn had been able to assemble a force large enough to defeat a body of men-at-arms on a particular day and under particular circumstances; he was not in a position regularly to confront the garrison forces, let alone contain them. By 1313 King Robert's men-at-arms would seem to have been able to counter their opponents on a daily basis if required to do so. By entering a truce with the community of Lothian he ensured that they did not have to, and therefore they could be deployed to another front, whereas the Edwardian administration in Lothian would have needed to maintain the strength of their garrisons for fear of the Scots breaking the truce and taking castles by surprise and also for the sake of their presence in the community as visible tokens of lordship. As long as King Robert was able to impose good observation of the truce by his troops, the disorderly conduct of the garrisons may have helped eventual acceptance of his 'peace' among Lothian men and women after the summer of 1314, since he would have demonstrated that he could offer, if not 'good lordship', certainly better lordship and more consistent protection than that offered by the Plantagenets.

It would be misleading to say that Robert I encountered no opposition from Lothian landholders throughout the rest of his reign: he did, but not on account of Lothian issues. Sir Peter Lubaud was forfeited of Cowden some time before 1316,[82] possibly for compromising a planned attempt on Berwick.[83] Sir Alexander Moubray and others entered the peace of Edward II in 1320–21 on account of the De Soulis conspiracy,[84] but these men were moved by 'national' political considerations; the location of their properties was not a factor. Although the De Soulis conspiracy was a failure, it was evidence that Robert I was less than secure in his kingship and may have encouraged Edward II to mount his 1322 campaign. If Barbour is to be taken at face value, De Soulis had a force of over 300 men in 'livery',[85] not an expression normally associated with the early fourteenth century, but perhaps in this context indicating men-at-arms bearing a device of their own as opposed to bearing the device of their leader, in which case De Soulis had mobilised a powerful force. The fact that he was taken at Berwick perhaps suggests that a considerable portion of his force might have been recruited from exiled Scots, the men who would later be known as the 'disinherited' and not, therefore, an indication of widespread opposition to the Bruce party among the existing political communities of Scotland. The very fact that this incident is known as the 'De Soulis' conspiracy is evidence of the success of Bruce propaganda[86]. The real rival for Scottish kingship was Edward Balliol, son of King John. His success at Dupplin Muir[87] enabled him to have himself made king at Scone and to hold a parliament at Perth, but the extent of his rule is open to question; he does not seem to have spent much time in Lothian during his brief kingship between Dupplin Muir in August 1332 and his flight from Annan at Christmas. In 1336 Robert de Byncestre claimed that he had been granted the lands of Sir Alexander Seton by Edward Balliol after his first battle and that he had enjoyed seisin of those lands until the cession of 2000 librates of southern Scotland to Edward III by Edward Balliol, who had since granted them to Sir William Eynesford.[88] Since Seton had joined the Plantagenet peace by December 1333 (though he had been forfeited again by 1335–36) when he served as one of the jurors making an extent of Berwickshire[89] and attended Edward Balliol's parliament at Holyrood in February 1334[90] there must be some question as to when exactly Sir Robert had enjoyed possession of the properties. Presumably he had not had them for very long given the short period between the forfeiture of Sir Alexander by Edward Balliol and his subsequent acceptance into Balliol peace in 1334 or his forfeiture by 1335–36 by Edward Plantagenet.

The extent to which Plantagenet government was established after Halidon Hill is impossible to ascertain. Since there was resistance to it, in the shape of William Douglas of Lothian among others, it evidently existed. In August or September 1334 the Guardian, the Earl of Moray, led his troops into Lothian to meet Douglas, recently released from prison, who had raised a body of troops and commenced operations against the English. Bower tells us that the exploits of Douglas would make a 'large and attractive book', and were evidently sufficiently impressive to make Douglas the chief focus of Bruce, or at least anti-Plantagenet–Balliol, sympathy in the sheriffdom. As such he was a natural ally of Moray in the sense that they shared an enemy. Moray could hardly avoid endorsing Douglas' rise to prominence so long as Douglas was harrying the enemy. Their co-operation was brought to an end by Moray's capture while escorting the count of Namur from the fight at Edinburgh. By the time Moray was liberated in the autumn of 1340 the English administration in Lothian was close to defeat and Douglas had established himself as a prominent war-leader among the Scots as a whole, not only in Lothian.

The large number of forfeitures made by Edward III in 1335–36 may be an indication of the success of the Bruce party in making themselves acceptable as a source of lordship. The promotion by Robert I of men like Alexander Seton or of John de Stirling[91] by Edward III to positions of some prominence as Lothian landholders no doubt provided, or was intended to provide, a source of leadership loyal to the crown. It is possible that since so many Lothian tenants held their property directly from the King, the introduction of such a figure would not necessarily be popular. The rights, responsibilities and privileges of free tenants may not have been very clearly defined, but it would not be surprising if the lairds of Lothian felt they might be compromised in some way by the rise of a great lord in their midst. It would not be surprising either, if a similar condition applied to the relationship between the Lothian gentry and the English crown. Under Scottish kingship Lothian freeholders might or might not approve of the king, but they could hope to get access to him should the need arise. Gaining the royal ear under English kingship might be rather more difficult. One attraction of Robert's kingship in 1314 was obviously military success. Lothian landholders – and the rest of the people of the county of course – had a vested interest in peace, however if they had to have war, much better that the focus of that war be southern Scotland or northern England or Ireland; in fact, anywhere but Lothian. As long as the Bruce party was in the ascendant militarily there were attractions for the martially inclined in Bruce adherence, and in the period of Bruce administration from 1314 to 1333 they had shown that while they could not *always* keep war out of Lothian, they could prevent *continual* warfare there if they could keep the focus of the conflict to the border areas. When circumstances allowed King Robert was prepared to offer, even force battle, but he was seldom in a position to confront large-scale invasions, preferring to adopt a 'scorched earth' policy. This can hardly have been popular with the people whose crops were destroyed, but it was certainly effective militarily. Any damage done to King Robert's political standing would have to be compared to how much the populace came to perceive Edwardian ambitions as the real source of their troubles.

Initially the position of Edward III's administration was similar in many respects to their predecessors under Edward II in the sense that for a while the presence of men-at-arms in garrisons at Stirling, Bothwell and Edinburgh by the winter of 1335 was sufficient to deter the Scots from mounting operations in Lothian, and in the sense that the ability of the administration to protect the community was eventually compromised by the inability to deploy enough men-at-arms to counter the Scots. Apart from the obvious consideration that only a strong force of cavalry can consistently impose its will on another body of cavalry it is worth noting that virtually all of the recorded actions (with the exception of a handful of general engagements and the capture of castles) which took place in Lothian throughout the Wars of Independence were, so far as we can tell, fought by men-at-arms. There is no doubt that there were archers and other infantry in the garrisons of the Plantagenet administration and we must assume that they took an active part in the defence of their establishments, but the task of an occupation garrison is primarily to exert control far beyond the perimeter of a castle or camp; not to man the walls but to exclude the enemy from the vicinity. Unlike the administrations of Edward I and Edward II, the garrisons of Edward III were apparently unable to fulfil that objective sufficiently well to exclude Bruce party forces from operating throughout Lothian after 1335 at the latest.

In the 1330s Sir John de Strivelin felt secure enough to leave his post, taking a large portion of the men-at-arms of the garrison with him, on an expedition to Fife to lift the Scottish siege of Cupar in May 1336,[92] but he was unable to prevent the guardian, Andrew Murray, from imposing a siege of Edinburgh Castle in June 1338.[93] The guardian appointed a Sheriff of Lothian, and while the siege was in progress, what Bower calls the 'community of Lothian' accepted his authority. It would seem, then, that the heavy cavalry element of the garrison was unable to confront their Scottish equivalents sufficiently to prevent the Scots leading a major force into Lothian. The Scots, on the other hand, do not seem to have felt confident of their ability to withstand intervention from another force. The approach of a relief column seems to have caused the Scots to lift the siege and move to Clerkington in order to meet the relief column, which they met and defeated at Crichtondene.[94] This was a tactical victory for the Scots, but their inability to restore the siege suggests that they had doubts about their ability to maintain a close investment in the face of English reinforcements, or, possibly, that they had expected the relief column to be stronger than it was, dispersed the infantry and detached a cavalry force to observe and/or disrupt the relief column. Finding that it was smaller than expected, the Scots offered battle successfully, but were not in a position to restore the siege. Although the garrison had obviously lost the ability to dominate the tactical situation in Lothian, they were not sufficiently intimidated to surrender, even in the wake of a battlefield defeat, which suggests that although Crichtondene was certainly a victory for the Scots, it did not materially alter the balance of power in Lothian. The acceptance of Laurence de Preston as sheriff should be seen in that context. The Bruce party, it would seem, could depend on the support of the Lothian community, or at least a significant proportion of it, if they could demonstrate military control. Once the siege of Edinburgh had been lifted the Plantagenet administration presumably reasserted its position to some degree.

How effectively is open to question; we might assume that the lack of sheriff court accounts in Lothian for 1337–38 (most of the records from 1338–41 relate to the administration of the garrison, not the sheriffdom) and thereafter is an indication that the Lothian administration had become an outpost of a forward policy of defence and obstruction rather than a serious attempt to retain Lothian as part of Edward III's domain. The outbreak of war between England and France in 1337[95] was obviously going to be a huge burden on Edward's resources and would almost inevitably reduce the effort that he could devote to his Scottish campaigns, but retention of castles in Scotland, particularly Edinburgh and Stirling, would help to keep the Scots occupied and reduce their ability to intervene effectively in support of the French and perhaps help to deny the Scots full lordship in Lothian and keep them from making further progress in Roxburghshire and Berwickshire.

The fighting in Lothian was not limited to operations connected with sieges. Sir Alexander Ramsay was able to conduct operations from Hawthornden,[96] the caves there providing what Bower calls an underground fortress. That Ramsay could base himself and his 'ioli' (gallant, or daring) company of men-at-arms[97] right in the middle of Lothian is a strong indication that the Edinburgh garrison was unable to carry the fight to the Scots effectively. The security of Hawthornden may have been a product of the nature of the force available to the Plantagenet administration, largely men-at-arms. Without adequate infantry protection, the men-at-arms of the garrison would be unable to close with Hawthornden without risking several excellent ambush positions whichever approach they chose, and the garrison did not have any close combat infantry at all so far as record reveals. The problem would seem to have been overcome by November 1338, when supplies were authorised for Sir Laurence Abernethy to garrison and provision 'the Castle of Hawthornden',[98] apparently recently captured from the Scots, though since that is the only reference to a Plantagenet force there it seems likely that the stronghold was recovered by the Scots shortly thereafter. The small complement of infantry allotted to the Lothian garrison suggests that the general tactical policy of the administration was to rely on the mobility of the man-at-arms element of the sheriff's force. Evidently that force was not sufficient to contain their counterparts in the Scottish army. In late 1337 Sir William

Douglas of Lothian offered battle to Sir John Strivelin at the Crags of Craigie (not located, but almost certainly in West Lothian, and probably in the vicinity of Torphichen) and was able to win the day, though Bower's claim that he did so with fifty men against 500 must be taken with a pinch of salt.[99] Sir John's garrison seems never to have amounted to as many as 500 men-at-arms, and even if it did, he would be most unlikely to lead the entirety of his force on a foray. He may have been able to call upon the customary military obligations of those Lothian landholders who were still in the peace of Edward III as well as those in paid garrison service so the limited number of men on garrison muster rolls should not be seen as the whole extent of his offensive capacity. Even so, the Plantagenet administration was clearly unable to maintain operational superiority over the Scots in mobile combat. Bower[100] patriotically records only one success (a fight at Blackburn from which Sir William Douglas was lucky to escape) for the Plantagenets against the success of the Scots in actions at the Crags of Craigie, Blacksollings, Burghmuir and Edinburgh castles, Crichtondene (where, according to Wyntoun, Douglas led a company of one hundred knights and men-at-arms in a successful attack against a wing of the English army), an unlocated action against Sir Laurence Abernethy which involved six different clashes, the defence of Dunbar Castle and the eventual capture, after a second siege, of Edinburgh Castle in March 1341.

Command of forces was by formal appointment in the Plantagenet party, but was, to some extent anyway, assumed by members of the Bruce party. Sir John de Strivelin's leadership role was a part of his general responsibility as an officer of Edward III, but that of Alexander Ramsay would have been the product of a number of factors. As a Lothian baron, Alexander enjoyed formal control over the men of his barony and a degree of influence over neighbours through his local prominence and familial relationships. But he was also a local focus for Bruce sympathisers, for those whose properties had been, or were at risk of forfeiture, for those who just resented the English and for those in search of adventure. The same is true of Sir William Douglas of Lothian, whose martial abilities allowed him to extend his influence beyond his tenants and relatives. By the time Edinburgh Castle fell to Douglas in 1341 he had established himself as one of the two most powerful men in Lothian (the other being Sir Alexander Ramsay), though in 1333 he had been only one of a dozen or more barons in the constabulary of Linlithgow.

The capture of Edinburgh Castle marked the end of Edwardian administration in Lothian, but not of military activity. Edward's interest in acquiring territory in Scotland would seem to have waned by the time he visited the Earls of Salisbury and Arundel at the Siege of Dunbar in 1337,[101] so to what end did he maintain expensive garrisons there for the next four years? In fact, Edward had little choice. The only way he could have relinquished Edinburgh without a fight or an ignominious withdrawal would have been as part of a general settlement with the Scots, who, in the military climate of the late 1330s, would hardly have been likely to accept any settlement presented by Edward. Perhaps more significantly he must have questioned the effectiveness of his administration in southern Scotland generally. The Earl of Dunbar had defected to the Scots more than three years previously, but his castle at Dunbar, surrounded by English-held castles, was still held against Edward III. Indeed, the fact that the earl had chosen to defect at all was a strong sign that the administration was not gaining the acceptance of the community, but was losing its credibility as an alternative to Bruce lordship. The failure of Edward III's officers at Dunbar is something of a curiosity. Evidently the administration was able to undertake a major siege without fear of serious intervention by the Scots, though they were unable to prevent a force of men-at-arms under Sir Alexander Ramsay of Dalhousie from entering the castle, mounting a sally against the siege force and departing again.[102] It is possible that Edward hoped to draw the Scots into offering battle to raise the siege, but the castle does not seem to have been in grave danger at any point.[103] This has implications for the confidence of the defenders. It was unlikely that the Scots would offer battle under such circumstances given their defeat at Halidon only four years previously. With no reasonable expectation of a relief force the defenders must have been confident that they could hold out beyond the ability of the administration to maintain the siege. This in turn throws a light on the state of the Edwardian government. If Lothian, Roxburghshire and Berwickshire were secure in Edward's rule it seems very odd that the garrison of Dunbar castle should undergo a siege of twenty-two weeks confident that the administration would be unable to force their surrender.

Regardless of exactly why the siege was abandoned, it must have been both an encouragement to Bruce supporters and a blow to the Plantagenet party in Lothian. Edwardian administration could hardly be

considered secure if there was a strong castle held by the enemy immediately to the southeast of the county. Lifting the siege amounted to an
admission that Edward's government was no longer consistently able to
direct the course of the war.

During the first period of Bruce administration in Lothian (1314–
33) Edward II continued to authorise officials to accept Scots into his
peace[104] and even to grant benefices in Scotland to petitioners.[105] The
latter perhaps helped men seeking other appointments; they could hope
for a sympathetic hearing if they could claim to have been ejected or
prevented from taking up their appointments by the Scots. To some
extent Edward's acceptance of Scots into his peace would have been a
means of fostering opposition to Robert I; the implication being that
men who crossed King Robert were very likely to find favour with
Edward II. Edwardian restoration in Lothian in particular and southern
Scotland generally must have seemed a far-fetched proposition in 1314,
but by adopting a policy of offering his peace to Robert's opponents
Edward perhaps helped to nurture support among minor gentry for
the party that would become known as the 'disinherited'.[106] Without
Edward's protection and, in some cases, financial support, a policy continued by Edward III until 1333, there might have been a rather smaller
body of men to accompany Edward Balliol to Dupplin Muir, though it
is worth bearing in mind that a large proportion of Balliol's 1332 army
was provided by English lords.[107] If such a 'constituency' of support
had developed it would seem not to have been important enough to
have made much impression on the situation after 1341. Even after the
dramatic victory at Neville's Cross in 1346, Edward made no move to
re-occupy Lothian.

Edward III's initial approach to the distribution of garrisons may be
an indication of how much effort he had originally been prepared to
expend on the task. When Edward took control of Lothian and the other
ceded territories he does not seem to have intended to build a network of strongholds across Scotland, but to have concentrated his efforts
on a relatively small number of centres. In Edward II's reign there had
been two major garrisons in Lothian, Edinburgh and Linlithgow, and
a number of smaller establishments, including a peel at Livingston, the
Hospitaller Preceptory at Torphichen, baronial castles such as Dirleton
and Yester[108] and whatever constituted the administrative presence
at Haddington. With the benefit of Bothwell, Stirling, Roxburgh and

Dunbar in the surrounding area, the lack of a Plantagenet-held strong-hold in Lothian may not have been considered an issue if the political community could be persuaded to support Edward III's rule; after all, Robert I had managed to keep Lothian securely in his power for nearly twenty years without a castle or, so far as we are aware, maintaining a force there. Edward's decision to re-fortify Edinburgh was not part of his original scheme of administration, but a reaction to events, primarily the defeat and capture of the Count of Gueldres there in 1335 which demonstrated the vulnerability of troop movements through areas without secure refuges and possibly to the capture of Sir Richard Talbot (who apparently had to find a ransom of £2000), Sir John de Strivelin and Sir John Felton[109] near Linlithgow. There may have been other pressures, not strictly military, which encouraged him to take on the expense of rebuilding a castle and providing it with a garrison. Edinburgh was probably already seen as the most significant town in Scotland, with the possible exception of Perth, which, in 1335, was ostensibly the centre of Edward Balliol's Scotland and a forward position of Edward III's military establishment. Without a strong castle and garrison Edinburgh would have been vulnerable to sudden attacks by the Scots; if Edward could not defend Edinburgh he could hardly hope to become master of southern Scotland. The absence of Linlithgow from his plans seems to indicate a different approach to both strategic and tactical considerations compared to that of Edward I and Edward II. They had developed a chain of fortresses that could rely on one another for support; Edward III seems to have adopted a similar policy for northern Scotland, installing royal officials or supporting the installation of those of sympathetic barons like Sir Henry Beaumont and Sir David Strathbogie, but in southern Scotland he made use of a much smaller range of locations. Perhaps in the hope that Edward Balliol would successfully assert his kingship and secure the transfer of the ceded counties to Edward III without meaningful resistance, he seems to have pinned his hopes on a more aggressive policy with a greater tendency to combat than the containment that seems to have been the objective of the garrisons in 1310–14. Edward's willingness to take large armies to Scotland can be seen as evidence that he still intended to achieve the cession of the southern counties, though he seems to have achieved little by the exercise.

We can be confident that had he been offered battle under circumstances that he felt suited him, he would have been quick to accept, but we should question whether he would have been likely to expect such an eventuality. The Scots had not developed a 'large army' tactical format that could counter the combination of the longbow archer and the man-at-arms, nor could they maintain a sufficient body of men-at-arms to force a purely 'chivalric' engagement on a large scale. The Scots would seem to have been able to raise a force of men-at-arms large enough to contain the man-at-arms element of a major garrison; they had been able to mount sieges of Edinburgh Castle in 1314, 1338 and in 1341. They could find enough cavalry to overcome even relatively substantial forces of men-at-arms at Roslin and Crichtondene, but could hardly hope to defeat the cavalry element of a major English campaign force. If the Scots were not likely to offer battle, they were still less likely to accept it and forcing battle on the Scots had proved difficult for Edward I and Edward II.

If it is hard to see any material military value in the massive expenditure involved, the political value is perfectly clear. By moving large bodies of men through Scotland Edward demonstrated his military power and expressed confidence in Edward Balliol. The former may have been counter-productive given the conduct of medieval armies, but without the latter Balliol would surely have lost his position more quickly than he did. The more time it took for the Scots to decide between Balliol and Bruce, the longer they would be too preoccupied with internal strife to pose a threat to northern England. Maintaining even a small field army under Edward Balliol would have been far too much of a financial burden to be adopted as a medium or long term policy and in any case, would have been a risky venture. Should that army be defeated the prestige of Edward III as a martial prince, and of English arms generally, would be severely diminished abroad, and the willingness of his English subjects to serve in and pay for a lengthy war of occupation and conquest might be seriously impaired. On the other hand the relatively small expense of maintaining a body of men-at-arms at Stirling that could intervene should Edward Balliol need immediate support would be money well-spent if it helped to keep the Scots in Scotland.

In opting, so far as we can tell, not to have any garrisons at all in Lothian between 1333 and 1335, Edward may have been making a political gesture, or rather two. By not stationing troops in the area he could be seen as having confidence in Edward Balliol's kingship and at the same time he could be seen as deliberately avoiding a potential source of contention with the community. There may even have been a policy motive in the composition of the garrison of Edinburgh; the 1335–36 muster roll is divided into two groups, Scottish and English men-at-arms, though at least two Scots served in the 'English' sub-unit, conveniently described as 'Anglici ad arma'.[110] The 'Scottish' component, almost all of whom would still be serving in the garrison in 1336–37 and a few in 1340, included several surnames to be found in the muster rolls of Edward I and Edward II's garrisons of twenty and thirty years before. It would not be rash to assume that some portion of these men were minor members of the 'disinherited' and other Scots who had either remained with, or joined, the Plantagenet cause after 1314.

The benefits of employing these men in garrisons would have been considerable. The garrison forces as a whole might not seem such an intrusion to the community if a large proportion of the establishment were Scots, the people who had remained in Plantagenet faith needed to be rewarded for their constancy and the garrisons needed men who would have to be paid. By employing Scots opposed to the Bruce party as men-at-arms Edward could be reasonably sure of loyalty from a garrison that had some understanding of the community in which they were stationed. The disadvantages were at least as considerable. The fact that such men were embedded in the community meant that they could negotiate defection to the Bruce party through their network of relatives and associates. William Fairley was pardoned, along with several other men who had served, or would serve in the Edinburgh garrison; including Alexander de Craigie Senior, Alexander de Craigie Junior, and William Dalmahoy,[111] for defecting to the Scots in 1335.[112] Fairley was serving in the Edinburgh garrison as one of the 'Scoti ad arma' in 1335–36,[113] but was no longer serving there by the summer of 1340,[114] and was involved in the capture of the castle in 1341[115] having defected to the Scots for a second time.

Installing a garrison and rebuilding the castle at Edinburgh undoubtedly strengthened Edward's position in eastern Scotland. Although the castle garrison was evidently unable to prevent Bruce forces from raiding in Lothian it would be unreasonable to think that its presence, let alone its activity, was not a factor for which the Scots had to make allowance. In a sense the Edinburgh garrison can be seen as a genuine 'subtracted reserve', that is to say, a portion of the force which has been retained to exploit opportunities or meet unexpected contingencies as opposed to a portion of a force that has not yet been deployed. The only clear example of the garrison in that role is Sir John de Strivelin's foray across the Forth to raise the siege of Cupar Castle.[116] The Cupar operation was a success in immediate tactical terms; the siege was raised and Sir Alexander had performed a notable feat of arms, both factors that would have encouraged the Plantagenet–Balliol party and discouraged Bruce supporters.

It would be rash to conclude that Edward never set much store by the cession of the southern counties by Edward Balliol. The cause of the disinherited gave him an opportunity to achieve the effective subjection of the Scots if he was fortunate or temporarily cripple them if he was not. Without the resources of most of Scotland south of the Forth and Clyde, and dependent on the ability of men who had been absent from Scotland for as much as twenty years to make good claims to extensive lordships in the face of Bruce opposition, Edward Balliol's chances of establishing himself as king were not good. If Balliol were unsuccessful, but could keep up a struggle, the garrisons at Edinburgh, Berwick, Stirling and elsewhere would keep the Scots occupied for some years to come while Edward pursued a campaign in France, from which the potential gains were much greater than anything he could hope to achieve in Scotland. Edward's Scottish operations may have initially been aimed at conquest, but by 1337 at the latest they had become a means of preventing the Scots from significant intervention in what would become the Hundred Years' War.

The effectiveness of Edward's occupation policy is revealed by the apparently large body of men-at-arms from south of the Forth who fought for the Bruce party at Culblean, exempted perhaps from the truce then in force[117] by the fact that they were going north to intervene in a contravention of that truce and by the fact that the Plantagenet administration was confident of success should the Scots adopt a combat policy. It is not necessarily the case that the forfeitures of 1335–36 were in any way connected with that battle, though if they were not that could be construed as evidence for a rather stronger Bruce sympathy than the forfeitures themselves suggest. Any men forfeited for reasons unconnected with Culblean would represent potential Bruce support additional to the men who *had* served there. It is of course possible that the situation should be read the other way round; that participation by Lothian men at Culblean was the product of forfeiture by Edward III, but that would still be an indication of a strong level of resistance to the

Plantagenet administration before November 1335, which, admittedly, is not quite the same thing as proof of strong sympathy for the Bruces.

The fall of Edinburgh Castle marked the end of Plantagenet rule in Lothian itself but the war continued to impinge on the community; Edward's 'burnt Candlemas' campaign in 1356 being the most significant example. The military aim of the campaign would seem to have been no more constructive than an attempt to disrupt the Scottish administration in the south-east and perhaps re-establish control of territory in Berwickshire and Roxburghshire; Roxburgh was regained by the English in 1346 and remained a symbol of English power in Scotland until 1460.[118] The campaign surely had a dramatic impact on the community of Lothian; it is called the *burnt* Candlemas campaign after all, but there would not seem to have been any real plan to achieve a strategic goal other than to disrupt the allies of his other enemy, France. At what point Edward decided to abandon the conquest of Lothian is unclear, though presumably his war in France made it necessary that he should do so. Bower at least was of the opinion that Edward's French war saved the day for the Scots, but by the time the French war started the Plantagenet administration was already well on its way to defeat. Edward Balliol's administration had virtually ceased to exist, the Plantagenet garrisons were at risk, the siege of a single Scottish castle (Dunbar) in the very centre of Edward III's Scotland was abandoned and the Bruce party retained the military initiative despite the concerted efforts of a larger and more prosperous kingdom.

Given Edward's enormous financial commitments and difficulties in recruiting men for service in Scotland this suggests that the entire project was beyond his means or at least that the candle was worth considerably more than the game. A battlefield victory on a grand scale might be enough utterly to disrupt the Scots for a brief period, but not to persuade them to accept a Balliol–Plantagenet division of the country. Then, as now, the ability to destroy the army of the enemy was no guarantee that an occupation government could be imposed successfully.[119] Success in battle, even when dramatic, was evidently not sufficient to cow enough Scots enough of the time into acceptance of the kingship of either Edward Balliol or Edward III. It would seem that the Bruce party – including perhaps an element of Scottish political society that saw the Bruces as no more than the lesser of two evils – were not convinced that the struggle was at an end merely on the strength of defeat in battle. As Clausewitz would have it, '[a defeated state]...often considers the outcome merely as a transitory evil' that can be overcome in future operations.[120] The Scots had 'lost' their war against Edward I in 1296, renewed the conflict in 1297, come to terms in 1304, renewed the fight again in 1306 and triumphed in 1314. There was no good reason for them to assume that they could not do so again in the wake of the campaigns of 1332 and 1333.

Indeed, there were reasons to believe that such a victory could be achieved. Edward III's failure to bring even Lothian under his control, the outbreak of the Hundred Years War, the knowledge that deploying large armies in Scotland had not, after all, brought Edward success, the failure of English arms to contain, let alone defeat, the Bruce party, was matched by political considerations. Prior to 1314 there had been no established tradition of Bruce lordship in Lothian, but in 1314–1332 Bruce sympathy would seem to have been on the increase. By 1333–35 there were two Lothian leaders (William Douglas and Alexander Ramsay) who identified with the Bruce party. To what extent they adopted the Bruce cause from personal political motives and to what extent they did so in order to further their influence as local potentates is impossible to say. If there had been no Bruce sympathy to tap neither Douglas nor Ramsay would have had much of a future as local leaders.[121] They may have been as much led by the local community as leaders of that community. Also, due to the efforts of the 'Good Sir James', the Douglas family had grown to magnate status. That status was derived from Bruce patronage, and would be unlikely to survive should the Balliol–Plantagenet cause prosper. In William Douglas the Bruce party had a figure of political influence and proven military ability from the political community of Lothian. The best Edward III could achieve was Sir John Strivelin, a man imposed on that community by an outside agency whose landholdings had been acquired through the forfeiture of local men and women.

2

RIGHTS AND RESPONSIBILITIES

By the close of the thirteenth century the descendants of the French, English and Flemish adventurers who came to Scotland in the reign of David I or William the Lion had long been assimilated into the nation of Scots.[1] Not all of the men and women who constituted the political community bore English or French names, and not all those who bore English or French names were members of it. The full range of factors which brought an individual into the political community, or kept them out of it, is not clear, but land tenure and military and court service obligations were part, and probably the most significant part, of the equation.

Very broadly we might assume that all barons and knights and a large proportion of landholders would be members of that community, though we might question whether extent of landholding was as important as traditions of political influence attached to particular properties. We cannot be sure that mere possession of land would necessarily bring acceptance into the political community, or even that the lack of it absolutely prevented membership. We can be confident that belonging to the political community was seen as a desirable condition and that landholding, particularly heritable landholding, was an element in obtaining or retaining membership. The privileges and potential for advancement pertaining to the nobility were considerable, but there were political, cultural, judicial and military burdens and obligations to be discharged as well the various duties involved in estate management. In varying degrees these issues affected all of the men and women who formed the political community: the secular landholders, clerics and burgesses whose allegiance was sought, cajoled and extorted by English and Scottish kings in the decades after the deposition of King John in 1296. This chapter examines in turn the relationship between the crown and the political community, the position of the lesser nobility, magnate influence and the extent to which the lot of the clerics and burgesses differed from that of their noble neighbours.

CROWN INFLUENCE

Royal recognition of the importance of locally prominent figures can be glimpsed among the witnesses to an 1136 charter of David I to Holyrood Abbey which was confirmed by Robert I between 1318 and 1327. The witnesses to the original charter include several men of national significance: the Bishops of St. Andrews and Glasgow, the chancellor and the chamberlain, but also William de Graham and Thurstan de Crichton, two Lothian landholders.[2] The witnesses to the confirmation, given between 1318 and 1327, include the Bishops of St. Andrews and Dunkeld and the Earl of Moray, but also Sir Alexander Seton and Sir Robert Keith, both Lothian landholders and both close to the King. Keith, admittedly, was the Marshal of Scotland and therefore had 'national' responsibilities, but Seton was first and foremost a Lothian man. The unnamed witnesses (those covered by 'et aliis multis') would very probably have been Lothian men. Similarly, in 1136, David I had felt it was appropriate to have a charter of local significance witnessed by men of his court, but also by a number of men of Tweeddale and Lothian to indicate approval of the king's actions (in this case a grant to Holyrood Abbey) among the local political community.

Those who were members of that community enjoyed access to the king's court when they sought justice, access to his authority when they sought preferment and access to the king himself when he was in the vicinity, the latter confirming or enhancing the individual's prestige. Since the crown was the most important source of patronage, access to the king at court, in councils and parliaments or in the field was highly desirable to those who sought to improve their position. For the most powerful men and women this access to patronage was generally direct and personal to the king himself. For the less exalted it was still personal, achieved either through direct service to the crown or through the agency of a lord to whom they were attached in some way, whether through landholding, marriage, family tradition or by adoption. Because of the absence of a great Lothian lord the significance of the crown as a source of lordship and patronage can hardly be exaggerated. Lothian may not have had a magnate in the thirteenth century, but the king's favour was highly desirable and could lead to positions of influence and specific families might manage to acquire particular offices in more than one generation. Geoffrey de Mowbray held all three sheriffdoms of Lothian until 1263 when he was replaced by another Lothian man, Sir William Sinclair; a generation later they were in the hands of Roger de Mowbray.[3]

Absence of a Lothian magnate does not imply that no magnates were Lothian landholders, nor that less important Lothian landholders permanently, or even habitually aligned themselves with important men outside Lothian or with the men that Edward I, Edward II, Robert I and Edward III would promote to positions of authority there. Duncan Earl of Fife and Patrick Earl of Dunbar were both significant landholders in Lothian[4] and lesser men and women held land from them, but it is not possible to demonstrate that either had an extensive customary 'constituency' of supporters within Lothian beyond their own tenants. Witness lists are less informative than one might expect; very few charters name more than a selection of witnesses – generally, it would seem, the more prominent persons present. It is not clear either that witnesses, named or unnamed, were necessarily tenants of, or closely associated with, the granter or the grantee. The witnesses described as 'et multis aliis'[5] may be no more than significant neighbours, men with an interest in the area rather than those with a direct relationship with the families or property concerned.

Even the power of the lord over his tenant is questionable given that Edward III empowered the Earl of Dunbar to take possession of the property of any of his tenants forfeited for supporting the Bruce cause in the 1330s,[6] suggesting that the earl could not rely on all of his tenants to follow his lead even in the period immediately after the two significant defeats at Dupplin Muir and Halidon Hill. We should not look for a simple relationship of instruction and obedience however. Even men who were heavily dependent on their lord were also influenced by a wide range of concentric and conflicting loyalties and responsibilities. Loyalty to crown, friends or family might override the relationship of landholder to superior in the same way that loyalty to the king might easily be overridden by the practicalities of the situation. Men who were undoubtedly loyal to King John, or at least sufficiently so to turn out for him in the campaign of 1296, can be found accepting Edward I's lordship, being restored to their properties, performing suit of court and military service throughout the Plantagenet administration of Lothian from 1296 to 1314. Similarly, men who served in Edwardian garrisons throughout the period 1296–1314 can be seen to have entered the peace of Robert I immediately after the Battle of Bannockburn, remaining in his peace until the erection of a new Plantagenet administration after the Battle of Halidon Hill, joining Edward III's peace and still being able to return to the Bruce party when they regained the military ascendancy in the mid 1330s.[7]

In short, kings had to accept that their subjects could not withstand the pressure exerted by the success of the other side. Lothian landholders, like the Morhams or the Setons, who wished to retain their position through changes of government naturally had to be prepared to support the de facto government of the day or be prepared to desert their property in order to give their overt support to the opposition. Some were prepared to do so. In the period between the campaign of 1296 and the Strathord armistice of 1304 a number of southern landholders[8] served against Edward I and in 1306 several were prepared to throw in their lot with Robert I[9] despite the apparent strength of the Plantagenet administration, and several more had joined the Bruce cause by 1312.[10] Equally, many gave military service for wages in Edwardian garrisons, and probably a very large proportion of them discharged customary military obligations attached to landholding. If there was a system for the commutation of such service for money payments no trace of it has survived, and it is reasonable to assume that the bulk of the service was performed (whether in person or by a substitute) since the overwhelming majority of landholders managed to keep their status despite changes of monarch. If they had not discharged their military obligations they would presumably have been forfeited for defect of service.

THE LESSER NOBILITY

Not all of the members of the political community were heritable land-holders, though clearly a great many were. At a more humble level, the men who are described as king's tenants[11] or bishop's tenants[12] on the Ragman Roll do, in some cases, appear as 'County' or 'Burgess' homagers as well, but the majority of them appear only in the former categories. Evidently their status was sufficient to admit them to the lower echelons of the political community, the 'worthy men' of Lothian, but it was not the same as the status of the 'county' homagers or there would have been no need to define their position. There may conceivably have been a distinction that extended to, or was even dependent on, military obligation. Of all the Lothian, Peeblesshire and Roxburghshire king's tenants and bishop's tenants who appear on the Ragman Roll, only one, Thomas Lillok of Roxburghshire, can be identified as serving as a man-at-arms. However Thomas was a county homager as well as a king's tenant so his military status may have been on account of his 'county' landholding. Thomas appears as a 'socius' or 'scutifer' of Sir Simon Fraser or of Sir Simon de Horsbrugh, a Peeblesshire landholder who was serving Edward I as a paid soldier.[13] Thomas' introduction to army service may have not have been connected to landholding at all, but to being a member of a family with sufficient wealth and status to support him in a career opportunity afforded him by a neighbour. Regardless of his career history, the fact that a man as obscure as Thomas Lillok could equip himself adequately as a man-at-arms is a pointer to the level of landholding that could carry, if not the legal obligation of man-at-arms service, the economic and social status to support it.[14]

In most cases men of Thomas' social and political stature seldom feature regularly in records. In part this is a reflection of the survival of documents, but it is also, perhaps more importantly, an indication of the ability of most people to be able to arrange their affairs in such a way as to avoid the dangers of not being on the right side at the right time. That most members of the political and landholding communities were is clearly demonstrated by the great many changes of allegiance which were accepted even at a second or third defection. Even men whose position would seem to have been heavily, or even utterly dependent on Bruce patronage such as Sir Robert Bruce (Robert I's natural son), Sir Robert Lauder and Alexander Seton were all able to make their peace, though in some cases only very briefly, with Edward Balliol or Edward III. Alexander Seton is an extreme example but virtually every prominent family in Lothian was in the peace of the Plantagenets at some point between 1296 and 1341. The majority of individuals either managed to avoid having to make a formal declaration of their allegiance (other than the Ragman Roll exercise of 1296) or crown records of their forfeiture or restoration have not survived. Even so, changes of political allegiance may have been a less regular occurrence than we might expect given the regularity with which historians have discussed the inconstancy of the Scottish medieval nobility in general[15] and the lowland nobility in particular.[16]

Defectors, members of garrisons and prominent members of society figure regularly in documentary record, but what of those, the majority of the political community, who, like William Bachelor, do not? William, a Haddington burgess sufficiently prominent to be one of the burgh's representatives in August 1296, was typical of Ragman Roll homagers in that he would seem not to appear in any other record. The reasons for this 'normal' incidence might be quite varied – death, decline into economic obscurity or forfeiture could all bring about this absence from documentary material, but the most likely explanation is that the individual (or family group for that matter) simply never did anything much that needed to be recorded. Even a relatively prominent member of society might turn up in record only as a witness to the documents of others but their rank and status would of course be more likely to bring them into record in some form. Less prominent men and women who managed to be consistently on the 'right' (i.e. currently more successful) side during the conflicts of the fourteenth century might never find themselves forfeited and would therefore never need restored. If they consistently paid their taxes and discharged their other burdens conscientiously they need never find themselves in court for failure to give service.

The manner in which families such as the Bachelors managed to transfer their allegiance is not made clear in documentary record, but self-evidently many, presumably the vast majority in fact, did so without incurring any serious damage to their status or wealth. Obviously the ability to change allegiance was desirable from the point of view of the individuals concerned, but it was also usually advantageous to the competing sources of authority. Whichever party was in the ascendant had nothing to gain from social or economic dislocation. Kings English and Scottish were primarily interested in furthering their own interests and therefore sought to achieve stability and good order, objectives that were more likely to be realised with the support of the existing structures of local power and influence.

It would be a gross over-simplification to directly equate forfeiture with defection. Men who declared for Robert I in 1306 were forfeited immediately it is true, and the series of forfeitures ordered by Edward II in 1312[17] was certainly aimed at men who had joined the Bruce party in the intervening period, but it is difficult to see a rationale for the delay between defection and pronouncing forfeiture that is explicitly stated in the document. Both of these exercises were undoubtedly intended to 'encourage' continuing loyalty in the political community but the much more extensive series ordered by Edward II in 1335–36 and 1336–37 would seem to have been more a question of disinheriting those land-holders who were not prepared to defect from the Bruce cause to the Plantagenet–Balliol cause and to indicate to the community a deter-mination on the part of Edward III that he would take a far harder line than his father on recalcitrant landholders. Edward II's government very probably disinherited rather more than the seven men whose properties were the subject of an inquisition in 1312,[18] but it would not seem likely that Edward II's forfeitures in Lothian were anything like so extensive as those of Edward III in 1335–36, when over one hundred men and women representing over one hundred properties, were the subject of forfeitures. Naturally several of those forfeited held lands in other coun-ties and their political actions must be seen in the light of their more 'national' role. Northern landholders with minor properties in Lothian might be more influenced by the fact that their main properties lay in areas under Bruce control than the fact that a solitary manor or annual was lost to them for the duration of English administration in Lothian.

One of the most striking features of the sample chosen for this book is the high incidence of actual performed military activity. Of less than three hundred people (of whom twenty-eight were women) at least one hundred can be positively identified as serving as men-at-arms. Many can be identified from garrison muster rolls and horse evaluations, but some from the evidence of their service, that is reports of their conduct in the field – such as being captured or killed in action – or by the fact that they appear as prisoners of war receiving subsistence allowances or being pardoned in exchange for service in the king's army. In all likelihood the figure of one hundred out of three hundred is, if anything, rather conservative. It would be likely, to say the least, that some portion of the men forfeited in 1306, 1312 or 1335 were actually under arms with the Bruce party and virtually none of these men would have served as common infantrymen. They have not been included in the figure of one hundred men-at-arms because their service in that capacity has not been demonstrated beyond question, though there is no doubt that some of them at least must have done so at some point in their career. Similarly, men who appear in record as the leaders of unnamed retinues have been counted as one man only as we have no way of knowing the origins of the members of the retinue. Only Lothian men serving in Edwardian armies and garrisons have been counted in the man-at-arms total of one hundred. This is a matter of some significance to our perception of the operational conditions prevalent in fourteenth-century Lothian.

Our traditional picture of Scottish medieval armies – a preponderance of spearmen with a small, almost token, element of men-at-arms and perhaps a few archers[19] – may not be even vaguely adequate when applied to particular theatres or periods of the war. Arguably, we might even find some support here for the view that part of Edward I's agenda in acquiring Scotland was to enlarge his recruiting grounds.[20] From his administrative relationship with Scotland in 1291–92 Edward would have had a far clearer appreciation of the economic and military potential of medieval Scotland than we can hope to achieve at a distance of over 700 years and without the benefit of the advice and experience of both English and Scottish administrators and nobles, not to mention access to records and registers. If more than one in three of the sample complied for this book can be shown to have performed military service in the period 1297–1341 we can be fairly safe in accepting that of the 300 -plus men that we can associate with Lothian in 1296 at least one hundred would have been socially and economically capable of serving as men-at-arms.

If anything this would be a conservative estimate. The Lothian forfeitures of 1335–36 involved at least a hundred landholders.[21] Not all were primarily Lothian men, though most were, and not all were necessarily forfeited because of their political alignment and activity, but it is clear that the majority must have been. Not all of the men forfeited would have been personally involved in the fighting, but, again, it seems likely that very many of them were and that that they served as men-at-arms in the Bruce interest in that year. During the same period at least twenty-seven men associated primarily with Lothian, such as William de Fairley, Alexander de Dalmahoy and Alexander de Craigie, served for wages in the Edinburgh garrison, and very likely more who served for land without pay if the Plantagenet government was capable of extracting customary military services from the local political community. Between the forfeited landholders, the men in Edinburgh garrison, men who were in the peace of Edward III and no doubt some men who managed to avoid involvement with, or forfeiture by, either side but were equipped to serve if they chose, it is almost unimaginable that there could be any fewer than one hundred men able to give man-at-arms service for land tenure in Lothian.

There were probably Lothian landholders who did not appear on the Roll in the Lothian categories and perhaps others who did not appear at all, and by the standards of medieval Scotland Lothian had a large urban population. Not only the towns of Edinburgh, Linlithgow and Haddington, but many nucleated villages, one at least (Seton) substantial enough to be held in 'free burgh' from the king and to support a weekly licensed market[22] despite the liberties of the Burghs. Certainly men from Edinburgh and Haddington served in garrisons as archers and hobelars for wages; to what extent and by what rationale they served as men-at-arms is not so clear since it is often impossible to be certain of the nationality of men named in payrolls and horse valuations. However John Wyggemore,[23] burgess of Edinburgh, was serving as a man-at-arms in the garrison in 1336–37 alongside at least forty-three other Scots, presumably men of a similar station to himself in terms of the capacity to equip themselves appropriately. John may have been an exceptional case but it would seem unlikely that men of substance would be excused the burden of army service just because they lived in a town.[24] We cannot be certain that people with surnames occurring in both garrison rolls and on the Ragman Roll were necessarily related to one another, but we can be confident that some proportion of them were. The Napiers (Napers) who appear on Lothian garrison muster rolls in 1312[25] and 1338[26] were, more likely than not, related to the Napiers who appear on the Ragman Roll, likewise the various Harpers and Butlers who appear in those, and other, documents.[27] These three family groups appear most often in record in connection with Edinburgh properties and affairs. We might reasonably see them as burghal rather than rural people and we might take this as a further indication that man-at-arms service was not the preserve of prominent freeholders owing knight service but a burden on a rather wider segment of society.[28] It is of course possible that the presence of burgh men in garrisons indicates a general enlarging of the class of men liable for (or expected to be capable of) man-at-arms service, possibly in order to ease the recruitment difficulties of the Edwardian government or possibly to spread the burden of service more widely in a period when casualties (in the widest possible sense, including prisoners of war and those avoiding service as well as those injured or killed) among the men-at-arms were probably high in relation to the amount of service required and the number of men able to perform it.

Man-at-arms service was definitely a very common experience for the nobility, and possibly for other members of the community, so should we consider service of that order of magnitude to be a product of more than traditional knight service obligations? Of more than 1,000 references to the 300 people chosen for this study only four are concerned with knight service and one of those, constituting almost half of the actual service requirements referred to, applies to a barony (Muscamp) in Northumberland. Certainly several of the men were knights, but the overwhelming majority of those serving as men-at-arms were definitely not. It has been pointed out elsewhere that the army service requirements for land tenure, even for very great estates, were not heavy in Scotland. Robert I gave the newly-created Earldom of Moray to Sir Thomas Randolph for the service of only eight knights.[29] Indeed, where knight service is stipulated at all it is often fractional – the service of half, quarter or even one twentieth of a knight.[30] How fractional service was practically expressed is not known, but it is clear that formal knight-service obligations were not sufficient to furnish Scottish kings with a large force of knights. All the same, one sheriffdom, admittedly a large and wealthy one, would seem to have been easily capable of furnishing at least one hundred men-at-arms.

Obviously land tenure obligations were not the only factor encouraging people to give army service; there was also the question of 'career development'. Some men, such as Pierre Lubaud or Sir John de Strivelin or *Scalacronica* author Sir Thomas Grey served in the hope of improving their fortunes through promotion for good service and were undoubtedly attracted to military service in the Edwardian administrations by the prospect of wages. The 12d per day paid to a man-at-arms would need to be accumulated for a long time before it would cover the outlay required for arms, armour and horse. The man whose status and background would enable him to serve as a man-at-arms for pay or for land would be likely to already own the necessary kit for the job. It might be more appropriate to view garrison service, for some at least, as a means of defraying the cost of an investment in horseflesh and armament that could not, in any case, be avoided if the man in question was going to be able to fulfil his traditional military service obligations. However attractive conditions or prospects might be, the overwhelming majority of the people in a position to give man-at-arms service were those with land tenure of some sort. Tenure might not be the reason for their service at a given point in time, but unless they came from the sort of family that did enjoy tenure of relatively high status they would be unlikely to have the skills or equipment required, though the likely presence of men from the burghal community in garrisons as men-at-arms would suggest that the commercial wealth of a family could perhaps confer, for military purpose anyway, the economic and social status which we associate with man-at-arms service.

The overwhelming majority of those Lothian people – almost all of them men – who appear in medieval records at all, do so only once or twice, but even such a slender presence is probably not typical of members of what Edward I called the 'middling' part of the society.[31] Only a fraction of those 295 people appear in record other than on the Ragman Roll, an indication that to appear at all in 'national' or 'crown' records was a rare thing, even in the lives of the prosperous. This should not be construed as evidence of a lack of administration – no doubt fourteenth-century Scots, like their counterparts elsewhere, felt that they were 'intensively' governed – but perhaps more an indication of some of the functions of government in the remit of the sheriff. If Edward I was prepared to authorise his sheriffs and other officers to accept 'middling men' into his peace at their discretion we might reasonably assume that Robert I or David II might empower their sheriffs to do the same thing. Certainly there is no extant Scottish instrument equating to the Ragman Roll recording the fealties of people previously in the peace of the Edwards, but it would be rash to assume that the local administrative structure of Scottish kings did not maintain registers of those due services to the crown. During Edward's administration of Scotland in 1291-92 he appointed commissioners specifically to examine the Scottish crown charters and rolls and mentions William of Dumfries, chancellor to Alexander III and custodian of his records.[32]

Although there are no extant examples from the fourteenth century, the existence of shrieval records and registers is not in doubt; there are several references to them in English crown documents.[33] Just what range of functions was covered by those registers is open to debate, but in the absence of other data we might reasonably conclude that the range included suit of court, military service, castle guard and such aids and taxation as might be imposed from time to time. Administrative effectiveness in any of these areas would be severely compromised if the sheriff was not able to make himself aware of who was or was not in the king's peace, what the extent of their liability for service was and when it was due to be performed.

Given that most of the men and women who were selected for this study do not appear in documentary record either frequently or regularly we might reasonably conclude that their relationship with central authority was adequately administered by the sheriff and other authorities (barons or ecclesiastical institutions) and that this was the experience of most landholders. We might ask then, 'what sort of activity brought the landholder to the attention of the crown?' Primarily questions of allegiance and service it would seem, insofar as a large proportion of the data consists of either forfeitures and restorations or references to prisoners of war; the latter usually relating to the payment of daily subsistence allowances. Virtually all of the record evidence relating to the parish gentry of Lothian can be seen as belonging to one of three rather broad categories: items relating to default of service, items relating to the discharge of service and items relating to legal procedures. The first category ranged from sentence of forfeiture to the payment of prisoner of war allowances, though one does not seem to have been contingent on the other; a man might spend years aligned with the opposition or as a prisoner of war without suffering forfeiture. The second group comprises pay roll or horse valuation entries, letters of protection and of thanks for service past or anticipated. The remaining category relates to matters like the acquisition of charters of land, office or pensions, appearing as a witness to crown charters and the discharge of suit of court obligations such as Post Mortem Inquisitions, Perambulations and criminal trials.

We should not conclude that these areas were automatically, or, particularly in the case of inquisitions, even normally, without the competence of the sheriff merely because particular examples happen to appear in what we might term 'crown' documents. Rather, for some reason obscure to us, these particular cases required the sanction of higher authority and are thus (or at least likely to be) somehow exceptional. This may not be the case with the 1312 forfeitures by the Plantagenet administration in Lothian. Since warrandice of title for lands held of the crown was obviously derived from the regal authority it might be the case that formal invalidation of that warrandice would be enhanced by the authority of the king in person. Should this be the case, we might conclude that the extensive series of forfeitures of 1312 was something of a 'tidying-up' exercise on the part of Edward II's government. The subjects of the forfeitures were people who had been active in the Bruce interest, in some cases for years, and were formally deprived of their estates in one administrative session though their properties had been taken into the king's hands to all practical intents and purposes at the time of their defection.[34]

There was no exercise by the Scottish crown comparable to the Ragman Roll. This may be a matter of the survival of documentation, but to have undertaken a similar exercise could have been seen as a tacit acknowledgement that the Plantagenets had had a case or that the Ragman Roll had some legal validity. No other document records such a large body of Lothian people as the Ragman Roll, but we can compile a fairly extensive sample of Lothian men and women four decades later from a variety of sources. Unlike the Ragman Roll this material gives us some information about political choice and activity. Edward III's administration of Lothian, as we might expect, kept records of garrison service, of retours to the crown and of forfeitures. By excellent good fortune there is an extensive body of information on all three areas for the years 1335–36 and 1336–37.[35] A compilation of the list of names of known Lothian men in English garrisons and of the names of the men forfeited in 1335–37 is not so extensive as the relevant portions of the Ragman Roll, but then it is probably a reflection of a smaller group – no mention is made of king's or bishop's tenants.

Most of the Ragman Roll homagers for Lothian were Lothian people first and foremost. Many of them were homagers for other counties or more than once for Lothian; sometimes in more than one capacity – 'county' and 'king's tenant' or 'king's tenant and Burgess'. The weight of evidence connecting them primarily with Lothian through property or service strongly indicates that in the Lothian sections of the Roll we see the Plantagenet administration's understanding of what constituted the political community of the county and, assuming that existing records were used to compile the roll, very probably that of the Scottish crown before 1296. The forfeitures and muster rolls of 1335–37 afford us a glimpse of that community after nearly four decades of intermittent war and the widespread famine that occurred across Europe in the early part of the fourteenth century. The material that can be extracted from those sources is of course a very partial picture; it comprises people known to be actively opposed to the Plantagenet administration, including several women, and people active in the service of that administration – all of them men and almost all of them men-at-arms in receipt of wages. Naturally those who avoided active participation on either side do not figure to any great degree. The administration had no call to forfeit them and if they performed military service for land the administration would not have paid them, therefore they would not appear on wages records or horse valuations.

Comparison of the two groups suggests that the political community managed to remain remarkably intact between 1296 and 1337 if we are to judge by the number of family names that are common to both groups. Precision over names is not always possible due to the vagaries of medieval spelling, but of approximately 260 surnames found as Ragman Roll homagers for Lothian and Lothian men who were prisoners of war or serving in Edward I's army in the summer of 1296, over eighty appear either as having been forfeited or serving as men-at-arms in 1335–37. Clearly at least one third of the families of Lothian were either giving military service for wages or had been declared forfeit on account of their political position. The remaining two thirds presumably discharged their various obligations to the Plantagenet government. A study of the comparable documents relating to Roxburghshire, Lanarkshire and Berwickshire would seem to suggest that the proportion of family names occurring in lists of forfeitures and of men-at-arms in relation to the Roxburghshire Ragman Roll names is not dissimilar. What is striking is the ratio of forfeited men to men who served in Plantagenet garrisons, virtually all of whom served as men-at-arms.

At least thirty-nine men who served in the garrison of Edinburgh 1335–37[36] bore names we can safely associate with Lothian, Roxburgh or Peebles in 1296 compared to at least fifty-three Lothian men and women who suffered forfeiture in the same period. Should we take this as evidence that the Plantagenet cause enjoyed a considerable level of support in Lothian in the period after the battle of Halidon Hill? Only in the same sense that we could say the Ragman Roll indicates a consensus of opinion among the nobility of south-east Scotland in favour of accepting Edward I as king. The forfeited landholders of 1335–37 cannot confidently be seen as the sum of Bruce support in Lothian, rather they represent that part of the political community willing to risk life, limb and property for the Bruce cause at a time when, it would seem to us, the Plantagenet government was secure. Superficially this would seem to have been the case. Edward III does not seem to have made any effort to restore Linlithgow as a base of operations. Indeed, he did not feel it was necessary to refortify Edinburgh until after the fight there in which the count of Namur was captured.[37] He may have felt that the victory at Halidon Hill had made the counties ceded by Edward Balliol (a grant confirmed by Balliol's parliament at Holyrood) secure. Alternatively he may have felt that he had to be seen to have confidence in Balliol's kingship and the establishment of a chain of castles would seem intrusive to his new subjects.

To what extent Edward III ever achieved acceptance of his authority in the southern counties of Scotland is difficult to say. Certainly the apparatus of shrieval government was in place in Lothian, Roxburghshire, Berwickshire, Dumfriesshire and Lanarkshire, but its effectiveness is questionable. The retours of 1335–37 do not merely list forfeited gentry. They contain a mine of information relating to the peacetime values of properties, but they also record the actual returns made. A good many were made in full, but the number of rents that could not be collected 'because of the war', 'because they are laid waste' or because they 'could not be raised for this compotus'[38] suggests that Edward's government could not provide 'good lordship' to the community even if the community was willing to accept it. The choice of phrases used to account for shortfalls in rentals may have some significance in itself. Lands 'laid waste'[39] were obviously just that; not an unusual occurrence in a war zone. Failure to collect the proper rent 'on account of the war' or the simple declaration that they 'could not be raised' is not explained. Presumably these properties had not been destroyed. Whether either comment implies that the area in question was beyond the control of the administration through the activities of the Scots, the resistance of the tenants or the garrisons could not spare manpower from operations for rent collection is open to question.

As far as we know neither Edward I nor Edward II made such a large number of forfeitures as those of 1335–37, perhaps indicating a change of policy toward the lesser nobility under Edward III. There must be a question mark over how people regarded forfeiture in practice. Theoretically it was an unmitigated disaster in a society that valued land ownership and inheritance rights so highly, so it seems odd that so many people were willing to risk the loss of their birthright to support causes (John and Edward Balliol in 1297 and 1332, Robert and David Bruce in 1306 and 1334) whose chance of success often looks very slender from a twentieth-century perspective. The men who were forfeited by Edward I in 1306 for their support of Robert I must have known that they risked forfeiture and been aware of the considerably greater military resources of England, the nature of Edward I and, significantly, that a very large part of the Scottish political community did not support Robert's kingship. Lothian men in particular must have been aware of the military power of Edward's government; since Edinburgh and Linlithgow castles were certainly garrisoned by his troops and it is inconceivable that he had not ensured that all the baronial castles were in the hands of loyal men. The Lothian landholders forfeited in 1306 must either have been awfully optimistic men or men with a very clear picture of weaknesses in Edward's rule that would allow the Bruce party to triumph despite their struggle with the Comyns and MacDougalls.

They possibly felt confident that even if they were defeated they would have a good chance of redeeming themselves and having their heritage restored. Prior experience may have encouraged such a belief. A number of the men who had fought Edward at Dunbar were freed and restored for service, or the promise of service overseas; the men who surrendered at Irvine in 1297 and at Strathord in 1304 suffered relatively lightly for their opposition. The 1335–37 forfeitures may indicate a different policy toward forfeiture itself as well as its distribution. Forfeiture by Edward I or Edward II tended to be of fairly significant figures in the community – not barons necessarily, but substantial landholders – though it is possible that other forfeiture records have not survived. Under Edward III the number of recorded forfeitures was very much higher, embracing some relatively trivial properties – even a field of seven acres was not below the interest of the escheator.[40]

MAGNATE INFLUENCE

Exerting administrative power would not seem to have been an issue for the Scottish crown in peacetime, but the inception of Edward I's administration inevitably led to a competition for authority as soon as the Balliol party started appointing their own officials.[41] In Ayrshire or Fife or Strathearn the local magnate could be a force in supporting or undermining the authority of the government of the day, but the lack of a local magnate whose priorities lay primarily in Lothian may have accorded an unusually prominent political role to barons. Dirleton Castle in East Lothian and Bothwell castle in Lanarkshire represent an enormous investment on the part of the owners – both barons – which cannot be ascribed simply to defence.[42] Both castles were built in the thirteenth century before there was any likelihood of a protracted Anglo-Scottish war and the incidence of baronial war in Scotland seems to have been insignificant. The construction of a great castle did, however, impart prestige to its owner. It gave him an imposing venue for his courts and for receiving his guests and perhaps lent an air of credibility to his military position as well being a conspicuous demonstration of personal success – castle-building was an expensive enterprise.

It is possible that Edward I, Edward II and Robert I all tried to improve their position by building local leadership groups through granting extensive lands and rights to men on whose loyalty they could depend, such as Sir Robert Hastang, Sir Pierre Lubaud and Sir Alexander Seton. Edward III may have continued this policy with Alexander de Strivelin. All four kings may have intended to install a magnate in Lothian, but Edward III may also have been attempting to replace local opponents with men that he could depend on not to defect.

The first of these men, Robert Hastang, Sheriff of Roxburgh for Edward I until 1305, was the recipient of various lands forfeited by Bruce supporters in 1306[43] which were restored to their owners when they returned to Plantagenet allegiance. In recompense Sir Robert was granted the properties of another group of Bruce partisans: Robert Keith, Thomas de la Haye, Peter Pontekyn, Godfrey Brun and Aymer de Hauden.

The sum of Sir Robert's holdings in Byres, Heriot, Ratho, Ladyset and Garvok in western and central Lothian, Easter Felton and Philipston 'in the barony of Musselburgh', Broxmouth, the barony of Cumbre Culstone, Cockpen and Wester Duddingston, made him a man of some substance among Lothian landholders in terms of acreage, but his properties were spread right through the sheriffdom, giving him greater influence because he had a 'presence' in several areas.[44] The distribution of his estates may of course have been simply the range of property available to Edward, but the concentration of grants in Lothian might have been a policy decision. As a major figure in any area of Lothian Sir Robert was bound to have some degree of influence beyond his immediate tenants and could get rid of his own tenants who failed to discharge their obligations. If Edward was consciously endeavouring to achieve security in Lothian by the introduction of a new layer of leadership by putting several baronies and properties into the hands of one man, the effectiveness of the policy must be questioned. An indication of the strength of the Plantagenet administration and of its acceptance in the community is the force of men-at-arms from Lothian who served at Bannockburn. Even if the 'gret menye' described by Barbour[45] actually only amounted to a few dozen or score men-at-arms the fact that they were there at all is testament to their belief that the war could be won, their continuing acceptance of Plantagenet lordship and their confidence that they would continue to live under that lordship after the coming battle (though many on both sides probably doubted that a major action would take place at all). The fall of Edinburgh Castle in March 1314 must have compromised the effectiveness of the administration, but it could still call upon and receive due army service three months later.[46] However, there seems to have been no extensive resistance to King Robert after June 1314. The political community of Lothian may have accepted Bruce kingship with reluctance, resignation, equanimity or delight according to inclination, but it would seem they did accept it, as no doubt they or their predecessors had accepted the rule of Edward I for the better part of two decades.

One man who evidently saw things differently was Sir Alexander Seton. Although he had served as a juror on the inquisition that had dealt with the forfeiture of Lothian Bruce supporters in February 1312,[47] he managed to effect a transfer of allegiance without damaging his career, defecting to Robert I on the eve of the main engagement at Bannockburn and, according to Sir Thomas Grey, encouraging the king to attack.[48] The extensive lands and superiorities granted him by Robert I in 1321 (at Gogar, Winchburgh and Pentland), with the properties he already held may not have been enough to make him a magnate on a national scale, but they would surely have made him a man of power and influence in Lothian. The other staunch Bruce supporter to benefit from the generosity of King Robert was Sir Robert Lauder who was granted Cowden in 1316 after the forfeiture of Pierre Lubaud in 1316[49] and Pencaitland and Nisbet forfeited by Sir Thomas Pencaitland.[50] Again, the availability of disposable land must have been a significant factor in the location of awards, but the concentration of several properties in the hands of two men may have been seen as a contribution toward binding the political community of Lothian to the Bruce cause. At a distance of seven centuries it is impossible to be sure that the advancement of these two men was a conscious policy, or if it was, to what extent it was successful. When a new Edwardian administration was erected in Lothian in 1334–35 it may, for all we know, have enjoyed widespread support, but the high incidence of war damage and forfeitures recorded in 1335–36 is a clear indication that a very large proportion of the landholders in the county were prepared to risk their lives opposing that government while a rather smaller portion were prepared to serve in its garrisons as paid men-at-arms. Obviously, since the majority of the political community figure in neither garrison pay rolls or lists of escheats, we must conclude that they were willing to accept a change of government, or at least not sufficiently moved to take up arms against it, presumably discharging their customary judicial and/or military obligations.

The new administration appointed Sir John de Strivelin of East Swinneburn, a Northumberland landowner, as Sheriff of Edinburgh, but on 12 July 1336 Edward also favoured him with a grant of 300 merks of land there, with the promise of 200 merks of land in England or 200 merks annually at the exchequer should the Scots regain Lothian.[51] Sir John then had the resources, not only of the sheriff's garrison, but, if he could enforce his lordship, of two significant baronies, Ratho and Bathgate – like Sir Robert Hastang before him – and a cash income from the mills of Dean on the Almond near Edinburgh. By 1337 Sir John's Lothian property included the 'lands' of Balnacreiff, Inch, Blackburn, Drumcross and half of the 'vills' of Cousland and Riccarton in addition to lands, breweries and mills at Bathgate. In sum, an extensive landholding concentrated in, but not limited to, the Linlithgow area. Although this choice of properties may have been a considered response to the operational situation, it may just as easily have been brought about by a relatively high concentration of Bruce supporters in that area whose lands could be forfeited. Edward may have believed that the combination of lands and office would make Sir John a major figure in the community, that his prestige – and of course his ability to remove tenants – would be instrumental in making practical possession of Lothian, formally ceded by Edward Balliol, King of Scotland, with the consent of his parliament, a reality. Edward was to be disappointed, and in due course Sir John was recompensed for his services with 200 merks of land around Newcastle and Hartlepool.[52] The bulk of the political community of Lothian, as noted above, seem to have accepted the Edwardian administration in 1335–37, confident perhaps that they would not be severely penalised for discharging their obligations to barony and shrieval authority during the occupation; they would seem to have accepted the re-imposition of Bruce lordship similarly. The Edinburgh garrison continued in existence until March 1341,[53] and Lothian men continued to serve in it,[54] but there seems to have been no resistance to David II after the fall of the castle, and Lothian men were present in strength at Neville's Cross.[55]

The three Edwards may have failed to make a magnate in Lothian, but magnates could wield influence beyond their own tenants and estates. However much of an advantage it was to the Plantagenets to have the Earl of Dunbar in their peace, his loss must have been a great disadvantage to the Scots, whose ability to conduct operations in Roxburghshire and East Lothian must inevitably have been compromised by his opposition. By November 1335 Patrick had returned to the Bruce cause, demonstrating his change of faith by leading his tenants to Culblean. Although the list of Lothian forfeitures recorded in 1335–36 comprises mainly free tenants, and some, perhaps many, may pre-date Earl Patrick's defection it is quite possible that the balance are indicative of local leadership of a sort. Local landholders may have been encouraged by Earl Patrick's defection because it gave a local focus for Bruce, or at least anti-Plantagenet–English feeling, because it gave them confidence that the war could be won (or else the Earl would not have changed sides) or that the war was *already* being won (in September 1334 Sir Richard Talbot was captured by the Scots near Linlithgow and in 1335[56] the count of Namur was captured at Edinburgh) and that the Earl's defection was a good indication that the autumn of 1335 would be a good time to change sides, lest the incoming government of King David took a less conciliatory position with Lothian landholders than that of his father.

Equally, the high incidence of forfeiture in Lothian between 1335 and 1337 may be a sign that the Bruce party enjoyed enough support among the minor landholders that the earl felt obliged to follow the political inclinations of his tenants and neighbours. The defections of both

Earls are indicative of the strength of their position; they might not have been so easily reconciled with Bruce or Plantagenet lordship if they had not been seen as desirable allies. The loss of the Earl of Dunbar seriously weakened the hand of whichever side had lost him. The defection to Edward I of Earl Patrick senior in 1296 would have strengthened Edward's position – a major castle, garrisoned and provisioned at Earl Patrick's expense against the Scots would have been highly desirable – but Patrick's absence was probably more of a problem to the Balliol party than his presence was an advantage to Edward. As the most significant temporal landholder in the south-east Patrick must have been a major influence in the political communities of Roxburghshire and Berwickshire and as long as he remained in the peace of the Edwards he would exert some pressure in the rest of the community. It would seem that after Patrick's return to Scottish allegiance in 1314 King Robert faced no real opposition in the south-east, which cannot be wholly ascribed to his success in battle, even in conjunction with a failure on the part of Edward II actively to support his erstwhile Scottish subjects.[57] Resistance to the Plantagenets had survived a massive defeat at Falkirk and smaller reverses both military and political too numerous to mention, resistance to the Bruce party cannot have utterly evaporated in June 1314, and we should perhaps see the example of Patrick as an indicator to the political communities of Roxburghshire and Berwickshire that the time had come to abandon the Plantagenets.

Patrick's defection to Edward III after Halidon Hill weakened the Bruces and aided the Plantagenet party, though there must be some doubt about the wholeheartedness of his defection, since, as we have seen, he was back in the Bruce party before the end of November 1335. Had he remained in Plantagenet peace and therefore been actively opposed to Douglas and Moray they would have taken a great risk in leading their southern tenants to Aberdeenshire leaving Patrick virtually unopposed in the south-east. Further, without the participation of the Earl, they would have had fewer men to lead there and might have been defeated at a time when the Bruce cause was in poor shape. March's defection and the victory at Culblean seem, from a modern perspective, a pivotal juncture, though March's adherence to the Scots will have certainly come about only through his conviction that the Scots were going to win the war and a desire not to find himself an isolated Scottish magnate in English peace. In 1334–35 he had enjoyed

Edward's confidence enough that he was allowed to upgrade his castle at Dunbar[58] or at least to be allowed to retain castleguard payments normally due to Berwick, but in the event of Edward having an opportunity to make peace with the Scots on good terms and thus free men and resources for campaigning in France, he might well have been prepared to abandon Earl Patrick to the Bruce party in the interests of achieving a secure northern frontier.

Despite the signal successes of Edward Balliol and Edward III against the Scots on the battlefield at Dupplin Muir, Halidon Hill and Neville's Cross, the cession by treaty of the southern counties and the detailed administrative structure erected for them, one has to question how serious Edward III was about his Scottish acquisitions, or at least how long he remained committed permanently to retaining Scottish territory. The Lothian garrisons in his father's day had been stronger and there had been more establishments; Linlithgow and Livingston peels do not seem to have been brought back into use by Edward III's administration. However confident Edward II or Edward III may have been about eventual success it is worth noting that at least two of the men that they appointed to the task of securing Lothian (Sir Robert Hastang and Sir John Strivelin) were both promised alternative rewards should Lothian fall to the Scots. Presumably this was a question of 'insurance' or warrandice[59] should the worst come to pass, though it might be construed as the 'real' promise of reward – particularly in the case of Sir John, who, unlike Sir Robert, knew that a Plantagenet administration of Lothian had already failed once – based on an assumption that the Scots would eventually displace the English administration.

By the time of Neville's Cross the general focus of the war lay in the south-west and in Roxburghshire and Berwickshire, but it did not cease to be a major factor in the lives of Lothian people. Edward made no effort to restore his administration there after 1347, but his troops made a destructive descent on the county after the battle of Neville's Cross and again in 1355 for the 'Burnt Candlemas' campaign. Apart from reacting to English operations Lothian men would have had to serve in the army of David II to reduce the English garrisons at Roxburgh, Berwick and Lochmaben as part of their general military obligation if they were to retain their property. Only a handful of those Scots who had served in the Edinburgh garrison between 1335 and 1340 appear in English records thereafter as recipients of allowances to compensate them for the loss of their lands in Scotland. Some, no doubt, had been killed in action and it is quite possible that some sought their fortune elsewhere, but it would seem quite possible, even probable, that the remainder found their way into the peace of David II in much the same way as Scots who had changed their allegiance from Balliol to Plantagenet to Bruce and back to Plantagenet kings over the preceding half century.

CLERICS AND BURGESSES

If we accept that the conflict in Lothian in the periods 1297–1304, 1306–14 and 1334–41 generally involved very small numbers of people and bear in mind the high incidence of man-at-arms service we would be justified in accepting that operational activity was, largely at least, the province of the landed classes, somewhat in the traditional division of medieval society into 'men who labour, men who fight and men who pray'. In fact, we should be aware that these groups were not so clearly delineated as all that. There are numerous instances of clerics being involved in combat or being declared forfeit for rebellion and Edward I found Scottish parish clergy enough of a problem that he attempted to resolve it by trying to reserve all benefices that fell vacant to Englishmen.[60] Martial activity among the clergy should not surprise us; the majority of benefices were probably held by men of the landholding class and several were landholders in their own right. They might be excused service for their charge,[61] but they would undoubtedly have to discharge it for any property held temporally. Holy orders did not save Richard, rector of Ratho, from forfeiture by Edward III.[62]

A possible indication that a cleric was involved in military activity may lie in the use of the term 'knight' with ecclesiastical titles.[63] The first incidence of this relevant to this study[64] is that of William de Balliol, Rector of Kirkpatrick, the only cleric described as a knight on the Ragman Roll. He may have been accorded the style of knight as a courtesy, though that must be considered unlikely given that none of the other senior clerics benefited from it. Another example from the same period includes Sir Thomas de Bridderhale[65] and a canon of Jedburgh, Sir Adam de Langchestre, who carried a letter to Edward I for William, his abbot.[66] The armigerous status of these men may have pre-dated their ordination of course. It is quite possible that Sir Adam was a man of knightly rank who had retired to a more spiritual life. Not all of the clerics involved in the war were knights; among the surrendered garrison of Dunbar there was one John Somerville, clerk, presumably a member of the Lanarkshire Somerville family. He may of course have been concerned with the spiritual welfare of the garrison, chaplain or secretary to a member of the company. That he appears as a prisoner of war surely suggests that he had been on active service, though that need not have precluded other duties. The chaplain of the Earl of Lennox was, apparently, another clerical knight. In the autumn of 1301 he had been 'out' for the Balliol cause but made his peace with Edward, who wrote to the Abbot of Paisley asking him to induct 'Sir Robert' to the vicarage of Kirkpatrick.[67] The Abbot responded that an appointment had already been made a fortnight before because Sir Robert had not yet entered Edward's peace. The vicar of Peebles and the rector of Skirling were both forfeited for rebellion[68] and William, Archdeacon of Lothian[69] confessed to his rebellion when he joined Edward's peace on 28 October 1305, more than a year after the surrender of the Balliol cause in February 1304.

When war broke out again in 1306 Edward was sufficiently convinced of the dangers presented by senior churchmen that he ordered the Bishops of Glasgow and St. Andrews to be kept in irons[70] partly no doubt as punishment for their defection, but presumably also to prevent their escape. The Archdeacon had left Plantagenet peace by April 1308, when he was receiving 3d per day as a prisoner of war.[71] Since the archdeacon was an officer of the bishopric of St. Andrews it is conceivable that his resistance to Edward I and Edward II was encouraged by the attitude of the Bishop. The examples of clerical forfeiture and/or imprisonment and attempts by Edward I and Edward II to install Englishmen or sympathetic Scots to parish vacancies are indicative of a level of opposition among those members of the secular clergy whose life in the community had a political dimension – for example those who were temporal landholders, and had obligations of social and military services. Despite the apparent failure of other attempts to provide Englishmen for Scottish vacancies, Edward II persevered, in making such appointments even after the loss of Lothian. He provided Richard Makaud to Yetham parish in the diocese of Glasgow in September 1316[72] and others to no less than ten Lothian parishes in July 1317.[73] What either Edward or the newly appointed incumbents hoped to gain is obscure unless there was a body of opinion (shared by the appointees) that the Scottish war was not yet irretrievably lost and that the appointments would be made good in due course when the Scots had been defeated.

Another clerical 'knight' was Sir William Bullock, chamberlain to Edward Balliol and constable of Cupar Castle.[74] He joined the Bruce cause in 1339, eventually filling the office of chamberlain for David II. Unlike other clerics who were accorded the title 'knight' there is perhaps a practical explanation for Sir William's accolade. As the constable of a castle he might have found some difficulty in asserting his authority over knights in the garrison. Conceivably Sir William's knighthood was a means of lending authority to his position as Edward Balliol's chamberlain, though knighthood would not generally seem to have been a concomitant of senior office under the crown. A final example of a clerical knight, Sir Robert Fraser, seems to be unusually clear-cut. Sir Robert was parson of Pencaitland,[75] but in 1336–37 he was serving in Edinburgh Castle garrison as a knight with a retinue of two men-at-arms (scutifers). We might assume that his service was a temporal tenure obligation; however, he was evidently serving for wages since he appears on a muster roll. Again, we might consider that Sir Robert's knighthood was given to enhance his authority among the men-at-arms of the garrison. As one of only six men serving with a retinue in a garrison of over eighty men-at-arms and one of only six knights it is very likely that he had a leadership role. The two groups are not identical, which would cast doubt on the possibility that any man serving with two companions was termed 'knight' as a courtesy.

The incidence of military service of any kind on the part of ordained clergymen might suggest a limited acquaintance with the relevant commandment, but it is not clear that that simplistic view would have been considered valid in the fourteenth century. The concept of a 'just war' was perfectly acceptable to mainstream medieval Catholicism on a number of levels. To fight 'God's foes' in the Holy Land was obviously highly acceptable, and at least one senior Scottish cleric, Thomas of Dundee, Bishop of Ross, preached that fighting against the English was just as acceptable.[76] Two others, William Lamberton, Bishop of St. Andrews and Robert Wishart, Bishop of Glasgow were sufficiently active in the Bruce cause to be held as prisoners of war at Winchester and Portchester castles respectively in 1307.[77] Clerics with temporal landholdings would be likely to have military service obligations no different to any other landholder. If those obligations were not discharged, whether in person, by a substitute or by payment, the clerical landholder was just as likely to lose his property for defect of service as his layman neighbour.

Burgess families were not divorced from the rest of the political community either. The position of individual burgesses was, arguably, more vulnerable than that of the landlords. Wealth based on commerce could be disrupted completely by damage incurred in one day. The destruction or confiscation of a warehouse, workshop or ship might well be enough to put a burghal family out of business permanently and thereby force them out of the political community. As long as a landholder could maintain or recover possession of an estate they would have a chance of restoring their fortunes even if the crops, livestock and installations had been destroyed or driven off. It is traditionally much easier to borrow money against the certain ownership of land than against the possibility of commercial success. That burgesses could be liable for military service is not in question. Clearly several members of burghal families served as men-at-arms. Not all of the Napiers, Botelers, Wyggemores and Harpers who appear in muster rolls were necessarily drawn from Scottish urban roots, but some, like John Wyggemore[78] certainly were. Presumably there was a qualification of sorts – perhaps membership of the burgess guild – which defined liability for service and clearly there was an expectation that townsmen could provide themselves with the necessary equipment: Robert I would seem to have expected that a burgh could supply 'armed' (meaning armoured) men to lead the town's contingent in time of war,[79] foreign merchants in Berwick were required to have arms and horses for the defence of the town[80] and Sir William Douglas was able to recruit from Edinburgh after the fall of the castle in 1341[81] but there is no definition of responsibility for arms and armour other than Robert I's 1318 legislation.[82]

In the absence of clear evidence to the contrary, and in the knowledge that Scottish men-at-arms could serve in or against the Plantagenet cause it would be reasonable to assume that the arms, armour, training and ethos attached to heavy cavalry service did not differ radically, if at all, between the two countries. Further, it would seem that the sources of such service – the nobility, the burgess community and appropriately-motivated members of the clergy – were at least broadly similar. This does not mean that these sections of society were the sole sources of men-at-arms, but they were surely the most significant ones.

3

LANDHOLDING IN FOURTEENTH-CENTURY LOTHIAN

Evidently Lothian men were prepared (or could be coerced into) serving as men-at-arms in the armies of Balliol, Plantagenet and Bruce kings, but, while it is clear that there was a 'national' political dimension, it is important to consider the driving force behind acceptance or rejection of particular lordship at particular times; specifically the retention, recovery or acquisition of land. The social and cultural pressure to keep property, especially heritable property, in hand is widely recognised, but it is valuable to examine the nature of the properties if we are to appreciate the condition of the landed classes that formed the bulk of the political community. This was not simply a matter of acreage and agricultural exploitation. Legal and military duties were all parts of the obligation of landholders, whether to another noble or to the king. The practical realities of landholding and the relationship between landholding and military service have obvious implications for this book, particularly in regard to the incidence of man-at-arms service that Lothian could contribute to the conflict.

LANDHOLDING AND ADMINISTRATION

Acceptance of Plantagenet or Bruce governance was not simply a matter of rents and army service. Participation in the administration and in the courts divided the political community from the mass of the populace. The sheriff's court provided the executive arm of the king in local affairs, chiefly the maintenance of law and order and the protection of the king's rights in the county. The men of the political community served as jurors in a variety of applications, including 'Post Mortem Inquisitions': inquiries into the estate of someone recently deceased to define the extent of their estate, the burdens on that estate, the rights of the crown in relation to it and the identification of the correct heir.

The Post Mortem Inquisition held for the estate of Robert de Pinkney in late 1296 is the earliest detailed inquisition surviving from the Scottish administration of Edward I and the only one that pertains to Lothian.[1] Why exactly it should have been recorded securely enough to have survived is open to question. Robert de Pinkney's estate was valuable, but hardly of great significance within Lothian, let alone in Scotland as a whole. Three distinct possibilities are worth considering. The 'new' administration may have considered it desirable to impose the same system as pertained in England and recorded the inquisition carefully to provide an example of how Scottish inquisitions were to be conducted in the future or, given Edward's apparent preference for retaining the established practices of Scotland, it may have provided an example of Scottish practice for the benefit of English administrators. The third possibility is that English and Scottish practices were not significantly different and that the report of the inquisition has been preserved simply through good fortune.[2] In the absence of a similar process recorded in such detail at much the same time it seems reasonable to assume that this document was acceptable to the jurors at least, and is probably reasonably indicative of Lothian practice at the close of the thirteenth century. Even if the inquisition itself was an innovation, the judgement is still valuable as an indication of the realities of landholding in the region.

On 26 October 1296 King Edward issued a writ instructing the Earl of Surrey to take the estate of Robert de Pinkney into his custody pending an inquiry as to the correct heir. A month later the Earl instructed the King's escheator for Scotland south of the Forth to hold an inquisition which convened shortly thereafter, presumably at Haddington, the caput of East Lothian given that the property in question lay in the vicinity of Aberlady and that the bulk of the jurors (if not all of them) were drawn from that area.[4]

The majority of the jurors had subscribed the Ragman Roll by the end of August 1296, the exceptions being John Purde and Adam de

Congilton. Neither of these men seems to make any appearance in written record other than as jurors to this inquisition. Adam may well have been the son of Mabille (Mabel) de Congilton and Walter de Congilton, both of whom were Ragman Roll homagers[5] so possibly Adam could be included as a juror on the grounds that if he was not yet a Lothian landholder it was reasonable to assume that he would become one in due course. The inclusion of John Purde is less easily explained, unless we assume that the political community extended beyond the ranks of the Ragman Roll homagers. This is very likely considering the range and extent of judicial and military obligation on the political community. The few hundred men who appear on the roll for the Edinburgh counties were obliged to serve as jurors for three of the king's courts, Edinburgh, Linlithgow and Haddington. With twelve people sitting on each jury, the three suits a year which seems to have been a fairly ordinary level of obligation would surely soon be exhausted by the demands of three busy courts, particularly when we bear in mind the extensive range of business that might come before those courts.

Alternatively of course Adam Purde may have failed to register on the Ragman Roll for a variety of reasons. He could have been out of the country, simply overlooked or a prisoner of war (a common experience apparently: at least twenty-one of the men selected for this study spent time as prisoners) or in service in Edward's army. Sir Simon de Horsburgh,[6] a Peeblesshire landholder, does not appear on the Roll, though Peeblesshire was one of the most intensively recorded counties and despite the fact that as a knight Sir Simon would surely have been a member of the political community of that county, suggesting the possibility that men serving in the field were not required to give their homage in a civil setting, or at least not in the rather unusual circumstances of August 1296.

The De Pinkney inquisition gives a report of the various lands and rights held by Sir Robert at the time of his death and the various burdens outstanding on the estate. These burdens show the fragmentation of the estate into several sub-tenancies or lettings of varying type. Robert and his ancestors had shown considerable generosity to the hospital of St. Cuthbert; a total of nine bovates, nine acres and twenty shillings a year from the two mills of the estate. The inquisition also mentions a group of cottar holdings with a fixed annual rental value of 112s 6d. These cottars, probably descended from men of servile status, presumably represented the main source of seasonal waged labour for the estate. Their rents represent a trivial percentage of the gross income of the estate so it is reasonable to assume that the acreage occupied by the cottars was minimal, probably not really enough to keep them fed and clad, hence the need for alternative sources of income, of which labour on the land of others would, in most cases anyway, be the only option. The cottars were undoubtedly 'thirled' to (that is to say they were obliged to use) the mills that provided £8 a year for the lord (including the twenty shillings paid to the hospital of St. Cuthbert) and to the breweries. These were worth 29s 4d per annum as fixed rents, but 13s 4d (or one merk) was paid to Alicia de Graham as a 'terce' from her late husband, Roger Lelman. How Roger Lelman came to have rights in the breweries of Robert de Pinkney's estate is not recorded, but it does serve to illustrate the potential complexity of medieval landholding.

A further six bovates were held by Henry de Pinkney, brother of the deceased.[7] Although that part of the estate was valued at £4, Henry's charter granted him the land for a mere 1d per annum, neatly demonstrating the means by which younger sons could be provided with a living. Henry's favourable rental is explained by the fact that the principal landholder was his brother, but the other major tenant seems to have fared even better, though he does not appear to have been a relative. John de Bickerton held the castle of Luffnoc (Luffness) along with three carucates and the demesnes of the castle as well as a further twenty marks of land at Bynyn in the constabulary of Linlithgow. The castle and the land attached to it was valued at £26 13s 4d, superficially a carefully derived figure, but in fact simply an alternative expression of forty merks. For these extensive properties John paid the paltry sum of 6d per annum. The most likely explanation of this generosity is that John had in fact provided a considerable lump sum in exchange for the permanent use of the land, but that Robert had been unwilling or unable formally to alienate the property permanently, the annual payment of 6d remaining as a token of the owner's rights. Since the castle, demesnes and the three carucates were held of Robert 'in capite', should John die without issue the property would escheat to Robert.

The two other significant tenants on Robert's property were Alexander de Lindsay, who held one carucate (though in two different parts of an area of the estate called 'le cotis') valued at £4 but paying only 1d, and Thomas de Coleville. Thomas's holding would seem to have been scattered through the estate; the value of his property being 'estimated' by the jurors at £10, though Thomas paid no money, instead performing the 'foreign service' (forinsec) of a quarter of a knight in the king's army. For all the property at Luffness and Bynyn Robert owed a total of one and three-quarter knights' service, but what he seems to have retained himself was the chief house at Ballencreiff with a garden and pigeon house within the enclosure with 10 carucates in demesne and fifty-four acres of arable with meadow and grazing and each valued at 21d, altogether some £95 14s 2d. The conclusion of the inquisition was that the issues of Robert's properties came to £112 10s, a sum that does not accurately accord with the amounts described in the document, but gives us a picture of the fiscal realities of landholding in Lothian. More significantly perhaps it demonstrates the fragmentation of estates among neighbours. Some of that fragmentation can be readily identified, such as the 'terce' holding, the gifts by Robert and his predecessors to the church and the provision made for his younger brother. Whatever the origin of the dispersal of the other portions of the estate it is clear that even a relatively small estate, though nominally a contiguous landholding belonging to, or rather held by, one individual might in fact be effectively held by several different people who might or might not be related to one another, but were bound to one another by what were essentially commercial considerations.

The de Pinkney post mortem inquisition provides a glimpse of the political community at work in a normal peacetime activity, but it is only one document among a collection of unrelated and fragmentary material. With little in the way of continuous record relating to specific subjects it is impossible to state categorically that any particular piece of material represents 'standard practice'. It is unlikely that all of the documentary evidence is the product of recording unusual or anomalous situations; therefore we might consider that a wide range of material might give us a generally valid body of evidence from which to draw generally valid conclusions.

In general there is very little evidence indeed relating to Lothian land prices in the early fourteenth century, and much of what there is tells us little about the actual value of the property. The return due to the crown might be stated, but not the extent, productivity or profitability of the estate in question.[8] Exceptionally, records of the Lothian administration of Edward III for 1335–36 and 1336–37 provide a remarkable snapshot

of the various properties, estates and baronies that comprised the sheriffdom, detailing not only the sums due from landholders, but the actual
returns received by the sheriff. Although we should bear in mind that
land prices were not constant in fourteenth-century Scotland – if only
because there had been intermittent war for nearly forty years before
Edward III's acquisition of Lothian after the battle of Halidon Hill – virtually all of the properties of Lothian would seem to have been held for
customary, rather than genuinely economic rentals. These rents were not
necessarily token payments in the strictest sense; no doubt many of them
had been economic at the time of their agreement, but had dwindled
relative to economic development generally. There are several examples
of rents of £5 or more, considerable sums of money, but not necessarily – and probably only rarely – anything like a commercially rational
return on the property.

In those instances where we can see what is, or at least appears to be,
a genuinely economic rental we should remember that the rent paid
by the tenant is not the same thing as the annual value of the land as a
production asset. The holding would have no value to the tenant if there
was no profit to be made from sub-letting or direct exploitation, and in
turn the sub-tenants or labourers would need to profit also.

LANDHOLDING AND ARMY SERVICE

Military obligation was often associated with land tenure in a way that is
easy to identify – estates granted for knight[9] or archer[10] (very occasionally
infantry[11] or 'armed man'[12]) service. Military tenures, seldom involving the
service of more than one knight and very often just fractions of the service of one knight,[13] can hardly have provided Scottish kings with an army,
but as we have already seen, experience of army service as a man-at-arms
was very widespread among the lesser nobility of Lothian. Dr. Prestwich
has observed that the financial rewards of a man-at-arms were more in
the way of a 'return on an investment' than wages.[14] The rate of pay was
not sufficient to justify the investment in horse and arms. However if the
purchase of horse and arms was an unavoidable duty anyway, there was
something to be said for enlisting to partially offset the cost.

Since we can identify over 100 men from a relatively small sample of
Lothian landholders serving as men–at–arms we must surely conclude

that heavy cavalry service of some kind extended well beyond provisions of knight service.[15] G.W.S. Barrow and A.A.M. Duncan have alluded to drengage landholding in Northumberland and Cumberland as a precursor of knight service[16] tenure and have suggested that a similar service may have been a condition of landholding in Lothian. If so it would seem to have left no readily identifiable trace by the fourteenth century, but it would be rash to assume that it was not part and parcel of many, perhaps most, of the properties that were big enough to encompass more than one farm merely because we have no record of it. If it was normal practice only exemptions would need to be recorded. Alternatively such duties may have been recorded in rather greater detail by the sheriffs and lords to whom such service was due, but the shrieval, magnate and baronial registers have not survived. If a military obligation on the tenant was part of the package of arrangements ranging from cash, produce and suit of court to hunting and military services that might constitute a rental agreement, that obligation obviously had an economic aspect or at least had at the time the agreement was made. If the tenant had to equip himself to a given standard, and take the time to learn and practice the skills of war, or devote some of his time to court duties, that might have been a factor in the rental that was likely to reduce the cash element.

A possible indication of the practical extent of cavalry service that might be expected from a particular area can be seen in a charter from the reign of William the Lion.[17] The King gave his sister Margaret one hundred librates of land at Ratho infeft with twenty knights; five pounds worth of rent per annum per knight. Of course the figure of £5 is indicative of the return to the landowner, Margaret. It was not of the value of the land to the knight, and the value of money had changed somewhat by the time of the Wars of Independence. An estate of £5 would hardly seem enough to sustain a man in 'knighthood' as we understand fourteenth-century usage; also, twenty knights is a very large number indeed when compared to the ten knights required of the Bruces for the whole of Annandale. However, if we think not in terms of knights, but rather of modest landholders – the parish gentry to use a phrase generally applied to a slightly later period – with an obligation to give service in the capacity of what in English record is called a valet, scutifer, or man-at-arms, and bear in mind that military obligations of this type were probably as little susceptible to change as any other aspect of land tenure packages, the number of 'knights' infeft at Ratho was probably not extraordinary when compared to Lothian generally. It would be premature to suggest that a £5 landholding was a 'threshold' figure for man-at-arms service in Lothian generally on the strength of one document from a hundred years before the Wars of Independence, but the incidence of that service among the parish gentry is sufficiently high to suggest that a large proportion of such landholders performed military service at that level.

Military service of any kind was not of course strictly and inevitably a product of land tenure in any sense at all. There were several men in English service with no particular association with Lothian other than army service, professional soldiers like the Gascon Pierre Lubaud. He served in Lothian as a man-at-arms from August 1298, when his horse (a 'rough liard' hackney) was valued at £20. He was constable of Linlithgow peel by September 1305,[18] and received a grant of lands at Bathgate and Ratho from Edward II in December 1311, by which time he had been promoted to sheriff of Edinburgh.[19] He defected to the Bruce party before the fall of Edinburgh Castle in March 1314[20] and was granted land at Cockpen, Lothian by Robert I[21] which he held for about two years before being convicted of treason. We might reasonably expect to see men on either side whose ambition was to achieve heritable landholder status as a reward for service but whose current service was not based on tenure.

MONEY RENTS

Perhaps the most significant factor in setting the rent of any property lay in the relationship between the principal and the tenant. Provisions of land for younger sons, friends or associates would not always be made at a commercial rate. If the tenure was heritable it would be difficult, if not impossible to alter the return. Money rents fixed in the early twelfth century would have lost a great deal of their value by the close of the thirteenth.[22] Perhaps more significantly the increase in the money supply and increasing velocity of exchange of that supply throughout the twelfth and thirteenth centuries had considerably improved the purchasing power of most, if not all members of the society other than those dependent on fixed rent incomes. Nominal rents are generally fairly obvious – men holding land for a pair of spurs or gloves or for a penny were not exactly heavily burdened – but tenants who paid more substantial sums were not necessarily, or even normally, having to find anything like the commercial rent value of the property. Generally we have no clear picture of the physical extent of particular landholdings, only the return due. From this information we can deduce that there were a great many properties throughout Lothian with a rental of ten pounds, ten merks or fractions or multiples thereof, [23] but we cannot tell if properties of identical values in different parts of Lothian were of similar value to the tenant. Tenant profits were obviously a function of productivity and demand for produce so we might reasonably assume that properties with a higher proportion of better land would be more desirable than others. However in peacetime proximity to the market might well make a less productive estate more profitable than a superior property with poor access to the market. In wartime the very properties whose relative isolation reduced their profitability in peacetime might be more likely to avoid the worst effects of the conflict. Thus the war, though not permanently affecting the customary rentals of the properties, may have affected their desirability.

A barrier to understanding the relationship of 'normal' rent values of properties compared to the actual returns is the propensity of medieval accountants to convert merk prices to sterling prices and vice versa. Superficially, the reductions for war damage to individual properties accepted by the administration of Edward III in 1335–37 seem to be quite arbitrary. Once the sums are converted to a particular account format there does seem to be a tendency for the return to be a 'round sum', one presumably agreed between the responsible officer of the crown (the sheriff, or at least his bailies) and the landholder. This is obscured somewhat by the use of the two terms for money of account. The seemingly arbitrary rentals can often be rationalised by conversion to the alternative method of accounting. If, for example the 'normal' return from a property was £26 13s 4d we might conclude that the odd nature of the sum is in some way a scientifically calculated value of property, and if the actual return from the same property in wartime was £6 13s 4d we might conclude that that too, since it is such a very specific sum of money, represents a rational calculation of some precision. If on the other hand the two sums are expressed in merks we find that the normal return was 40 merks, and the actual sum paid was 10 merks. This suggests that the initial sum is a customary and perhaps quite arbitrary rental, probably of considerable antiquity, such as we might expect for any 'feudal' property, and that the actual return, being one quarter of the usual 'peacetime' return, may be arbitrary or represent an agreed composition, that the landholder and the bailie had agreed – or that the bailie had decided – that war damage and commercial dislocation had reduced the value of the property by 75%.

The barony of Keith,[24] valued at 100 merks in peacetime was assessed at £40 (60 merks) in February 1312. In 1335–36 a property at Garmilton, normally worth £5 per annum to the crown made a return of only ½ merk (3s 4d) in 1335–36.[25] It would seem, then, that each of these properties made a return that was almost token. On the other hand the barony of Glencorse, forfeited by Sir William Abernethy and normally valued at £13 6s 8d (20 merks) made a return of only £2 18s 6d in 1335–36.[26] The latter sum cannot be expressed conveniently in merks or as an obvious rational fraction of the normal return. It might therefore be reasonable to assume that the bailie acting for the Plantagenet administration had investigated the condition of the property and had made a realistic assessment of its current value; a 'fair rent' in effect. However in 1336–37 the return from the same property was £3, suggesting a rather more arbitrary approach.[27]

The evidence does not support a conclusion that the returns demanded were all necessarily of this pattern. A property normally returning 13s 4d (one merk) but returning only 12d does not make any immediate sense as a simple extrapolation for comparative value. The 12d is, obviously, one shilling, a unit of account rather than of specie, but there is no direct relationship between merks and shillings that can be expressed as a fractional function. A merk is two-thirds of a pound and a shilling one twentieth of a pound; the arithmetical difficulties of the multiplication, division and rationalisation of complex fractions would have presented a considerable challenge to people who did not have the benefit of Arabic numerals. Certainly the shilling was a generally acceptable unit of account – there was no shilling coin, nor merk or pound coin for that matter,[28] but it was not a simple fraction of a merk such as a quarter or a tenth. In the absence of any evidence of a specific calculation it may well be the case that a return of a shilling was agreed with, or imposed by, the mechanism of the state in the shape of the bailies of the sheriffdom as much as a formal recognition of responsibility as anything else – a token of the continuing landlord–tenant relationship.

It is not universally the case that the returns demanded for different properties can be readily expressed as round figures in either pounds or merks, and some at least of these demands may well represent economic rentals based on the real productivity of the estate in question. Many, perhaps the majority, seem to be based, or to have been based in the past, on ideas of the value of a property sufficient to maintain a person of a particular social status in the economic condition deemed appropriate to their station and to enable them to provide the services demanded of such a person. This is often seen as a function of the military aspects of medieval landholding, and there is a good deal of merit in this. However, the social duties of landholders extended well beyond any question of the ability of the landholder to provide themselves with the necessary equipment – armour, weapons, horses, staff – to follow the king to war. The full extent of suit of court obligation is quite impossible to judge given the loss of sheriff court records other than a mere handful of inquisitions, but they were probably seen as a considerable burden to those who had to discharge them. Court duties often required the subject to travel distances that seem trivial to us but would have been a considerable burden seven centuries ago. In poor weather conditions, or in short winter days it might well have taken a whole day to travel to court to discharge their obligations as jurors, and, having done their duty, another whole day to return home. One day in court, therefore, might well take up three days of their time. For a man with property and judicial duties in two or more sheriffdoms the burden might be increased by longer journey times amounting to twenty or thirty days a year.

In the absence of a clear indication as to a rationale that might explain the variety it is probably reasonable to assume that a rent set at a round sum such as ten merks or thirty pounds or fifty shillings, is likely to be a sum set on the basis of the relationship between the landholder and the superior as indicated above, but this can be misleading. A rental of 33s 4d might seem to be a carefully calculated sum reflecting the real value of the property. It is also the sum of two 'simple' units of account (one pound and one merk) and therefore might just as easily represent the rent of two different properties combined or simply an alternative expression of two and a half merks. Such a rental might be the product of the division of a property at some time in the past (for example a quarter share of what had originally been a 10 merk property), and some of the more curious-seeming sums may well be the result of division and subdivision and amalgamation of estates over generations resulting in what might seem like curious, random rentals that are in fact a half of a third or a fifth of a half of an earlier rental agreement brought about by the requirement to provide for younger sons, or to fund terces and dowries or by the partition of estates between daughters. Division of property to provide income for dependants was commonplace, but not permanent. Land allowed as terce, dower or dowry from heritable estates returned, generally at least, to the estate on the death of the holder. Life tenures of this sort do not seem to have been automatically affected by the forfeiture of the principal landholder. The forfeiture of William Douglas[29] did not prevent his widowed mother, Joanna, from retaining her terce holding in 1335–36; on the other hand her gender did not prevent her from being forfeited in 1336–37,[30] presumably for her political convictions if not activities.

BARONIES

The application of the term 'barony' is not entirely clear in any way, other than that baronies were in some sense, though not necessarily in an aspect common to them all, different from other landholdings. That the barony was not a single block of territory owned outright by a baron is clear from the number of properties described as being 'in the barony of...'. That description is surely indicative of more than geographical location. Barony would seem to have formed a level of local administration in various spheres most significantly judicial and military responsibilities. It would seem that those responsibilities were not necessarily tied permanently to the land and that administrative functions, and no doubt privileges, could be negotiable items in their own right; hence we see Alexander Seton acquiring the 'superiority' of Dundas and Wester Craigie in Lothian.[31] One of these properties may have already belonged to him since the Craigie family would seem to have been among the disinherited. Sir Alexander Craigie and his son both served in the Plantagenet garrison of Edinburgh from 1335–40,[32] so evidently the superiority was worth having in addition to, or separately from, actual tenure. A strong possibility must be that superiority conferred judicial authority; that the residents of the property became subject to the court of Alexander Seton and presumably were removed from the jurisdiction of a different baron. The profits of justice in the barony court accrued, unsurprisingly, to the baron, making 'ownership' of such a court an attractive proposition.

At least thirty baronies existed in Lothian in the late thirteenth and early fourteenth centuries.[33] What administrative relationship, if any, they bore to the constabularies in which they lay is unclear, though it would be likely that both military and judicial responsibilities were involved. In turn it is not clear that there was a specific relationship between baronies and properties. A particular location might be described as lying in a particular barony and the barony may have been a unit of court juris-diction, but we cannot be sure that all properties lay in the sway of one or other barony. King's tenants for example might, for all we know, fall within the scope of the sheriff for all purposes from taxation to military service and not be in any legal sense attached to a barony at all.

Beyond judicial and army services it is difficult to identify a feature that is common to fourteenth-century baronies and separates them from properties without baronial status. This is a topic that has received very little attention from historians apart from Professor Duncan's con-cise description,[34] but it would not seem that barony was either land tenure, judicial rights or military leadership, but that elements of all three were constituent parts, though not always universally. The scope of judicial power varied from one barony to another[35] and there is no reason to assume that military leadership could not be a variable. In 1321 Sir Alexander Seton was granted the superiority of Elphinstone though he already held the barony itself.[36] If that superiority included rights of leadership in war we must assume that some figure other than the baron of Elphinstone had had the responsibility of leading the Elphinstone men when required before 1321 and that 'superiority' was a thing desirable in itself or Robert I would not have granted it or Sir Alexander would not have gone to the bother of acquiring it. It may be that 'superiority' was a vital component of 'barony' holding; that other rights, powers, privileges and property might form part of the 'barony' package, but that superiority conferred the actual status of barony and thus had to be specifically stated to erect (or perhaps restore) a property to barony status.

As a general rule we can safely assume that the rights implied by a grant 'in barony' were clearly understood by the donor, the recipient and the existing tenants of the barony and that grants of superiority separate from the baronial property were something of a rarity. The military service burden attached to the barony was not the same thing as leadership of the men of the barony in war. Each property within the barony would have a military obligation, as did the 'baron' for his property within the barony. Jurisdiction and military leadership might lie elsewhere, but generally the 'baron' would hold these powers and his tenants would provide him with the manpower to discharge his obligations to the king. The leadership rights of a favoured individual might be extended to exclude the customary rights of others. This might well be the case in the granting of the 'superiority' of a property separately from the actual landholding. It was certainly the case for Sir James Douglas, who, in 1369 received letters from David II which gave him the leadership of all of the men who lived on all his lands 'throughout our kingdom'.[37] The clear implication is that men who lived on estates belonging to James, who in the past had been subject to the military command of sheriffs or of other lords, would now come under his direct authority.

The nature of service demanded was not consistent. Knight service predominates, but there are examples of grants made for archer service. The instances of relatively heavy demand from baronies, such as ten archers for half of Manor, Peeblesshire,[38] or thirty archers and an armed man from Bowden, Roxburghshire,[39] should remind us that our perception of archers as an element in Scottish armies – that they formed only a very small proportion of the force – could easily be compromised by the discovery of just a couple of similar grants since the demand for knight service is so low. Similarly, although there is a popular perception that Scottish archers hailed from Ettrick Forest, the relatively high incidence of archer service from Roxburgh and Peeblesshire in military service tenure grants may be a matter of document survival and the numbers involved are not large. A couple of archer service charters from other areas would, superficially at least, invalidate the perception that the Forest was the chief source of archers for Scottish armies.

Although military tenure grants are a significant proportion of the surviving charters of Robert I, the number of knights involved is not large. As we have already seen in Chapter 2, it would seem that in Scottish armies, like their counterparts elsewhere in Europe, the number of men-at-arms available in Lothian was considerable for a government that could effectively impose its lordship. Even a very superficial survey of the incidence of paid man-at-arms service recorded in muster rolls[40] and horse valuations[41] and of forfeitures in 1335–36 and 1336–37 [42] among the landed families of other southern sheriffdoms would strongly suggest that Lothian was not exceptional. It therefore seems reasonable to conclude that there were extensive cavalry service obligations attendant on land tenure well below the social status of knights. That service may not have been part of the leadership obligations of barons, but it was certainly discharged at some level. As an example of what might be expected in the way of such service from a particular property we might look to David II's grant of a charter of entail for the estate (not even a barony) of Pettynain in March 1352 for the service of four 'armed men' and four archers.[43] Unarmed men would not be at a premium obviously, and in general 'armed' in a medieval document should be understood as 'armoured'. Men who could provide themselves with armour were unlikely to be men who would serve without horses; even though they might actually fight on foot should the tactical situation require it. The service of eight men trained to arms (as Professor Duncan has pointed out,[44] there was clearly a considerable difference between an archer and a man armed with a bow) would seem to be a considerable burden, but it is quite possible that the light military obligations attached to the majority of properties and baronies for which we have evidence are exceptional, hence the need for their burdens to be defined, and that the eight soldiers from Pettinain or the thirty archers from Bowden or the ten archers from Manor are actually more indicative of normal levels of obligation attached to landholding. That does not mean that the military service of all of the parish gentry in Lothian took the form of cavalry soldiering, though clearly a considerable portion of it did. The archers from Bowden and Manor might fall into the same sort of category in social and economic terms as the man-at-arms from Lothian but serve, perhaps by tradition, in a specialist capacity. Dr. Morgan has shown that men from Cheshire,[45] whose social status would make them likely to serve as men-at-arms if they came from a different county, served as archers in the reign of Edward III if not earlier. The same may hold true of the Manor men.

The size of force available from a particular area does not seem to have been a factor in conferring baronial status. The four 'armed men' from Pettynain and the thirty archers (with an 'armed man' to lead them) of Bowden may represent unusually heavy burdens or the ten archers required of Kilsyth or for half of Manor unusually light burdens, but whether or not they bear any relationship to the physical size of the barony – in gross acreage or perhaps arable acreage – or its financial value or whether it was derived from traditional burdens is impossible to say. Assuming that the barons were responsible to the sheriff we must also assume that the sheriff held some form of register to ensure that the correct level of service was being demanded and discharged.

Beyond the duty to provide men as required, the army function of the baron is open to question. In battle we could expect that the majority of men-at-arms of all ranks would serve with the cavalry if a mounted force was being deployed at all, which would preclude them from fulfilling a 'junior leader' role among those of their tenants called to arms, but combat is only a very tiny facet of the life of an army and the administration of sentry, ration and work parties might have been provided through baronial leadership under his superior sheriff or magnate. If so, the disparity in size and nature of the commands of the individual barons must have made the assignment of tasks and responsibilities and of provisioning something of a challenge for senior officers, but maintaining the prestige of the baron among his tenants might demand that his civil status be reflected in his military status. We might wonder whether the existing social and judicial hierarchy of landholders, barons and sheriffs would provide a viable structure for the tactical and administrative articulation[46] of Scottish medieval armies. Self-evidently a large army must have articulated leadership in some form and the advantages of leadership figures already familiar to the rank and file are obvious – those being led might not like their landlord or baron, but at least they would know who he was and that he held the relevant authority.

The extent of military obligation and of judicial power was peculiar to each barony. The latter is more surprising than the former since each barony will have had a different value and population, but there would seem to have been considerable variation in the nature of the jurisdiction of barony courts. Obviously their physical jurisdiction in terms of area varied one to the next, but they did not all have the same range of powers in relation to which crimes they might try and who they might try and what sentences the court could pass. Professor Duncan[47] has demonstrated that the absence or presence of infangandthef and outgangenthef or of capital powers did not unite baronies as a class of landholding, nor does value of the property seem to have been a crucial factor; the peacetime valuations of Lothian baronies varied.

Barony, then, did not convey either judicial or military rights of itself, but those rights were among the range of easements that might be, and mostly were, attached to a barony. The range of easements, like the range of administrative power, was by no means universal, but broadly we might expect that they might include fishing, fowling and hunting rights, advowsons and the rather elusive 'free tenant services' and 'usual services', which were sometimes specifically included or excluded but usually not mentioned at all.

Barony tenures may have varied in detail one to the next, but one of the factors they shared was obviously tenants, men who held their property from the barony. The free tenants, largely rentiers, owed the baron service of varying natures and extents depending on their individual relationship but generally a package of obligations and responsibilities that included military service, suit of court, money and produce. To varying degrees this held true for all the tenants, but the degree of security of tenure and the nature of obligation depended on status. The free tenants of one barony need not have automatically enjoyed exactly the same rights and privileges as their counterparts in the neighbouring barony, but, like those holding in barony, elements of that status were likely to be broadly similar.

ESTATES AND FARMS

The 'land' or 'lands' in this barony and in that sheriffdom and held by this man from that did not farm themselves. The rents that the free tenant and the baron drew from the land were the product of labouring men, but they, like the barons and the free tenants, were not all equal in status or in the nature of their landholding. The smallest level of landholding of which we are aware is that of the cottars. It is not impossible that the status of the cottars varied, and not only according to the extent of their holding. A two acre cott was obviously less valuable than a six acre cott of similar quality, but the status of the person from whom the cott was held may have had a significance. A cottar holding directly from the king was, if only in a very technical sense, a tenant 'in capite', and though the holding was not officially heritable (as far as we know) one would wonder what motive the king would ever have for the removal of a tenant and it would not be surprising if such holdings effectively were inherited as long as there was a male heir to take up the lease. The cottar must have been in a more comfortable economic condition than the landless labourers, and it is surely more than likely that virtually all of them will have been included in Robert I's army legislation of 1318 as being men with goods in excess of the value of a cow, and thus liable to serve with bow or spear at need.[51] How regularly this liability was called upon is hard to judge, but probably only very infrequently since the majority of day-on-day military service seems to have been performed by men-at-arms.

The incidence of cottar holdings may have been quite high in order to support the considerable numbers of people needed for regular day-labour on larger farms and estates and to supplement the efforts of landless day-labourers. Many of these cottar properties may have had their origin in *villein* holdings providing the upkeep for the labour on the lord's fields, but the apparent disappearance of servile status in Scotland by the middle of the fourteenth century suggests that it was economically advantageous for both lord and tenant to convert their relationship to a more commercial format. Evidently the cottars were an important part of the economy, otherwise they would have ceased to exist for the same reasons that drove the agricultural revolution of the eighteenth century. Small holdings tend toward lower productivity – though not necessarily lower production – than large fields. A far greater proportion of agricultural land was occupied by larger farms, many, probably the majority, with multiple tenants sharing arable and pasture. The practices of Scottish medieval agriculture cannot be examined in detail here, but we should assume diversity rather than uniformity perhaps even more in Lothian than other areas.

One of the factors that distinguished the free tenants from the others lay in their relationship to the barony court. Both free tenant and sub-tenant might serve on the barony court; the free tenant was probably less subject to it but either could take their cases to the king's court if they felt that they had been denied justice.[52] The most important distinction however was that a free tenant held his or her property heritably, in 'fee and heritage'. As long as the 'fee' side of the equation was fulfilled properly the 'heritage' side was guaranteed. The financial burden on the tenant might or might not be substantial, but the services due to the superior could be extensive. Attendance at the barony court, military service and the obligation to help with the hunt would demand a lot of the tenant's time and if he held more than one property the demands could be very heavy indeed. A man with three such properties might have to discharge nine days' court service, 120 days' army service and a quantity of hunting days that cannot be ascertained, though presumably there were customary limits. If the properties were extensive the tenant could reduce his personal obligation through subinfeudation, but if the properties were modest that might not be financially realistic and the alienation of property generally and of heritage property in particular save in the utmost necessity was contrary to the *mores* of the time.

The bulk of property held by free tenants, barons and religious houses in Lothian was set to rent in the form of farms, burgages, tofts, orchards, gardens and cottar holdings. A burgage was more than simply a house in a burgh. The property could be extensive enough to include a garden which could grow enough to make a real contribution to the family economy and possession brought a share in such fields and grazing as belonged to the town. The term garden would seem to imply a different sort of property, possibly more akin to what we would think of as a market garden. Orchards we can reasonably assume to have been made for growing fruit, potentially in some quantity since we can see the monks of Coldingham seeking compensation for damage to their orchard which had previously generated 100s a year in addition to the needs of the community.[53] What is less clear is the significance of tenure terms with a financial rationale, librates and marcates. Each term obviously derives from a relationship between time and money, that is to say a librate would be land that was worth £1 per annum and a marcate land worth 1 merk per annum, but at what point was the value assessed? Land for which the king received £1 a year could potentially be very extensive given the number of valuable properties held for 1d or 6d per annum. Land that generated £1 per annum in rent from the farmer to landlord would inevitably be considerably smaller than that. If the librate represented the amount of land adequate to generate £1 worth of produce per annum it would be smaller yet.

Discrete farms were generally held in multiple tenancies from the free tenant or baron on a notionally annual basis,[54] though continuity of tenure was very probably more the rule than the exception since landlords anywhere are traditionally inclined toward stability. Perhaps more significantly there was very possibly[55] already a decline in the population of Western Europe and there is no reason to assume that Scotland was not affected; even before the sharp reduction occasioned by the Black Death in the late 1340s tenants may not have been too easy to come by.[56]

As we have seen in the case of the orchard of Coldingham priory, the properties of the religious houses were not insulated from the war. Although the centres of the foundations may have escaped the worst effects of passing armies, and though they might be able to get compensation for damage, the heads of the houses could hardly avoid acceptance of the more powerful party of the day. This must have been apparent to both English and Scottish kings, since ecclesiastical institutions seem never to have suffered for their acknowledgement of either party when a new administration took over. Both English and Scottish governments were happy to make use of the administrative capacities of religious foundations to achieve military aims. The Abbot and Convent of Jedburgh offered to match Edward I's investment of up to 500 marks per annum for five years to repair Jedburgh Castle and provide a 'sufficient bachelor' to command it.[57] Local religious foundations were required by Edward III to fund improvements to the fortifications at Perth in the 1330s and the Priory of St. Andrews was relieved of responsibility for collecting money to support the Scottish army during the siege of Loch Leven Castle.[58] With a few very prominent exceptions; Bishops Lamberton, Wishart and Sinclair under Robert I and Sir William Bullock under Edward Balliol and then under the government of David II, few senior churchmen seem to have been very actively involved in warfare. This does not mean that the actions of the heads of religious houses were without political significance. Like any other great landowner they would inevitably affect local opinion as well as reflect it. An approach to the new government, perhaps for a particular favour or the confirmation of charters, would be an act of recognition and acceptance of his lordship. That recognition would have an impact on the tenants of the house; if they wished to retain their tenancy they would be obliged, pro tem, to accept the validity of the new government since their tenure was dependent on that of their landlords.

There is a great deal that we should like to know about fourteenth-century landholdings in Lothian, not least some definition of various terms and their practical significance. King's tenants, bishop's tenants and sergeanties are all classes of land tenure that occur sufficiently often or prominently to indicate that they had specific meanings; presumably clearly understood by the holders of the tenancies and their landlord, whether crown or prelate. It would be very desirable to have a better understanding of the practice of agriculture, particularly the proportion of arable land devoted to wheat, barley, oats, rye and maslin,[59] but also the incidence of other crops. There would seem to be no incidence at all in record of either legumes, brassica or root vegetables as field crops in the thirteenth or fourteenth century, but that should hardly be taken as evidence of their absence from the diets of the wealthy at least.[60]

The only surviving description of the produce of specific farms is from the group of estates in the Cramond area whose output is recorded in the returns of Edward III's administration in 1335–36 and 1336–37.[61] Although they may well have been absolutely typical of Scottish farms it is by no means certain that they were. Apart from the obvious difficulty of assessing what exactly constituted a 'typical' farm, it seems very possible that the farms in question provided very carefully specified quantities of particular produce, wheat, barley, oats and hay, to fulfil a particular need in the crown income of the Lothian sheriffdom, such as the requirements of the garrison of the sheriff, and thus may have differed substantially in their output from neighbouring properties. What is clear is that in general Lothian property was profitable and therefore desirable. If we accept that agriculture in Lothian was probably not radically different from agriculture in Yorkshire, though perhaps (and even this is by no means certain) with a smaller proportion of the arable devoted to wheat, we should consider the opinion of Jean le Bel, who, resident in York for over a month in 1327, commented on the great 'abundance' of produce.[62] There has perhaps been too great a tendency on the part of historians to concentrate on reports of famine, but then this may well be due to the chronicle accounts from which so much of our information is gleaned. Years of outstanding productivity might draw comment, but years of great shortages would probably loom larger in the minds of compilers.[63] Years of 'ordinary' productivity would hardly be worthy of comment at all.[64]

CONCLUSIONS

The relationship between landholding, income, status and military obligation was, self-evidently, idiosyncratic. The size of an estate might not, indeed generally did not, have any relation to the extent of service and/or money due from landholder to superior. On the other hand, the nature of the service and of the tenure would, in general, have implications for the status of the landholder. Tenure with military obligations was more 'honourable' than tenure based simply on money rents. Military service, even as a man-at-arms, need not have been strictly dependent on landholding. Although we cannot be absolutely positive that the Napiers[65] and others who appear in garrison payrolls and horse valuations were in fact members of burghal families it seems very much more likely than not. However men like the Napiers and Botelers[66] were serving for wages and we cannot be certain that their status would have obliged them to give such service in normal 'peacetime' circumstances. Sir William Douglas of Lothian added recruits[67] from the burgesses of Edinburgh to his following in 1341 when he captured the castle and appointed his half-brother, also William, as sheriff. Unless the burgesses could serve as men-at-arms Sir William would not have had too much use for them given the nature of the fighting. Similarly we cannot be absolutely positive that all landholders had a military obligation attached to their tenure, though again, it seems probable that in practice they did. Certainly there is good cause to believe that the overwhelming majority of landholders did perform military service and mostly, if not universally, as men-at-arms.

The enormous variation in the financial details of their tenure does not seem to have been a significant factor in their obligation compared to their social status and their ability to carry the burden. It would seem certain that the bulk of unpaid service as men-at-arms was provided by the rural political community, partly a matter of customary obligation, partly of financial capacity, partly perhaps of maintaining social status, but for the majority of men-at-arms these three conditions would have been a function of their position as landholders. This is not to say that these men were in some way separated from those for whom military service was attractive as a means of increasing their income, furthering their ambitions or simply because they liked soldiering. There was no clear distinction between those discharging service because they had to and those serving in the hope of gaining property or ransoms[68] or making a chivalrous reputation. The latter, with very few exceptions, were drawn from the ranks of the former. Almost all of the operational activity of the Wars of Independence south of the Tay was conducted by men-at-arms discharging obligations attached directly to their landholding or to social status which was at least largely dependent on landholding. It is important to have some picture of the land they held, since that was what they were fighting to retain, either directly, in the sense of recovering their property from occupation, or indirectly in that failure to discharge service would be likely to result in forfeiture.

The loss of land through forfeiture obviously deprived the landholder of his income. Those incomes were primarily derived from the rents of tenants. Since there was no consistent relationship between return owed to the crown and the actual rental income of the property to the land-holder it is impossible to make any general statement about the wealth of landholders even where their return to the crown can be identified. Bernard de Hauden owed the service of one knight and 20s castleguard for his property in 1316–17[69], but his income from rentals was estimated at 853 shillings (£42 13s)[70] at his defection to the Scots in 1356. A selection of Robert Lauder's forfeited properties was valued at £86 by an extent in 1335–36[71] and the barony of Dirleton at £140 in the recover or retain them same year[72], but these are the existing nominal cash rents of tenants and take no account of produce or casualties or, in the case of the barony, profits of justice in the barony court. Knowledge of income is not of itself knowledge of wealth. The material may not exist to construct an adequate picture of the value of money in fourteenth-century Lothian, and certainly not to give even a dim impression of the financial liabilities of landholders, but it would seem that Lothian properties were considered desirable enough that people took great risks in their acquisition.

4

EDWARDIAN GARRISONS IN LOTHIAN, 1296–1341

An examination of the nature, incidence and effectiveness of men-at-arms serving in the cause of John Balliol, Robert I and David II must, for practical reasons, include an examination of the practices of the forces committed by Edward I, II and III to their Scottish projects. The operational policies of the Scots were, naturally enough, a product of the nature of the resources available and the prevailing military traditions. They were also – inevitably – conditioned by the response of the English. Had Edward I and Edward II adopted a policy that was essentially ethno-centric[1] they might well have dispensed with garrisons and concentrated on controlling the means by which the structures of Scottish society were supported. The deployment of an infantry-based army with a remit to starve the population into submission through confiscating or killing live-stock, trampling crops in the field and burning produce in barns,[2] would have required the Scots to adopt a very different approach. It should not be assumed that the policies of Edward II and Edward III were identical to those of Edward I, though initially at least the desired outcomes were broadly similar. Edward I and Edward II hoped to bring Scotland under their direct rule on a permanent basis. Edward III hoped to acquire per-manent possession of the southern counties – including Lothian – and he was certainly prepared to accept Edward Balliol as a sub-king, but by the later 1330s he may have seen his Scottish campaigns as a means of preventing the Scots from becoming a more serious impediment to the conquest of France. Edward III's failure to even attempt to prevent the fall of major fortresses in Scotland – Edinburgh in 1341, Roxburgh and Stirling in 1342 -strongly suggests that he was not completely committed to maintaining an administration north of the River Tweed.

PART 1: KING JOHN TO ROBERT I

The function of garrisons would not be achieved adequately simply by stationing men in centres of power in the fourteenth century any more than at any other point in history. In order to retain secure possession the new administration must demonstrate not only the ability to retain control of specific locations within the territory but the ability to prevent incursions and insurrections on the part of any resisting power that remains after conquest. This was not simply a military consideration for Edward I's government in 1296. If the new administration were to make itself generally acceptable to the population it would have to be able to impose or maintain the wider functions of government throughout the territory as a whole. In addition to suppressing armed opposition to the government the normal conditions for stable administration need to function adequately and consistently if the occupation is to be successful in the long term. There can be little doubt that both Edward I and Edward II had every intention of adding the entirety of Scotland to their realms on a permanent basis, and to that end the provision of garrisons, initially on a fairly modest scale,[3] was part of their general war policy throughout the period 1296–1314.

The military function of the garrisons is fairly self-evident. The force committed was responsible for preventing armed opposition from gaining momentum throughout the region, in this case Lothian, and in particular to prevent such opposition from gaining control of the towns and castles of the sheriffdom. This was not simply a matter of ensuring that the castles had a complement of troops adequate to defend the castles and towns themselves but to maintain a visible presence of armed strength throughout the sheriffdom sufficient to deter resistance. In this, the garrisons were rather more successful than might seem, superficially, to be the case given that all of the towns and strongpoints did fall to Robert I by the summer of 1314. It is worth bearing in mind that the major centres of power (at least) were taken through the intervention of elements from outwith the area or fell to the Scots after the Battle of Bannockburn when it became obvious that Edward II was not in a position to enforce his rule through military effort. This is not to say that the garrisons were completely successful at all times in preventing the Scots, whether under the Guardians or under King Robert, from conducting operations in or around Lothian, but they were successful in preventing consistent Scottish military activity. Nor is it the case that the garrisons could always be considered secure as installations. According to Walter of Guisborough, in 1298 Edward I was obliged to commit a force[4] under Anthony Bek, Bishop of Durham to capture castles in East Lothian, Dirleton and two others, possibly Yester and Hailes.

It would seem very unlikely that any of these castles had remained in Scottish hands in the period after the battle of Dunbar in 1296. Yester had been put under the command of Peter de Dunwych and its provisioning and 'arming' had been the responsibility of Henry de Greneford in 1296.[5] It is therefore reasonable to conclude that they had fallen to the Scots at some point in the intervening period, though whether they had been taken by the Scots, been abandoned or been turned over to the Scots through the defection of the owners is not clear. That the Scots were able to enter Lothian is demonstrated by the fact that Wallace was able to issue documents from Haddington,[6] but it would seem that he could not maintain a sufficient presence to form an alternative administration, or at least he does not seem to have appointed a sheriff of Lothian in competition with the Edwardian government. As far as we are aware Wallace was unable to threaten either Edinburgh or Linlithgow. The former was protected by a major castle. If Wallace were to lay siege to it and not succeed his prestige as a military leader would be compromised and his political power rested primarily on his martial reputation, but Linlithgow had not yet been developed into a major stronghold. Since it was obviously more exposed to Scottish threats we might wonder why Wallace chose to make an incursion so deep into the territory under occupation as Haddington.

It has been observed[7] that when Wallace offered battle to Edward I he chose to do so on the very borders of Lothian, at Falkirk, and this might be seen as an indication that the garrisons were not equal to the task of preventing Scottish military activity. The required scale of intervention would have been beyond both the remit and capacity of the various garrisons posted since 1296. When Wallace deployed at Falkirk he had command of a major field army, one concentrated for the specific purpose of fighting a large engagement with the main force of the enemy. Even if all the garrison troops of Lothian had been brought together they would hardly have been equal to the task of defeating Wallace's force, and such a concentration would have compromised the function for which the garrisons had been deployed in the first place. If the castles were denuded of troops how were they to be kept secure against the enemy and how was the business of government to be conducted? Providing a secure environment for Edwardian government was, after all, the chief function of the garrisons.

With the possible exception of 1296–97[8] the English administration of Edward I and Edward II does not seem to have imposed heavier burdens on the community than the due and accustomed practice under Alexander III or King John. Nor, generally, do they seem to have had any particular difficulty in collecting the issues of the county or maintaining civil order during the first few months of the occupation. The difficult circumstances of 1297–1304 and 1306–14 meant that a far greater military presence was required than had been the case under Alexander III. The small numbers of what appear to be knights in receipt of cash allowances and the fees authorised to constables of castles[9] during Edward I's administration in 1291–92 would hardly have been sufficient to provide a large force. The initial level of success may have been more apparent than real. Even in Berwickshire, where the local populace must have been all too aware of the extreme violence of Edward's sack of the town in March 1296,[10] it was proving impossible to collect the issues of the county by the summer of 1297.[11] The level of military presence maintained by Alexander III and King John cannot be accurately assessed from the surviving documentary record, but that does not mean that there was no military presence at all. In 1291–92 payments were made to the commanders of several Scottish royal castles from the Scottish exchequer under the authority of Edward I, to whom these castles had been entrusted pending the resolution of the succession dispute that arose on account of the death of Margaret, Maid of Norway, the heir of Alexander III. The castellan of Edinburgh castle, Sir Ralph Bisset received the considerable sum of one merk per day (13s 4d).[12] Given that the 'field service' rate of pay for a senior knight with a leadership responsibility (a banneret) was 4s a day in English armies it would seem unreasonable to assume that Sir Ralph's 13s 4d a day was intended simply as salary, but rather more likely that he was obliged to supply a retinue, however small, to support him in his duties and provide security for the castle. It is of course possible that such an arrangement was a novelty in Scottish affairs and that it was an innovation of Edward I, but Edward does not seem to have been in the way of reorganising any aspect of government practice in Scotland. In fact he was committed, at least in theory, to the continuity of existing administrative practice under the terms of his agreement with the Scottish political community.[13]

A small retinue was presumably considered an adequate complement in peacetime since a force of ten men-at-arms (plus three for his lands in Scotland) was considered sufficient for Sir John Kingeston's retinue in August 1302.[14] If, in addition to that one merk per day, the commander of Edinburgh Castle had the benefit of castleguard income from Edinburgh and Haddington (there was no royal castle at Haddington) there would probably have been adequate funding available to the commander for both his retinue and the normal upkeep of the castle itself, though significant improvements to the fabric of the castle would very probably require additional funding from the king. This was certainly the case under David II, whose exchequer supplied funds for various military stores for the castle.[15]

Strong garrisons might not prevent Scottish operations, but they would certainly have reduced the frequency of such operations to a minimum. In the sense that keeping the war out of the counties held for King Edward allowed the people to get on with their daily business in relative peace, garrisons like Ayr, Aberdeen and Linlithgow may have helped to make the presence of Edwardian government more acceptable to the community and even if it did not do so, there was really very little the community could do to change the situation without taking the risks of forfeiture attendant on armed resistance. Even if such resistance was undertaken, there was no guarantee that it would be successful in the long term. Local military activity might reduce the ability of the garrison to carry out the functions of government, might even eject the garrisons from the towns and castles, but would be very unlikely indeed to repel the advance of a well-found field army intent on restoring the situation, which would undoubtedly be the response of King Edward to a 'revolt' that successfully dislodged his administration. Perhaps just as significantly, the ejection of the garrisons would not of itself be a source of stability, let alone bring about better government unless there was an alternative source of lordship ready to take the place of Edward's administration and, just as importantly, capable of preventing its return.

The Edinburgh garrison establishment of thirteen men-at-arms under Sir John de Kingestone authorised in September 1302 seems to conflict with another ordinance of 1301–2[16] which had authorised a force of thirty men-at-arms plus officers. It is possible that this is a comparison of two different establishments: the force of ten men-at-arms being a 'unit' dedicated to the security of Edinburgh Castle and the force of thirty representing the requirements of the sheriffdom as a whole. Records of the garrisons in Scotland compiled in September 1302 indicate that there were 386 men-at-arms serving for wages and a further seventy-three serving for lands granted to them in Scotland. The report includes forty-one men-at-arms and a further forty infantrymen (half of them crossbowmen) in Sir John de Kingestone's garrison at Edinburgh.[17] The wording of the document is ambiguous but it seems to indicate that the garrisons were collectively about ninety men-at-arms short of the theoretical establishment: fifty who should have been serving for their lands and another forty who should have been in the retinue of Sir John de St. John. The indentures[18] of the various garrison commanders give slightly different figures to the report, indicating that of 508 men 113 were serving for their lands in Scotland and 395 were receiving wages; very few had Scottish names.[19] Those men serving for lands are specifically described as having been granted lands in Scotland by the king, presumably lands that had been forfeited by others. The military obligations attendant on the land were in all probability identical to those due from the previous owner. Since these grants had been made in recent times – they could hardly have been made before the spring of 1296 – it seems remarkable that as many as fifty men who had received grants of land in Scotland for military service should fail to discharge their obligations in 1302.

The fact that the garrison of Edinburgh Castle would appear to have been at three different sizes of complement authorised in a period of only two months may be a product of misdated documents or administrative confusion caused by the arrival or departure of contingents of men; equally it could be the product of a rapidly-changing military situation. The most likely explanation surely lies in the difference between what was considered adequate in the light of the practices of Scottish kings before 1296 and the realities of the prevailing conditions of 1302.

This does not necessarily mean that the garrisons were intended simply as a means of retaining control of the sheriffdom or even of keeping the war out of the area, although these were surely important considerations. Strong 'depot' forces at important centres like Dundee or Stirling could provide temporary reinforcements for other establishments when required, but they could, in theory at least, also provide or contribute to mobile formations carrying the war to the Scots in other areas without compromising the security of local deployments and assets. Thus the complement of the Edinburgh garrison over and above the ten men-at-arms assigned to Sir John (plus the three from his own resources) may in fact have been accounted at Edinburgh for administrative reasons only, their task being the support of Edward's government in a rather wider sense than the defence of the castle and county.

The eventual collapse of the Edwardian administration in Scotland is not proof-positive that the garrison policy itself was an outright failure. The field successes of the Bruce party were not a product of incapacity or incompetence on the part of the garrisons so much as the product of a consistent inability on the part of central government to obstruct the development of an alternative source of lordship powerful enough to contest the authority of English kingship. Superficially it might seem that the Lothian garrisons were in fact reasonably successful throughout the period from 1296 until the fall of Linlithgow peel in march 1314 when compared with those in the north and west. The Bruce party may have been able to extort money and truces from Lothian in 1311–12, but apparently could not extend their rule into the sheriffdom. On the other hand it would seem that the operational capacity of the Scots was identified as a real threat in 1304–5 when the Hospitallers were guaranteed entry to Linlithgow peel in the event of their preceptory at Torphichen being attacked.[20] The possession of castles does not of itself necessarily imply the control of the surrounding countryside; although Edinburgh fell to the Scots in the spring of 1314 through the efforts of a force from outwith the area under the Earl of Moray, the garrison was evidently not able to prevent the deployment of a Scottish force strong enough to institute a siege. Nor would it seem that the Edwardian administration was able to raise much in the way of issues from the sheriffdom, or at least not enough to be able to forward a balance (after local expenses) to contribute to Edward I's exchequer. Nonetheless the garrisons were strong enough to deny effective possession of Lothian to the Bruce party.[21]

Paid service in Lothian garrisons, and no doubt, throughout Scotland, seems to have been a 'career choice' rather than a function of the 'normal' military responsibility associated with land tenure. The majority of the men whose service is dated seem to have been in more or less continuous service the whole year round – the Edinburgh garrison account for 1312 is a particularly clear example – for fixed rates of pay. There are references to men-at-arms serving 'for their lands' (see above), but this provided only a small proportion of the manpower needed to staff the establishments.[22] Additionally, most of the men serving in that category were serving 'for their lands in Scotland granted by the king'. The implication is that these were lands granted by Edward I or Edward II in the hope that these grants would become permanent through eventual success in war against the Scots, and while some of the recipients of these grants were very possibly Scots, it would seem reasonable to assume that the majority were Englishmen trying to further their careers. This assumption is reinforced by the incidence of senior figures (such as Sir John de Kingestone, see above) in the English administration supplying men for their garrisons or retinues over and above the troops receiving the king's wages; the implication being that these men had received lands through subinfeudation in order that their superiors could fulfil the army service commitments attendant on their Scottish titles. Presumably those tenants who had remained in Edward's peace retained their property and continued to be liable for the appropriate military service. No doubt the officers of Edward's Scottish administration who were the main beneficiaries, Robert Hastangs, John de St. John, Robert Clifford and others, made a point of demanding the service of their new tenants in order to fulfil their own military obligations to the king.[23]

We can reasonably assume that that obligation was quite carefully defined. Although we can be sure that the autumn of 1302 was hardly 'peacetime', nor was it a period of deep crisis for the Edwardian administration, so it would be rash to assume that Edward's troop demands were either unrealistic or exceptionally heavy. It is perfectly possible that a force of 100 or more men-at-arms could be raised from landholder obligations in Lothian alone, a suggestion that is supported by the high incidence of man-at-arms service among those who appear in English records. Men serving 'for their lands' were not, it seems, generally recorded by name in central government documents relating to garrisons, though obviously their discharge of service was recorded in some way. If the men who owed that service were rotated on the basis of forty days of duty – or even perhaps fractions of forty days in the case of those owing fractional knight service – it would be an unnecessary inconvenience to maintain a nominal register of men serving for land at any given moment. The sheriff or constable would need to keep a register of who had or had not discharged their obligation – if only in order to identify and deal with defaulters – but the king's lieutenants would only need to know that the service was being performed. In a sense the modern observer is in the same position: we may not know the names of the individuals or the properties for which they served, but we can identify that service being performed.

Making grants of land as a reward for service past or an incentive to serve in the future was obviously an attractive option to Edward since it encouraged serious commitment to the future of his administration in Scotland. It did, of course, depend on the availability of land to be granted. Although Scots could be, and were, forfeited for adherence to the Balliol cause (and of course the Bruce cause after 1306) forfeiture was something of a last resort, since it would discourage defections among the Scottish nobility. Further, should forfeited men join or return to Edward's peace, any of their lands that had already been granted to Edward's supporters might have to be restored to the defector.

Documentary examples of grants of land in Scotland to Edwardian soldiers are few and far between, no doubt because the military successes of the Scots eventually rendered them worthless, but since as many as seventy-three men were serving for land grants in September 1302,[24] it is obvious that such grants were being made. It may be the case that grants were made for the service of archers or other troop-types – Kilsyth was granted for the service of archers,[25] possibly an unusual but traditional arrangement since it was continued by Robert I – but the primary concern seems to have been to increase the heavy cavalry element of Edward's forces. Certainly all of the seventy-three men referred to above were serving in that capacity. The men in question were obviously the recipients of lands forfeited by Balliol supporters or of crown property, but the significance is not so much who the men were or where their properties lay; this information does not seem to have been required in garrison reports. Regardless of who held the land the burdens that were attached to it still had to be discharged, and it would seem that in 1302 the administration was able to take advantage of some portion of the service due from Scottish estates.

Most of garrison men-at-arms were in the king's pay, receiving 12d a day or two shillings (24d) if they were knights. Whether or not those serving for lands got paid is not clear from the source material, however it is clear that service for land became less common than service for wages throughout the Scottish wars of the three Edwards, as it did in their other conflicts, since the incidence of men recorded as 'serving for their lands in Scotland' would seem to have disappeared entirely by the time Edward II came to the throne. This may, of course be a reflection of the inability of the administration to retain territory. The success of Robert I, and of the guardians in the period 1296–1303, in ousting the Edwardian administration would obviously have compromised the tenure of men who had been granted Scottish estates in locations no longer under English control and of course would reduce the willingness of men to serve for grants of lands which were still in that control but that might fall to the Scots at any time. Perceptions of security would naturally vary according to the wider political and military situation. Men granted land in Lothian by Edward I might have felt quite secure after the settlement of 1304; they had probably felt less so in the days after the fight at Roslin. Arguably men like Robert Hastang and John de Strivelin, respectively recipients of grants predominantly in Lothian from Edward I and Edward II before 1312 and from Edward III before Culblean might have felt more secure in their acquisitions, but both men took the precaution of obtaining a guarantee of compensation if their properties fell to the Scots.

It would seem probable that the Edinburgh Castle garrison included a number of retinues, all of them rather small, as well as a number of men enlisted individually, hence the differentiation between, for example, Thomas de Morham, recorded as serving with two esquires and Pierre de Lubaud, recorded as an individually enlisted man-at-arms. This may indicate a distinction between men provided by a lord as a feudal obligation and those enlisting for wages, but the distinction, if it existed, was not a permanent social condition. There were very real career opportunities for professional soldiers due to a seemingly endless demand for men-at-arms, so a man who served for a given period for his lands might well have the option of serving for longer periods in addition to that obligation for the sake of the wages available. Army service potentially offered more than just daily wages; a successful soldier like Pierre de Lubaud could rise in status from man-at-arms[26] to the rank of sergeant-at-arms[27] and eventually knighthood and appointment as a sheriff.[28] Once promoted, Lubaud provided a retinue of his own, either as a product of landholding or as a commercial supplier of troops. The latter would involve entering into a contractual arrangement – an indenture – whereby, for a given sum of money, he would provide a specified number of soldiers for a defined period. In 1312 Lubaud commanded thirty men-at-arms in the Livingston garrison,[29] six of whom he retained personally and at least thirteen of whom were Scots. Unusually, the muster roll for that garrison seems to differentiate between men-at-arms and scutifers; the men retained by Lubaud are listed as men-at-arms, the others as scutifers. The significance of this, if any, is unclear. All of the men were paid at the usual man-at-arms rate of 1s per day, an indication that they were not serving for their lands and, incidentally, of the quality of their equipment. The full 12d a day wage for a man-at-arms was dependent, not only on having arms, armour and a suitable horse, but on having appropriate armour for the horse.[30] Given the general trend of the war by 1312 thirty men-at-arms might seem to be a slender garrison, though it should be borne in mind that Livingston was within easy reach of the far larger establishment at Linlithgow and that although Robert I was unquestionably in the ascendant militarily he had yet to seriously challenge the Edwardian administration in the south-east. It would seem possible that Lubaud was not able to maintain the strength of the garrison since the sum expended on wages – £439 12s – fell considerably short of the £517 that would have been required to pay 30 men 12d each for the entire pay term of 346 days,[31] though of course to some extent the disparity is likely to have been a product of men going on leave or serving terms at other garrisons.

The few garrison infantry soldiers serving in Edinburgh garrison in 1312 who can be readily identified as Scots – six out of twenty-four crossbowmen and ten out of twenty-seven archers who had served a full year, would seem to have been recruited from the immediate vicinity. Robert de Vallibus (de Vaux), Walter del Inche (presumably the 'Inch' area of Gilmerton), Johanis de Nodref (Niddry), William de Redehale (Redhall) and Walter de Pentland among the crossbowmen, and Serlonis de Edenburghe (Edinburgh), Johannis de Lithcu (Linlithgow), Hugo de Blacknesse (Blackness), Thomas de Craumont (Cramond) and Adam de Prestone (Preston), all bore names with strong Lothian connections and other members of the group might very well have been local men. It would seem, then, that some proportion of the troop requirements of the administration in Scotland could be raised in Scotland, a minimum of sixteen men out of a particular group of fifty-one members of the Edinburgh garrison in this instance and at least thirteen out of twenty archers in the Livingston peel garrison of the same year.

Local recruitment was certainly significant, but would hardly seem to have been dominant in the composition of the most important garrisons. However it is important to bear in mind that military service was not necessarily recorded. Men serving for land would not normally be paid, nor would they have their horses appraised for the 'restauro' roll. Such men might serve in large numbers without leaving any trace in surviving records. The muster rolls from 1312 are not after all descriptions of the full complement of the garrison, merely a record of those receiving pay for their services. If the Edwardian administration was able to make landholders discharge their obligations the amount of unrecorded man-at-arms service might be very considerable. In addition it is quite possible that some landholders might have chosen to perform castleguard services instead of paying money to avoid them. Although the money saved would not be genuinely concomitant with the time committed, it would still be money saved and an additional man-at-arms would very likely be more welcome to the sheriff or constable than the money lost, insignificant sums when compared to the overall cost of the garrisons.

Assuming that Sir John de Kingestone's fee as constable of the castle excluded him from the garrison wage bill, and that the remaining knights, men-at-arms, archers and crossbowmen were in receipt of the usual pay rates of Edwardian garrison troops (2s/day for knights, 1s/day for men-at-arms, 4d/day for crossbowmen[32] and 3d/day for archers) the daily total would come to £7 16s. The garrison also included a considerable number of non-combatants, amounting to 202 out of a total of 347,[33] so the real daily expenditure on garrison wages was obviously a much larger sum. Some deductions about the function of the garrison may be made from a consideration of its membership. It is clear from a comparison with wages of other garrisons and with field armies that the archers and crossbowmen of the garrison of 1300 were not expected to maintain horses. Archers would of course fight on foot, but the mounted archer would seem to have enjoyed the same rate of pay, 6d/day, as the hobelar, a light cavalry soldier. It should not be assumed that the archers and crossbowmen never took part in operations outwith the castle, but it is fair to assume that their primary role was defensive. The fact that the largest combatant group within the garrison was the men-at-arms and the careful detailing of the availability of suitable horses shows that mobility of force was seen as an important factor in the design of the garrison complement. Mobility was obviously of limited value for those manning the walls of the castle so we can conclude that the men-at-arms were stationed at Edinburgh with a view to conducting operations throughout the sheriffdom; otherwise they would be an unnecessarily expensive contribution to the complement. That expense was not simply a matter of higher wages. The non-combatant element of the garrison included large numbers of grooms and the logistical effort required to maintain horses for the men-at-arms, and one should bear in mind that the number of horses required to keep the man-at-arms force would generally greatly exceed the number of men[34] and would obviously call for a considerable expenditure on large quantities of hay and hard feed.[35]

Since Edward I was prepared to support an expensive force of men-at-arms in Edinburgh it seems reasonable to assume that he meant them to make a useful contribution to his policies, and since Edward had a considerable experience of imposing his lordship in newly conquered territories,[36] we might further assume that he was confident that that contribution would bear results. The possession of castles would not have been sufficient to enforce Edward's government if the sheriff of the county could not deploy sufficient force to discourage disorder, and while ten or thirty men-at-arms[37] was hardly likely to constitute an adequate counter to incursions by a Scottish army, it would surely have been more than a match for any local opposition. This is not to say that the garrison men-at-arms were deployed to perform 'policing' duties as a general rule. There seems no good reason to assume that the 'peace-time' law and order systems in the form of 'local' courts that had existed under Scottish kings prior to 1296[38] were swept away by the occupying power after the Battle of Dunbar. The fact that we have very limited information about the administration of justice through baronial courts or sergeanties[39] in early fourteenth-century Lothian does not mean that these aspects of government had disappeared or that they had become ineffective. We might more realistically see the garrison troops in the role of 'aid to the civil power' rather than as a substitute for the existing systems of government, in which case we might envisage the troops being deployed to deal with situations beyond the capacity of local officers rather than providing a defence against activity by the enemy. This might explain the different levels of force assigned to Edinburgh Castle or to Linlithgow peel in the late summer and autumn of 1302 (see above) i.e. that one 'unit' of ten men-at-arms was intended for aid to the civil power in the form of the sheriff's retinue and the other of thirty (plus 'officers') for more belligerent operational purposes, thus, for administrative purposes at least, giving Sir John de Kingestone a total of forty-one men-at-arms.[40] What exactly was the status or remit of the 'officers' of Linlithgow garrison is not clear, but their existence does indicate a formal command structure at levels of responsibility below the garrison commander. Edmund de Caillou serving in the Edinburgh garrison of 1312 was described as the 'king's sergeant-at-arms', a rank or status he shared with two others, George Saunford and Arnaldo de Sancto Martino. Each of these men may have been the commander of a permanent sub-unit within the cavalry element of the garrison; the lay-out of the rolls suggests that this was so, but the title might indicate that the officer could be entrusted with a particular level of responsibility as and when required.

Whatever the practical function of the garrisons, Edward plainly saw them as a necessary expense. Even if his judgment was faulty, and there is no reason to assume that it was, the fact remains that he was prepared to make the provision of men and materials a long-term commitment. Presumably he did not envisage maintaining such large or expensive deployments indefinitely, but we should be wary of assuming that a reduction or increase of garrison manpower or a change in the constitution of garrisons was simply a product of the requirements of the military situation. If the only perceived threat to the security of the castle was a siege by the enemy's field army, and not from any possibility of local disorder, the number of men-at-arms might reasonably be reduced in favour of archers. Availability of men may or may not have been an issue, but the strength of Edinburgh and Linlithgow garrisons did not remain static throughout the period 1300–1302. The muster roll of 1300 represents the actual service of individuals, but the two subsequent documents are more in the nature of statements of intent, i.e. that the garrisons of Linlithgow and Edinburgh should in the future comprise so many men-at-arms and so many archers as a matter of policy rather than being a reflection of the number of men actually available for service.

The reductions of strength envisaged in these documents compared to the Edinburgh muster roll of 1300 may have had a financial basis, but there must also have been an operational justification of sorts. This does not mean that the Scots were perceived as less of a threat in 1302 than they had been in 1300, although that is certainly possible. The Scots may have been improving their position generally, but failing to threaten the English administration in Lothian. Changes in the structure of garrisons could be the result of a number of military factors. The men-at-arms in the Berwick garrison of 1300 were expected to take part in operations against the Scots, but not to confront large bodies of them in the field day-on-day. Twenty-five men-at-arms were evidently considered an adequate force for the maintenance of law and order; however the garrison also included 270 archers and sixty crossbowmen.[41] A force of such magnitude would not have been assigned carelessly; a reasonable explanation would be that while the administration was not concerned that the sheriffdom of Berwick was at risk of being overrun by the Scots it was still necessary to maintain a strong force of archers to deter attempts by the Scots to take the town and castle by storm.

The number of men-at-arms recorded as serving at a particular location is not an infallible guide to the level of perceived threat in that vicinity; we must consider the purpose of the deployment. The Linlithgow garrison of 1301–02 included eighty-five men-at-arms, ten of whom served as the retinue of the sheriff, Sir Archibald Livingstone.[42] The fact that ten men-at-arms were considered adequate for the needs of the sheriff surely indicates that the other seventy-five men served a different function. In the absence of any other clear operational objective the conclusion must be that their purpose was to carry the war to the enemy and thus away from Lothian. We should, therefore, see Linlithgow, not as a frontier garrison whose primary function was to keep the Scots out of Lothian, but as a secure base from which operations could be mounted into the Lennox, Menteith and Strathearn in complete confidence that the peel would not be vulnerable to the Scots.

No doubt the huge sums of money required for wages had some effect on the numbers of men assigned to particular establishments, but it might be the case that experience had indicated that the lower numbers were adequate to the task and that men could be re-deployed to other establishments without compromising the security of Lothian or that the civil government functions of the sheriff no longer required the same level of military commitment or even that the Edwardian government believed that the size of the garrisons had a political dimension. If the government retained large forces in Lothian castles they would be tacitly admitting that there was a need to do so; that the Lothian constabularies were at risk from the operations of the Scots. Alternatively the government may have believed that the presence of a highly visible force might produce resentment in the community. It may be the case that Edward's officers simply could not recruit men in sufficient numbers to maintain the garrisons at the levels of manpower committed in 1300 and that troops had to be re-deployed to areas where the demand for men was more pressing than in Lothian.

Despite the defeat of Wallace's army at Falkirk in 1298, the Scots enjoyed a remarkable degree and consistency of military success until 1303, securing the north-west and driving the English from Invernesshire, Aberdeenshire, Badenoch and Angus, and this may be reflected in the apparently small numbers of Scots serving in Lothian garrisons compared to either 1311–12 or 1335–37. The ability of the Balliol party to mount operations virtually anywhere in Scotland – even if only at a relatively trivial level – and to carry on the business of King John to the extent of being able to appoint officials and even hold a Parliament at Rutherglen[43] was hardly an indication that the Edwardian government was successfully 'settling' Scottish affairs. In 1300 the position of the Edwardian government may have looked very insecure indeed in which case enlisting in the military service of that government would not have been a very attractive proposition for Scots even if their political sympathies lay with the Plantagenet cause.

The garrison rolls for 1311–12 show an apparent rise in the proportion of Scots serving. It may be the case that there are simply more names recorded and/or that a greater proportion of the names are evidently Scottish. However there may be a political element present. In February 1312 Edward II forfeited a number of landholders as 'enemies'.[44] Some of these men had been in the Bruce camp for years by this point and quite why they should be forfeited at this juncture is unclear. Other than the fact that they had all defected and that they were all either Lothian men or at least men with extensive interests there, there is no obvious connection between the seven men concerned. Had their properties lain close to one another there might be an argument that these forfeitures were a direct product of the military situation, possibly that that particular area of Lothian was no longer in the control of Plantagenet government, but since those estates were widely scattered throughout Lothian that would suggest that very little of the Lothian sheriffdom actually remained in English hands in February 1312. Given the relatively large numbers of Scots serving in his garrisons Edward, or his advisors, may have felt that it was desirable to make an example of those who had left his peace, either as an incentive to those serving in his garrisons and Lothian land-holders generally to continue in his allegiance or to demonstrate his appreciation of their continuing support.

In 1312 the Bruce cause was certainly enjoying a substantial degree of success, but a considerable body of Scottish opinion was clearly aligned against it as we can see from the garrison muster rolls of that year. At least twelve out of the thirty-five men-at-arms in the Stirling garrison and fourteen out of eighty-eight at Linlithgow were Scots, though only John de Maleville, Thomas de Ramsay, John, William and Nicholas de Lithcu (Linlithgow) and Gilbert de Duddingston can be confidently associated with Lothian other than through military service. The Edinburgh garrison of the same year included eighty-one men-at-arms of whom twenty-three were Scots. It must be stressed again that the number of Scots and the number of Lothian men should be regarded as absolute minimums; both categories are likely to have been rather larger, perhaps even of the order of Bothwell garrison where at least forty-three out of one hundred and thirteen men-at-arms were Scots.

The reasons for this were wide-ranging. Robert was a usurper and it is quite possible that men who had favoured the Balliol cause saw the Edwardian government as the lesser of two evils. Sir William Oliphaunt had commanded the garrison of Stirling castle against Edward I in 1304 for the guardian administration of King John until the pacification of Perth, and even after the surrender of the Balliol party continued the defence of the castle, allegedly in the name of 'The Lion', the heraldic symbol of Scotland, rather than surrender. But he was remarkably steadfast in his service to the Plantagenet cause thereafter, to the extent that he was the commander of the Perth garrison when it fell to the Bruce party in 1312[45] and Sir Ingram de Umfraville served as Guardian for the Balliol party, but fought against the Bruce party at Bannockburn. It is clear that not all Scots equated the Bruce party with the 'patriotic' cause. Bruce's attempt on the throne certainly drew men from Edward's allegiance, but it probably enabled him to recruit others who had previously opposed him, men like Sir John Graham who had fought Edward on behalf of the Balliols until 1304 but was serving Edward as a man-at-arms at Ayr in 1307.

A practical consideration might lie in the nature of the Bruce struggle. King John had undoubtedly been the legally constituted king prior to the invasion of Edward I. Since John had been deposed by force, his heir, Edward Balliol, would have a legitimate claim to Scottish kingship. King Robert had no legitimate male heir other than his brother Edward and both of them were active in the field. If they should both be killed in action or captured and subsequently executed the Bruce cause would cease to exist. In 1312 it may well have seemed to the majority of Lothian Scots that the chances of an eventual Bruce victory were still slim. The local garrison system seems to have been able to provide the administration with the stability and order necessary to conduct government. Resistance to that government was likely to provoke forfeiture at the very least, whereas service to it might help to preserve Lothian from the worst effects of a war in which that government had clear advantages in terms of manpower and money.

Admittedly Edward II had not been able to force battle on Robert. In fact it could be argued that before the summer of 1314 he had made little serious attempt to do so, but in general it was clear that the military capacity of English kings, should they choose to mobilize it in earnest, was unquestionably superior to that of Robert Bruce. In all probability most contemporary observers would have expected that should a major confrontation occur, Edward would be in a much stronger position. Also, although the Bruce party had enjoyed a considerable degree of military success prior to 1314, they had not been able to make permanent inroads into the south-east of Scotland generally. Although they were able to force county communities to buy truces, they do not seem to have been in a position to retain territory. As long as that continued to be the case it would be rash for Lothian landholders to join the Bruce cause. While it is true that some Lothian men did join King Robert, even in the early part of his kingship,[46] the majority chose not to do so. According to Barbour,[47] a considerable number served Edward II at the Battle of Bannockburn, an indication that despite the fall of Edinburgh Castle, the English administration could still count on some degree of support from the political community of Lothian. Superficially this might suggest that the retention of castles was not a crucial factor in maintaining government; however it may not have been clear to Lothian landholders that the Edwardian government was suffering anything more than a temporary setback. Edinburgh Castle had fallen to a coup de main operation rather than through a formal siege that Edward was powerless to raise, and while we might identify King Robert's failure to garrison and retain the castle as part of a general policy of reducing the value of such installations, the Lothian community may have construed his slighting of the castle as an indication of weakness, that Robert did not feel that he would be able to keep the castle in the face of an English counter-offensive. The fact that the war had gone in Robert's favour for some time was no guarantee that it would continue to do so.

In 1303 the Scots had been in the ascendant militarily for some years, notwithstanding a signal English victory at Falkirk, but they capitulated in 1304.[48] Lothian gentry would be positively rash to assume that a similar state of affairs could not come about as a result of Edward II's expedition of 1314. Edward had initiated preparations for his attack before the close of 1313 and had written to supporters in Scotland on 28 November to assure them that he would be making an intervention in Scotland by midsummer of the next year.[49] Men who deserted his cause before that intervention would face a bleak future if Edward were successfully to derail the Bruce party through a major victory in the field. The fall of a castle would not be sufficient of itself to convince the community as a whole that the relatively stable administration that had ruled Lothian for most of the preceding twenty years was moribund; a castle that had fallen to an enemy could be regained.

The proportion of man-at-arms service performed by men identifiable as Scots in the Edinburgh and Linlithgow garrisons is not particularly high, assuming that the number apparently identifiable as Scots is a reasonably accurate expression of the numbers who actually were Scots, but it is hardly insignificant. As in Livingston, it is more than likely that some portion of the named members of the garrisons were in fact Scots. John le Marechal and Roger de Merleye may well be the same men whose names appear on the Ragman Roll,[50] but we cannot be absolutely certain that they were. Since this applies to a considerable proportion of the muster roll names it may be the case that Scottish men-at-arms formed a rather larger part of the whole than we might expect since only a relatively small number, such as Thomas de Wobourne and Nicholas de Paris, can be safely assumed to be not Scottish. It could be that as few

1. Stirling Bridge. A view from the battlefield from the top of the Wallace Monument. The leading elements of the English Army were trapped in a loop of the Forth and were forced onto the area now occupied by the rugby club whose pitch can be seen in the middle distance of the photograph.

2. The Battle of Stirling Bridge. A view from Stirling Castle, across the battlefield toward the Wallace monument.

3. Torpichen Receptory. In the thirteenth century the headquarters of the knights of St. John in Scotland was at Torpichen in West Lothian. The Knights of St. John, like the Templars, had long lost their military role and had become an international commercial concern. One of the few surviving instruments issued during Wallace's government, a grant to Alexander Scrymgeour, was made at Torpichen.

4. Incholm Abbey. Walter Bower wrote his *Scotichronicon* at the island abbey of Incholm on the River Forth in the mid-fifteenth century.

5. The Wallace Monument. Built at great expense, and plenty of controversy, in the nineteenth century, the Wallace Monument overlooks the field of William Wallace's greatest triumph, the Battle of Stirling Bridge.

6. Linlithgow Peel. Edward I commissioned the erection of a large 'Peel' or fortified camp at the Linthglow which incorporated the parish kirk. The peel was the base for a large mobile force of men-at-arms until it fell to the Scots c.1313. In addition to the peel at Linlithgow, Edward constructed a small satellite peel at Livingstone, a larger peel and horse hospital at Selkirk and planned another peel at Dunfermline.

7. Blackness Castle. Blackness was an important depot for the English occupation between 1296 and its recovery by Robert I c.1313. Great quantities of grain, ale, wine and beef were delivered here for the supply of strongholds such as Edinburgh and Linlithgow.

8. Edinburgh Castle. Although Wallace was able to mount an operation into Lothian in 1297, he was unable to bring the sheriffdom under his control, due chiefly to the strength of the castles held by English garrisons.

9. Trebuchet. For many decades after the introduction of gunpowder, kinetic weapons – catapults, ballistae and trebuchets – continued to be a major element in siege warfare. Edward I obtained gunpowder for the siege of Stirling Castle in 1304, but as an explosive thrown at the target rather than as the propellant in a firearm.

10. The catapult exhibit at Caverlock Castle.

11. Men-at-arms in combat. Both of these men carry equipment typical of the later thirteenth century. By the time of Bannockburn most, if not all, of the men-at-arms on either side would have acquired plate armour for the arms and legs as well as the lighter bacinet helmet. The figure on the right bears the arms of Sir Aymer de Valence, Earl of Pembroke. Pembroke spent much of his considerable military career in Scotland.

12. Men-at-arms and infantrymen (photo by Lydia Diamond).

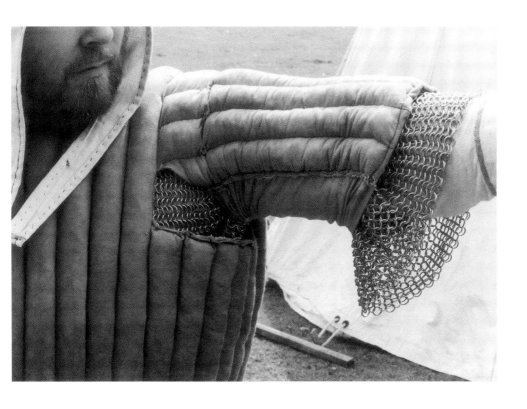

13a & b. A jack may be worn over chainmail or underneath it.

Above: 14. The term spearman should not be taken too literally; since men were generally responsible for providing their own weapons there would inevitably be quite a variety of polearms in use. The experience of re-enactors would seem to suggest that spears and polearms were rather more robust than the slender and elegant weapon shafts of Victorian artworks.

Left: 15. Liveried archer. Livery was becoming increasingly common by the mid-fourteenth century.

16. King Robert's encounter with de Bohun by a Victorian artist.

17. Spearmen standing and kneeling to receive cavalry. This is very much the general conception of Scottish tactics during the Wars of Independence, however the Scots were, in the main, offensively-minded, and were inclined to attack rather than stand on the defensive.

18. English troops at Stirling Bridge and Falkirk were confronted by large bodies of spearmen. As long as the integrity of the formation was maintained, these *schiltroms* were virtually impossible to defeat, however they were extremely vulnerable to archery.

19. Chapel-de-fer, or 'Irn hat'. These were widely used throughout later medieval Europe, and appeared in a variety of styles.

20. Another style of Chapel-de-fer, or what the 1318 legislation of Robert I referred to as a 'good iron', was probably the most expensive article that the rank and file needed to invest in if they were to fulfil their military obligations.

21. Cambuskenneth Abbey. Only one tower remains of what was, in the thirteenth century, an extensive suite of buildings. Close to Stirling Castle, Cambuskenneth would have been a likely venue for the deliberations after the battle of Stirling Bridge in 1297.

22. The first recorded instance of glass windows in Scotland is of their purchase for King Robert's manor house at Cardross. This modern reconstruction at Blackness Castle, Midlothian, is probably quite similar in design and construction to those purchased for Cardross.

23. Looking towards Culblean Hill, just to the left behind the tree line.

24. View north from Halidon Hill. The English position was virtually impregnable.

as one in four of the Edinburgh men-at-arms were not in fact Scots, and since only one of them, Archibald de Livingstone, is described as a knight. This may have implications for our assessment of the numbers of men-at-arms that could be recruited from Scottish counties and there-fore for the military capacity of Scottish armies in periods when there was no serious competition from Edwardian administrations for recruit-ment. In terms of battlefield roles there was little if any real difference between men-at-arms and knights and there is no obvious correlation between the number of knights and the number of men-at-arms that might be enlisted from Scottish resources.

The nationality of Linlithgow garrison members may have been rather different to either Edinburgh or Livingston. Only thirteen out of eighty-seven named members can be readily identified as Scots, and one of those is Sir Archibald de Livingstone, who, as we have already seen, was also on the roll of Edinburgh, an indication that he bore some responsibility in both installations. We cannot discount the possibility that two separate individuals are indicated, though this is less than likely. If there were two knights of that name the rolls would surely differentiate between them, possibly as *junioris* and *senioris* if they were father and son or by including a geographical reference if they were not. There could be an operational significance should it be the case that the Edinburgh garrison consisted chiefly of Scots and the Linlithgow garrison did not. Given the lesser political and economic significance of Linlithgow it would seem safe to assume that the duties of the garrison extended to a greater range of activity than simply the immediate defence of the establishment, pre-sumably raiding and interdiction operations. The administration might feel that it would be more effective to deploy men from outwith the area to the more aggressive role; men who could safely be considered to be less at risk of defecting to the Scots should they become pris-oners or through the persuasion of their friends and relatives serving under Robert I. Arguably, the complement of Linlithgow might be more exposed to contact with the enemy and, if they were locally recruited men, might be more vulnerable to persuasion or blackmail than English regulars.

The small garrison at Livingston, being mainly, perhaps exclusively, Scots would seem to militate against this, since they might choose to defect *en masse*. However if that garrison was manned by men in the per-sonal retinue of Sir Archibald Livingstone it would not be unreasonable for the administration to assume that he was utterly convinced of their dependability, and in any case, the Livingston peel was not as significant an asset to the administration as Linlithgow, nor would it seem to have been regarded as a base from which offensive operations were mounted. If they were to defect they would not be putting a major asset in jeopardy, nor would they be likely to compromise operations in hand.

The rate of expenditure required to support the Lothian garrisons was obviously a heavy burden on the finances of Edwardian governments throughout the periods of occupation. Even when the garrisons were at their smallest it would seem to be the case that the cost of wages alone was more than could be collected from the issues of the county. Prior to the 1296 campaign the cost of garrisons was theoretically covered by the collection of castleguard money from the community and the fees paid to the commanders of castles,[51] but it would seem unlikely that the payments were sufficient to cover the costs. In the period 1291–92, when Scottish royal castles were entrusted to Edward I pending the settlement of the succession dispute, the commander of Edinburgh Castle received the considerable sum of 1 merk per day (13s 4d), a total of £243 6s 8d per annum,[52] a figure greatly in excess of the recorded castleguard demands from the constabularies of Edinburgh and Haddington. Although it is quite possible that the fees paid in the period of Edward's government were greater than the customary costs under Alexander III there is no clear evidence that that is the case. The daily payment of 13s 4d was designed to do more than pay the sheriff's wages: out of that sum he would be obliged to cover staff wages and at least some proportion of the general running costs of the castle and its garrison.

The record of castleguard payments is not necessarily complete and even if it is complete there may have been customary demands of produce. This would seem to have been the case in other castles. Paisley Abbey accepted the burden of finding five chalders of oatmeal for the garrison of Dumbarton Castle in exchange for being excused various exactions by Robert I; the Abbey was presumably going to make a contribution to an existing system of supply.[53] Evidently the Abbey had been making this contribution in the past, or there would have been little point in acquiring a charter to free it of the responsibility. The Edwardian administrations continued to collect castleguard, and King Robert did so as well, even though he had slighted Edinburgh Castle in an effort to render it indefensible, so he did not maintain a garrison there. Although castleguard was theoretically what we might call a 'hypothecated' government income, that is, one dedicated to a specific purpose, we should not assume that it was adequate to that purpose. No doubt when the payments were first levied in the twelfth century they constituted a serious proportion of the cost of garrison support. The customary castleguard payments uplifted by Edwardian administrations[54] were hardly sufficient to make a noticeable contribution to the cost of manning the castles. However, although the continuation of government business in general was an important part of the function of the garrisons we must bear in mind their significance to the general war policy of the Plantagenets in Scotland, and indeed in France and Flanders, if we are to understand why three successive English kings were prepared to expend their resources so freely in an area that was unlikely to yield any material profit in the foreseeable future.

The successful conquest of Scotland, or even the effective control of a portion of it, could be seen as a useful operation in a number of ways. In 1295 King John had demonstrated that he was prepared to combine with the king of France against the interests of Edward I, and though it has been remarked that medieval English kings were not always particularly interested in the well-being of their northern counties, a recurring threat of Scottish incursion could not be ignored, particularly since that threat would be most likely to become a reality in periods when England was at war with France.

A war on two fronts is always a dangerous situation, and although events of the fourteenth century would indicate that the defence of the border could generally be safely entrusted to the communities of the northern counties in preventing Scottish annexations, this may not have been so clear at the close of the thirteenth century, particularly if the attentions of English kings were focused on their interests on the continent. The neutralisation of Scotland did not need to take the form of annexation and perhaps eventual integration of Scotland into England, though clearly that would be potentially the most attractive option. If, however, the Plantagenets could secure tracts of southern Scotland and retain them without making a major commitment of men and materials, any Scottish administration would be likely to have to concentrate their efforts on regaining those areas rather than on making anything more than rather transitory incursions into northern England, thus compromising the effectiveness of the Scots as allies of the French. Further, if the garrisons that would be needed to retain a foothold in Scotland could, to some extent at least, be paid for and manned from the resources of Scottish counties, the strain on English crown resources would be reduced accordingly. If it was going to be necessary to fight the Scots due to their commitments to France, and if it was going to be necessary to establish strong garrisons to hold castles against them, then those deployments might as well be made in Scotland in the hope of containing conflict there rather than having to campaign on English soil. In any case it would do no harm for the prestige of his kingship if he were to extend his rule.

PART 2 – EDWARD BALLIOL TO DAVID II

Edward III was not opposed to the idea that he might incorporate Scotland into his realm. After the success of Edward Balliol at Dupplin Edward called a parliament to consider what course of action he should take in relation to Scotland. Renewing his father and grandfather's claims to the Scottish throne was certainly one of the options he entertained.[55] Balliol was ejected before the end of 1332 and Edward gave his overt support to the continuation of his war against the Bruce party at the Battle of Halidon Hill. The price of that support was the cession of a large proportion of southern and eastern Scotland to the English crown in perpetuity, the balance to be held as a kingdom by Edward Balliol with Edward III as his feudal superior.[56] In a sense this reduced Edward's claims in Scotland, but it also made the apparent objective a more manageable proposition. If Edward Balliol could occupy the attentions of the opposition by campaigning in and for Scotland north of the Forth, Edward Plantagenet could concentrate his efforts on Scotland south of the Forth. Not only would that make occupation of the southern counties a more realisable ambition, but it would mean that should Edward Balliol fail in his endeavours there would be less damage to Plantagenet prestige than if the King of England tried again to gain all of Scotland and failed. Further, should the Bruce party succeed in ousting Edward Balliol, they might be prepared to accept an armistice with Edward III on the basis of his retention of southern Scotland, particularly if a large part of the political communities in those counties could be brought to the Plantagenet party. In the short term, the resources that would need to be deployed to garrison Lothian and the other ceded counties would obviously be much less than what would be required to provide garrisons for towns and castles throughout Scotland as a whole, even if continued support for the Balliol cause were to require the intervention of field armies from England. As things turned out Scotland did in fact become a drain on the financial and manpower resources of Edward III, a drain that was much larger than any direct gain he could hope to make from the acquisition of the ceded counties, but it is safe to assume that it was not his intention to squander men or money. Edward I had apparently been close to achieving a favourable settlement of Scottish affairs in 1304 so why should Edward III not be able to bring matters to a satisfactory conclusion?

In the brief period between his victory at Dupplin in August 1332 and his defeat at Annan in December that year Edward Balliol would seem to have made little headway, possibly because castle and peels had been rendered indefensible by Robert I. The outcome of Halidon Hill initially provided a rather more secure basis for his kingship. In February 1334 he was able to hold a parliament at Holyrood.[57] However his security may have rested on the fact that Edinburgh was included in the settlement he had made with Edward III[58] and he could rely on the presence of English troops as much as on the inability of the Bruce party to act against him.

Edward III's hold on his recent acquisitions soon proved to be less than secure. On 8 September, less than two months after the appointment of officials in the Edwardian administration, Sir William Keith and Sir Godfrey Ross forced a Balliol party under Sir Richard Talbot to surrender after they had tried to defend themselves in a church near Linlithgow.[59] It soon became obvious that the incorporation of several southern sheriffdoms of Scotland into Edward III's domains was not going to be achieved by the transfer of lordship from the Scottish crown; a more positive military effort was required. To this end Edward III raised an army for service in Scotland and kept it in being throughout the winter of 1334–35, perhaps in the hope of forcing a settlement on the Scots in the way that his grandfather had in the winter of 1303–04. The army was based at Roxburgh, but undertook operations throughout lowland Scotland. The Bruce party did not oblige Edward by offering him battle and the result of the campaign would seem to have been no more than the rebuilding of Roxburgh Castle and widespread looting and burning.[60] Reconstruction at Roxburgh gave Edward a means of maintaining a secure military presence in that county and possession of a fairly significant town, but the actions of his army probably did more to push Scots to the Bruce party than to intimidate them.

A second army was raised for a summer campaign in 1335, this time entering Scotland in two divisions, one under Edward III and one under Edward Balliol.[61] The Scots were not strong enough to offer battle to such powerful forces, but equally, those forces were unable to prevent Scottish operations in their rear. On 30 July 1335, the day before the two Edwards united their armies at Glasgow[62] and marched to Airth, a Scottish force under the Earl of Moray captured the Count of Namur after a fight in the ruins of Edinburgh Castle while he was on his way to join Edward III at Perth.[63] Namur would seem to have had a force comprising 100 men at arms and as many archers.[64] Since they had been pursued for some distance,[65] we could reasonably assume that Moray's force, reinforced by the arrival of the Earl of Dunbar, Sir William Douglas and Sir Alexander Ramsay,[66] was rather stronger than that and that the force available to Edward's administration in Lothian was insufficient to prevent Scottish operations in the sheriffdom even though Edward had a powerful army less than forty miles away.

Moray had the misfortune to be captured himself while escorting his paroled prisoner to English held territory,[67] but that was more a matter of Moray's misfortune than evidence of an adequate English military establishment in south-east Scotland. Obviously the retention of Lothian was going to require a greater investment of money and manpower and to this end Edward embarked on a programme of reconstruction at Edinburgh Castle to provide a base for a more extensive garrison. On 14 September Edward concluded an indenture,[68] with Sir Thomas Roscelyn for the wardenship of Edinburgh Castle and the office of sheriff of Edinburgh, posts handed on to Sir John Strivelin on 2 November. The indenture relating to the transfer of the office[69] makes it clear that the castle was in a very poor state of repair. This can hardly have come as a surprise to Edward since he had been in Edinburgh himself in September.[70] On the positive side, Edward's administration was able to raise revenue from the sheriffdom in the years 1335–36 and 1336–37. However the revenues were much reduced 'on account of destruction through war' in 1335–36, amounting to £122 13s 4d halfpenny from Edinburgh constabulary, £73 2s 9d from Linlithgow and £81 17s 6 halfpenny from Haddington.[71] The income from Lothian may have been trivial throughout 1335–37, but the cost of supporting the garrisons there was enormous.

Edward's administration, like that of his predecessors, did not install a garrison at Haddington, though we can be confident that existing baronial castles in the area such as Linlithgow and Luffness were integrated into the military establishment of Lothian, but the garrisons at Edinburgh and Linlithgow were considerable and therefore costly. In 1335–36, no doubt for a valid reason that is not known to us, the Edinburgh garrison was enrolled by nationality in some sense. The knights of the garrison are divided into 'Scots' and 'Germans' (apart from a solitary Englishman, Sir Edmund de Berkely), an indication that Edward was prepared, or obliged to deploy mercenaries from overseas to protect his Scottish lands. The assignation of nation to individuals would seem to have depended on a rationale unclear to the modern observer. 'Lord' Dedricus de Almayne and his two scutifers appear among the *Milites Scoti* rather than the *Milites Almanni* (Germans), as does Thomas Libaud. Thomas was presumably a descendant, if not the son, of Pierre Lubaud, formerly commander of Edinburgh Castle for Edward II, who had defected to the Scots before Bannockburn, but had been forfeited and executed for treason sometime before March 1316 when his property at Cowden was regranted to Sir Robert Lauder.[72] A possible explanation for the appearance of these men among the *Scoti* could be that they had been granted lands in Scotland by Edward III and by serving in the Edinburgh garrison were discharging obligations due for those lands, though it would be unusual for men to appear by name in payrolls unless they were serving for wages. Interestingly, although six of the twelve knights of the garrison hailed from Germany, possibly only two of the seventy-five scutifers did, and even this may be an exaggeration; the two men in question are not named, they appear as the two scutifers of Lord Dedricus de Almayne, who in turn is described as a Scottish knight. If Dedricus was discharging obligations due from lands in Scotland it is perfectly possible that his two scutifers were in fact his tenants, and therefore very likely to be Scots. The thirty-four men-at-arms in the *Scoti* section of the roll did not represent the full complement of Scots in the garrison. Additionally there were six 'Scottish' knights, including Thomas Lubaud and Dedricus de Almayne, each of whom served with two scutifers. Assuming that apart from Sir Thomas and Sir Dedricus they were all 'Scots', a total of forty-seven Scottish men-at-arms (including the apparently misplaced Roger de Dalmahoy and Mungo de Buttergask) and four knights served in the

1335–36 garrison.[73] This accounts for well over half the entire force of eighty-eight men-at-arms and is probably as high a proportion, if not higher, than at any previous point during the Edwardian occupations. In the following year the proportion of Scots had become even greater, a minimum of fifty-one out of eighty-five men-at-arms. In 1335–36 the rest of the garrison comprised seventy-one hobelars and archers, apparently all Englishmen, little different from the next year when all but a handful of the sixty-four hobelars and archers were Englishmen. The high proportion of Scots men-at-arms would seem to suggest that the Edwardian administration in 1335–36 was reasonably acceptable to the community of Lothian – certainly several Lothian men were in service. However, by January 1339, although the ration strength of the garrison was much the same as it had been three years before, the proportion of Scots in service had dwindled considerably to two of the Scottish knights, William Ramsey and Alexander Crag, and twelve men-at-arms; less than a quarter of the total. The 1336–37 garrison may not reflect 'normal' circumstances. Although the roll bears a large quota of Lothian men, probably at least twenty-nine, there are several Scots who do not normally appear in Lothian garrison documents such as William de Prestwick, William Syward, Gilbert de Lumsden and William Olifaunt. Their presence, and that of others, may be an indication of the contraction of areas under Plantagenet and Balliol control: as towns and castles fell to the Bruce party there would obviously be fewer places in which men in Balliol or Plantagenet allegiance could serve.

It would seem, then, that less than two years after Edward's acquisition of Lothian, and despite the efforts of Edward Balliol against the Bruce party, the English administration in Lothian was already under sufficient pressure from the Scots that the communities of Lothian were unable to conduct their business in safety. In 1336–37 the situation deteriorated further. The rents of Edinburgh constabulary fell to £88 10s 7 halfpenny[74] – a reduction of approximately one third. Although this was offset by escheats through forfeiture amounting to £46 8d,[75] Edward's grant of 300 merks of Lothian land (which would otherwise have been in the hands of Edward III and contributing to the income of the sheriffdom), to Sir John Strivelin[76] obviously more than accounted for any profit from that source. Superficially there would seem to have been some improvement in the situation at Haddington which generated £102 3s 4 halfpenny and £10 3s 4d from new escheats in that constabulary for the financial year 1336–37.[77] Examination of the compotus shows that many of the properties in the section apparently relating to Haddington escheats were in fact in Edinburgh or Linlithgow constabularies. The significance of this, if any, is unclear, but there can be no mistaking the general trend of falling returns from issues throughout the sheriffdom. Overall income may not have been radically different, but the value of individual properties had fallen dramatically in the period 1335–37. Since it is perfectly clear that the reduction in income from these properties was due to war damage – the record tells us so repeatedly – it would seem equally clear that the Edwardian administration could not provide the stable and secure government, the 'good lordship' that would be necessary if Edward III was going to make his rule acceptable to the community of Lothian.

The forfeiture of Lothian landowners in 1312 may conceivably have been a reflection of the tactical situation in the sense that Edward II's government forfeited Lothian landowners who had joined the Bruce party only when the lands in question were no longer under Edwardian control and thus of no material significance. It would not seem to be the case that the Scots in 1335–37 were capturing and retaining territory in Lothian, but were chiefly occupied in gaining control of northern Scotland while at the same time conducting operations in Lothian (and Fife) with the sole objective of denying the produce – in the widest sense of the word – to the English. Sir Thomas Grey, author of *Scalacronica* claims that Edward III lost his possessions in Scotland for want of 'good lordship',[78] but it is perhaps misleading to assume that Edward still believed in 1336–37 that he could make good his claims to the sheriffdoms that had been ceded to him by Edward Balliol: rather that he saw his Scottish operation more as an exercise in preventing the Scots from recovering to the point where they could make a positive intervention in his plans for France. Edward's efforts to restore his rule in southern Scotland after the fall of Edinburgh Castle 1341 were unambitious and ineffective. Even after the signal victory of Neville's Cross in 1346 he seems to have made no serious attempt to install a new administration in Lothian. Edward Balliol led an army as far north as Falkirk in May 1347,[79] but retired to Galloway almost immediately having made no attempt to recover Edinburgh. Edward III's final campaign in Scotland, the 'Burnt Candlemas' saw him spend ten days at Haddington, during which time his troops caused extensive damage throughout Lothian, but he seems to have had no intention of forming any sort of government there, and, like Edward Balliol in 1347, he seems to have made no effort to capture Edinburgh Castle. Edward's failure even to attempt to restore his rule in Lothian may have been the product of experience: a decision that the investment required to enforce his rule there was greater than any likely return or an acceptance that he simply could not recruit enough men willing to commit themselves to service in Scotland when there were better opportunities in France. Further, we should not discount the possibility that the capacity of the Scots to man and maintain garrisons had improved beyond the offensive capabilities of the forces that Edward could afford to commit in Scotland. In 1338 a major siege of Dunbar Castle had failed despite a brief visit from the king himself. Edward's lieutenant, the Earl of Salisbury withdrew from the siege, allegedly, in order to follow his king to the continent, but the operation had been an expensive and humiliating failure.

Similarities in the approaches of three Edwards should not lead us to assume that their policies were identical. Edward I intended to secure the entirety of Scotland, which, in the main, called for a persistent and expanding occupation policy which was successful inasmuch as it brought about the surrender of the Scots in 1304, but clearly the Scots still had a stomach for the fight in 1306. The position of Edward III's administration was rather different. Edward might hope that Edward Balliol would be successful in his bid for the Scottish throne, but if he was not, Lothian would always be vulnerable. Possibly Edward saw the ceded counties as no more than a buffer zone and perhaps, given the experience he gained between 1333 and the end of 1335, only a temporary one.

In 1335–36 the Edwardian administration was unquestionably endeavouring to govern southern Scotland for the King of England, but by 1339–40 the duties of the garrison had been reduced to denying territory to the Scots. The ability to launch sudden attacks or ripostes was of greater significance than the ability to provide a secure environment for Plantagenet lordship. The final muster roll of the Edinburgh garrison,[80] detailing the complement at the time of the surrender, is broadly similar in form to that of 1339–40. Of forty-three men-at-arms (Bain puts the figure at forty-nine, six more than the original document[81]) at least five, Adam de Berwick, John de Abernethy, Roger Dalmahoy, Thomas and Adam de Pontekin, and possibly a sixth, William Bachelor, were Scots, as were at least five of the sixty mounted archers, namely Alexander

Elphinstone, Robert Conyngham, Walter Dalmahoy, Adam Preston and another, unnamed, member of the Pontekin family. Curiously there would seem to have been no knights in the garrison at all, suggesting that the Scottish knights serving there before 1340 (Sirs John Lockhart, William Ramsay, John de Crichton and both of the Alexander Craigies) had become casualties, defected to the Scots or had been redeployed to other posts.

The possibility that Edinburgh had been reduced to an outpost in 1339–40 having been a centre of local government in 1335–36 does not mean that Edward III saw the castle as a disposable asset. Improvements to the fortifications there and at Stirling were still being made until at least January 1340, when the cost of building work and garrison wages for the two castles was computed at over £2000.[82] The normal issues of Lothian and Stirling, even if they could be collected, would hardly cover such expenditure, but Edward presumably saw it as money well-spent in keeping the Scots busy enough to reduce, if not prevent, their intervention in his war with France.

THE LOGISTICS SITUATION

In the strictest sense it would seem that, in general, the maintenance of a consistent provision of produce and ordnance did not pose a severe, or at least not an insuperable, problem for Plantagenet administrations in Lothian, either in 1296–1314 or in 1333–41, though it was clearly an issue in other locations. With the possible exception of the three unspecified castles which had fallen to Wallace in 1297, none of the castles in the sheriffdom seems to have been surrendered through failure of provisions. Even so, the maintenance of a supply system was obviously of critical importance to the administration. It would seem to have been easy enough to ship stores to Leith or Blackness,[83] but once the goods were unloaded from the shipping it would be necessary to transfer them to Edinburgh or Linlithgow in the first instance, and then possibly to satellite installations such as Dirleton Castle[84] or Livingston peel. In some stages of the war this would not have been a great burden: so long as the Scots could be kept out of Lothian the security of a supply column travelling through the sheriffdom could probably be trusted to a handful of men to discourage banditry. Similarly, during the purchased truces of 1312–14 it is reasonable to assume that the Scots did not regularly interfere with the provisioning arrangements of the Plantagenet government, or that if they did, the results were not sufficiently significant to draw comment from Edwardian officers.

The apparent ease of maintenance must have been, in part, a product of the relationship between the community and the administration. The notion that Lothian people were particularly amenable to English rule and were uninterested in or inimical to Scottish kingship cannot reasonably be sustained (Lothian had, after all, been part of the Scottish kingdom for some time before 1296), but it is clear that the majority of the community were not prepared to oppose Edwardian government actively before the Strathord agreement of 1304, and very few indeed between Robert I's accession to the throne in 1306 and his victory at Bannockburn in 1314. Acceptance into Edward's peace would undoubtedly entail being prepared to discharge various obligations to the crown, including military service. The burden of military obligation fell most heavily, or at least most frequently, on the political community, since they were most likely to have an obligation to serve as men-at-arms. It could be argued, in fact, that the Lothian community not only accepted and supported the administration; but even staffed it with soldiers and jurors. Their service in Garrisons has certain implications for the logistical structures of the Lothian administration and for any assessment of the forces available based on analysis of recorded demands for, or receipts of, materials required for the army.[85] The extent to which such men had to provide their own provisions is not clear from record sources, and though it is probably realistic to assume that men serving for land 'messed' with men serving for wages and were considered part of the ration strength of the establishment, it is quite possible that they were obliged to deal with all of their own supply needs, or at least some portion of them. A man giving service for land was not, for example, entitled to a restauro payment should he lose his horse in action, but it would be reasonable to assume that the fodder for his horse (and perhaps himself) could be supplied by the administration since individual provision would be ridiculously inefficient and would lead to logistical difficulties if every man had to have his own facilities. Bearing in mind that the administration would have had a vested interest in making military service acceptable to the local military tenants, making the burden less irksome by providing messing and fodder for those serving for their lands would surely be well worth the relatively trivial expenditure involved.

The garrison complements initially authorised by Edward I, in Lothian at least, would not seem to have been greatly in excess of the sort of forces available to the sheriff of Lothian and his constables at Haddington and Linlithgow under John and Alexander III. Presumably these very tiny forces had been supported through the fees paid by the crown to the officers in question, castleguard payments from the community, the income accruing to the sheriff from judicial processes and perhaps through the produce of particular crown properties permanently allocated to the purpose. The extensive description of income due from crown tenancies in the Cramond–Corstorphine area as listed by Edward III's administrators in 1335–36 and 1336–37[86]indicates a planned system of goods and money, including wheat, oats, barley and tiny sums of 'hen' and 'hearth' money from the minor tenants, presumably the cottars and others who provided the day labour for the properties. The proceeds from these properties may not have been traditionally applied to the support of the customary (and minute) peacetime garrisons of Scottish kings before 1296, but the men and horses would have to be fed somehow and the hypothecation of crown income from a local source would be a simple means of ensuring the delivery of rations.

Since there was already a system of some sort in place to support the sheriff and his staff there is no reason to assume that Edward I did not intend to retain it as the means of supporting his own administration. If he could make his lordship acceptable to the community there would be no great need to have larger complements than was customary. Indeed installing large forces might well be politically counterproductive, particularly if the garrisons were an economic drain on the community. Keeping the garrisons at traditional peacetime strengths and making only the customary demands for military service, castleguard and rents (whether in cash or produce) might even help to lend an air of 'business as usual' to the political situation. It would be very much in Edward's interests to promote the idea that the Dunbar campaign had brought about a change of kingship, but that that should not be a great concern to the political community. The practical advantage of being able to fund the administration from local resources would obviously have been very real to Edward; he did not invade Scotland with the intention of pouring money into the indefinite maintenance of his troops there – quite the reverse. It would have been infinitely preferable to him if the structures of government in Scotland did not make demands for military and financial resources that he could make use of elsewhere.

It is abundantly clear that the administration in Lothian could not be secured on the basis of traditional levels of locally available force and revenue from the frequent demands made for provisions from English towns and counties and the many receipts issued by garrison commanders.[87] However it is difficult to make firm observations from the very limited data available. The nature of the material demanded can, in some instances, be a very fine guide to the purpose of the demand. A purchase of sulphur and saltpetre can hardly indicate anything other than an intention to use a firearm or an explosive or combustive weapon. The provision of large quantities of food, however, is not clear evidence of the consumption of the garrison to which it was sent. Many English and Scottish men in Edwardian service received large quantities of provisions as 'prests' on their wages or as gifts. The incidence of these prests and gifts is impossible to estimate, but it is safe to assume that those recorded in *Calendar of Documents Relating to Scotland* or *Rotuli Scotiae* are not the sum total.[88] Such supplies were generally to be collected from the stores of specific garrisons so clearly the stock issued to those garrisons was required to do rather more than simply feed the complement. It is quite possible, even likely, that the major garrisons were centres for the distribution of supply to castles held by Lothian barons and lords in Plantagenet peace, such as Luffness or Dirleton. The disparity between the amount of supply provided to Edinburgh or Linlithgow and the actual consumption of the garrison may have been very substantial. Additionally, the stocks of produce held at a particular garrison are not a good indicator of the consumption of supply. In June 1311 at least three baronial castles in Lothian, Luffness, Dirleton and Yester, were in the charge of constables in Plantagenet peace. The garrisons of these castles may have consisted entirely of local landholders discharging customary castleguard obligations, though it is clear that two men-at-arms resident at Yester with Sir Adam Welle in late 1302 were liable to ride out with Sir John de Kingestone, constable of Edinburgh Castle, 'at his command'.[89] Dirleton Castle was certainly considered a logistic responsibility of the Plantagenet administration in 1300, given the estimates of the 'victuals required' for the maintenance of a garrison there from January to June of that year.[90] This is not clear evidence that Dirleton was regularly replenished by the Plantagenet government at all, let alone through a particular supply head such as Edinburgh, but the possibility that it was cannot be discounted. There was certainly a Plantagenet garrison of twenty men-at-arms there in 1300, four of whom were serving for lands in Scotland,[91] and it was under the command of Sir Robert Mauleye in October that year at the start of a truce with the Scots.[92] The additional cost of supporting a handful of very small garrisons in baronial castles would be trivial in the overall expenditure required to support the administration as a whole and would help to maintain confidence in the administration among those garrisons.

If the major installations, Edinburgh and Linlithgow, acted as the supply depots for a number of outlying minor strongholds, it would have been sound practice to have retained adequate stocks against two contingencies for both Linlithgow itself and the satellite installations: the possibility of a siege that would require larger stocks to be retained and the possibility of accidental damage (fire, flood, decay) to existing stocks.

The nature of the supply demanded is a clear indication of the perceived need of the garrison, but it is not necessarily a reliable guide to the local availability of produce or goods. Wine certainly could not be produced in Lothian and so had to be imported, but most of the produce purchased, purveyed or requisitioned was of a more basic nature: wheat, oats, barley, and bacon could all be produced locally. Since the transport of money was, in general, rather easier to achieve than the transport of high volume goods, grain for instance, it would surely seem to have been more efficient to provide funds for local purchase. Instances of demands for particular supplies are not, however, a clear indication of what was, or was not, generally available from local sources.[93] Demands for hay in late 1301,[94] for example, are not evidence that hay was unavailable, but that there were practical reasons for importing it at a particular time. With a higher proportion of land devoted to arable than pastoral production, Lothian may well have been an expensive place for hay at the best of times so one unseasonably wet month in the summer of 1301 might have pushed up prices to a point where it was economically preferable to import hay, even though the cost of transport may well have been greater than the value of the product. Further, if there was a shortage of hay in the Lothian market, it would not go well with the community if the supply was bought up for the needs of the garrison.

A garrison at a town would itself become part of the local financial structure in that people from the town served in it, and some portion of the wages paid to the garrison would feed into the economy of the town through the purchase of goods and services. According to Bower,[95] eighty garrison members (in keeping with his nationalistic and moral standpoint Bower states that they were all Englishmen) were killed in 1338 when they were caught in the brothels of Edinburgh. They were, no doubt, making a positive contribution to the fiscal state of the community. It is clear that local markets and merchants could not be relied on to supply all the needs of the garrisons, but local provision must inevitably have been of some significance since local merchants were clearly trading with the garrison on a regular basis throughout the periods of Plantagenet rule.

The logistical support structure of the Plantagenet administration was a sophisticated and successful operation. Supply was evidently reliable enough to prevent the fall of strongholds through failure of provision. Most of the chief castles of eastern Scotland – Perth, Dunbar, Dundee, Berwick, and Edinburgh (as long as the garrison controlled Leith) – could be easily replenished by sea, but Linlithgow, and perhaps other installations would have required the delivery of supply by road from depots where goods could be unloaded from shipping. To this end it would seem that Blackness was regularly used as a delivery point for as long as Linlithgow peel was held for Edward II.[96] It is not clear whether there was a permanent installation there. The earliest extant parts of Blackness Castle date to the early part of the fifteenth century, but it would seem likely that there would have been an establishment of some kind, though not necessarily manned on a permanent basis. The business of unloading a ship and re-packing the stores into wagons would take some time, particularly if the stores had to be transferred to lighters rather than directly onto a jetty. Since such transfers, the movement of supplies from Linlithgow and perhaps the further distribution of supplies to minor strongholds, were evidently achieved reliably (or at least reliably enough to prevent the fall of Plantagenet strongholds to the Scots), it is fair to assume that, in the main, the administration was strong enough to prevent regular Scottish operations against the logistic structure that maintained those strongholds. The Scots could certainly mount operations within and around Lothian, even at times when the Plantagenet government was quite firmly entrenched, as seen from the engagements at Roslin in 1303, the capture of Talbot and Strivelin near Falkirk in 1334 and the fights at Edinburgh Castle, Blaksollings and the Crags of Craigie in the 1330s, but from 1296 to 1314 and, perhaps to a lesser extent in 1333–41, they could not achieve the consistent local dominance required to prevent the replenishment of Plantagenet garrisons. The two situations were not the same however. In the first period of Plantagenet administration there were three major permanent installations, Edinburgh and Linlithgow with powerful garrisons, and Livingston peel with a very minor force. In addition to these there were an undeterminable number of baronial castles such as Luffness and Dirleton and, though not a castle, the Hospitaller Preceptory at Torphichen. To what extent these were supported in either period of Plantagenet administration is unclear, but they would seem to have been a more important part of the military structure in 1296–1314 than in 1333–41. The evidence is very sparse indeed, but the little that exists suggests that in the earlier period at least, the owners or constables of private castles could look to the Edwardian government for some degree of logistic support.[97] There may have been rather fewer functioning castles in the later period due to the slightings attributed to Robert I, but Edward may have adopted a policy of a smaller deployment in fewer locations for fear of being unable to prevent operations against his lines of communication.

The ability of the Bruce party to field men-at-arms was probably greater in 1333–41 than it had been in 1306–12 (at least) due to their improved level of support in parts of the country where man-at-arms service was the customary form of noble military activity, particularly the eastern seaboard counties. During the early years of his kingship Robert I was heavily dependent on troops from the west of Scotland, where there was no great local operational demand for, and therefore no established custom of, cavalry service. Without sufficient men-at-arms to achieve local superiority on a regular basis, Robert I could not intervene in Lothian, Roxburghshire or Berwickshire until the last year or so before Bannockburn, so the supply system of the Plantagenet garrisons could be maintained by relatively small numbers of men-at-arms. How the structure fared between the fall of Edinburgh Castle in March 1314 and Bannockburn three months later is open to question. It would hardly be surprising if castles in the sheriffdom had surrendered to King Robert immediately after either event. However, given that some Lothian men-at-arms served against Robert[98] at Bannockburn, it is clear that Edward II was still able to exert lordship (or rather, command fealty) after the fall of Edinburgh Castle. It is possible that some privately-owned Lothian castles were still being held in his cause throughout the intervening period, as Dunbar was. On the other hand the fall of towns and castles in the north such as Urquhart, Inverness, Aberdeen – or in the west, Dumfries, Ayr, and Rothesay – seems to have brought the fall of minor strongholds.

Shortage of supply was a much less critical factor in the security of the Plantagenet administration of Lothian than military and political failures. The military dominance of Edward I's government was enough to keep Lothian in English hands, but after his death, the failure of Edward II to mount operations that would effectively stop Bruce expansion, and his inability to save his supporters from blackmail, eventually undermined confidence in the Plantagenet cause. The same applied in 1333–41. Edward III could not provide the 'good lordship' necessary to retain control over Lothian. To some extent this was a product of his operations elsewhere. His resources were drained by his French campaigns. The Balliol cause did not enjoy enough popularity across Scotland to win power without a large commitment of English troops and money. Scottish military success in 1335–41 can hardly have encouraged Englishmen to enlist for service in Scotland. Casualties, and defectors, among the disinherited would have been very hard to replace. The properties of men killed in action might, in theory, pass to their heir, assuming that they had one, or escheat to Edward III or Edward Balliol if they did not. In practice, as the Bruce party achieved dominance, there was little chance of securing effective possession. In turn, that dominance enhanced the attractions of defection. If the Bruce party could offer a reasonable accommodation and more secure lordship, there was little value in adhering to the Balliol cause. Even by 1337 or 1338 it must have been increasingly clear that the Balliol cause had been lost and that the Plantagenet administration was failing. Under these circumstances it must surely have been a challenge to attract men who would give service for the unlikely possibility of becoming an established heritable landholder in Scotland. This does not indicate that Edward III was *never* confident that Scotland could be conquered. Like his father and his grandfather, he definitely favoured the formation of one British kingdom under one English king. Unlike them, he was prepared to adjust his political aims to conform to prevailing tactical and strategic realities.

5

ALLEGIANCE AND SERVICE

The concepts of allegiance and service were inextricably entwined in the lives of medieval landholders, no less so in Lothian than anywhere else. If a landholder wished to retain their property they had to accept the authority of whichever party was currently in a position to exert governance. In return for accepting the authority of the government the landholder would naturally look to that government to provide a stable and secure environment and the government would expect the landholder to discharge the various obligations attached to the property. From 1296 until the 1350s the most significant of those burdens was military service, not simply because of the obvious value of armed men in time of war but because it was a clear indication of allegiance. Naturally this cut both ways. Those who lost their inheritances under the Plantagenets would have an incentive to join the Bruce party on the understanding that a Bruce victory would lead to the recovery of their property and those who lost their estates under the Bruces would be likely to join or remain in Plantagenet peace in the hope of an eventual Plantagenet victory. Either way, if an individual wished to gain, retain or recover lands, they would almost inevitably be obliged to discharge military service for a superior, generally the person from whom they held the property.

In much of southern Scotland the high incidence of 'in capite' landholding meant that for a large proportion of the political community military service was owed directly to the crown rather than to an intermediate level of authority. This chapter is concerned with the operational and material realities of that service: operational in the sense that it examines the extent of military obligation and the actual activity of those called upon to discharge service, and material in the sense of examining the nature and cost of the equipment required for an individual to fulfil their contractual and/or customary military obligations.

ARMY SERVICE

The duty of every man to perform 'Common Army' service was unquestionably in place long before the Wars of Independence[1] but so little is understood of the terms of service and the organisation of the troops raised that we can say virtually nothing about any aspect of the army it produced. We cannot even say whether the system of enlistment, the equipment or the tactical application of the force raised was good, bad or indifferent. The army that was raised to oppose Edward I in 1296 did not come to blows with the enemy, but simply disintegrated in the wake of the defeat of the heavy cavalry element of King John's army near Dunbar. It would seem that the Scottish cavalry had been making an attempt to raise the siege of the castle but were intercepted by a formation of English men-at-arms and quickly beaten. The defeat led to the surrender of the castle and the end of effective resistance to Edward I until the risings of William Wallace, Andrew Murray and the magnate-led revolt that fizzled out at Irvine in 1297.

If we hope to gain any insight into military affairs in southern Sotland c.1300, we must look to English records, simply because there are so few Scottish ones. Naturally, this tells us much more about the forces of the Edwardian administration than it does about their opponents, but Edward's garrisons contained many identifiable Scots and probably many more that cannot be identified. These men would not seem to have been any different from their peers among the petty nobility, free tenants and burgesses who comprised the local political community. Military service obligations were part of their lives regardless of which king was in power. The contention that the fear of losing property in England was always sufficient to keep Scottish landholders loyal to Edward I does not bear examination given the number of people who were forfeited of English estates – Hugh and Margaret de Penicuik for example. What we can learn about the Lothian men in English service is likely often to hold true for their neighbours in the Balliol or Bruce camps. There seems to be no evidence of forfeitures of pro-Plantagenet Scots by the Balliol party between 1297 and 1304, an indication perhaps that they did not feel confident about using forfeiture as a weapon, either because the absence of a king deprived them of sufficient authority to do so, because they did not feel that they could enforce such forfeitures or because they felt that forfeiture might alienate potential supporters among the uncommitted.

The lack of a document listing forfeitures of Plantagenet supporters in similar vein to the forfeiture of Bruce supporters in 1306 and 1312 is not proof that forfeitures did not take place. Several of the properties granted by Robert I to his supporters had been at one time the property of Plantagenet supporters or of men implicated in the de Soulis conspiracy. Not all of the grants made by King Robert would necessarily have been the product of politically inspired forfeitures (estates could, for example, fall to the crown through failure to produce an heir), but several were. Sir James Douglas[2] and Sir Robert Lauder[3] benefited from the forfeiture for treason of Sir Peter Lubaud sometime before 1316, Sir Laurence de Abernethy benefited from the forfeiture of Ingelram de Guines,[4] Hugh de Vickers profited from the forfeiture of Adam de Mindrum and William de Dalton[5] and Melrose abbey from the death in exile of Sir John de Soulis,[6] all of whom had been active in the Plantagenet or Balliol causes.

It is distinctly possible that for the campaign that led to the Battle of Dupplin Muir the disinherited party were able to enlist significant numbers of men (out of an army of only 1500 to 2000 admittedly) from minor landholders who had left Scotland, or been driven out, in the period after Bannockburn and had not made their peace with King Robert. In order to attract men to his service, Balliol was obviously under some pressure to restore those men to their property, or, at the very least, provide them with comparable alternative prospects. The drawback to restoration was that it required either the acceptance of the current landholders or their removal. The former might be a viable matter for negotiation, but Edward can hardly have expected to be able to remove men from property granted them by Robert I in order to restore his own supporters and still attract the dispossessed men to his allegiance. Bruce grants of forfeited property were calculated to promote loyalty and exclude opposition. The best prospect for the permanent retention of such properties therefore lay in the success of the Bruce cause since the ambitions of the Balliol party were so dependant on restoration of the disinherited and thus on the forfeiture of those who had gained land from King Robert. The whole process of granting land was both a means of encouraging support, and, just as importantly, of discouraging defection. A man who had profited by his service and allegiance to the Bruce cause might be dissuaded from defection by the prospect of having to surrender land to a member of the disinherited who (or whose forbear) had lost that land during the previous conflict. We might consider that the sources of lordship, Bruce, Plantagenet and Balliol had an interest in raising the stakes for landholders who wavered in their allegiance. From the Bruce standpoint the large numbers of Scots who served in the Plantagenet administration between 1296 and 1314 must have been an incentive to bind the political community as closely to the Bruce party as could be arranged and hopefully prevent them from joining any future Plantagenet or Balliol campaign.

Edward I had been able to recruit men for his garrisons and collect the military dues of some proportion of the Lothian landholders within a matter of months of Dunbar. Presumably he would not otherwise have been restoring men to their forfeited property.[7] It would, however, be surprising if absolutely no Scots served quite voluntarily in English armies in other theatres in search of adventure or a military career. Some served to procure release: eleven knights and fifty-three scutifers, prisoners of war after Dunbar, were released to serve in Flanders in the autumn of 1296,[8] and others, including Patrick, son of the Earl of Dunbar, were intending to join Edward there in May 1297.[9]

Although the imposition of service in Edward's armies in France and Flanders seems to have been a concern of the Scots in the period of insurrection before the pacification of 1304 there seems to have been little if any pressure on the populace as a whole to perform that service.[10] The fears of conscription that were alleged by the leaders of the 'noble' rising of 1297 (the Bishop of Glasgow, Robert Bruce and John the Stewart) to have fuelled resistance seem to have been without foundation, though several Scots who had become prisoners of war after the fight at Dunbar and the fall of Dunbar Castle chose to serve Edward in Flanders as a means of achieving release from prison and of earning the restoration of their lands.[11] There is no evidence to suggest that bodies of troops were raised in Scotland as discrete parts of Edwardian armies in the way that they were in Ireland or Wales.[12] This is perhaps surprising given the perennial manpower shortages that curtailed Edward's military policies.[13] The principle of recruiting defeated enemies for service elsewhere was hardly a revolutionary concept, but in practice Scots were chiefly enlisted for service within Scotland. This might conceivably be a product of Edward's experience in the use of such forces. Large contingents were raised several times from Wales for service in Scotland, but their reliability was open to question. The failure of Edward's logistical effort in 1298 caused rioting and near mutiny among the Welsh troops on the eve of the battle of Falkirk.[14]

Once the Edwardian administration was in place any Lothian landholder who wanted to retain his position in society would have to discharge the various burdens attendant on that position, and that would inevitably include some degree of military obligation. Army service obligations took a number of forms; indeed all male members of the society from age sixteen to sixty were theoretically liable for army service twice over. The obligation on all men to serve the king for up to forty days at their own expense was not the whole extent of anyone's burden because they could be called out any number of times in addition to those forty days in the event of a military emergency.[15]

CASTLEGUARD

The more prominent members of the community had to be prepared to carry a good deal more of a burden than that. The majority of landholders were obliged to perform military service for the person from whom they held their estate. This service took two forms, knight service in the field, or at least in the retinue of the superior, and castleguard. The latter term is ostensibly self-explanatory, but should not be taken too literally. Performing forty days' castleguard, which would seem to have been the normal requirement, would have been an irritating obligation for most, if not all, tenants, but it was probably less than totally practical for the superiors to whom it was due. Certainly it would have been very difficult indeed to rely on castleguard obligations to provide the entirety of a garrison even if the total of service due would have been theoretically sufficient to furnish the necessary manpower. In practice it would be enormously difficult to maintain good security if the membership of the garrison changed every forty days, and what would the service of forty days performed personally really be worth if the vassal owing the service were a child or too aged to serve? Obviously there must have been a system for substitution or for payment in lieu.

That castleguard payments were collected is not in doubt. Castleguard had been collected by Alexander III[16] and, presumably, by his predecessor, since it is from his reign that Bernard de Hadden's (or Hauden) confirmation of castleguard (and other) obligations dates.[17] The chamberlain's accounts from June 1328 to September 1329[18] show an income of £40 from this source and this is remarkably close to the £34 2s 8d collected by Sir John de Strivelin for the administration of Edward III in the period 1335–36. Sir John collected a further £30 from Haddington and £7 5s 6d from Linlithgow.[19] Castleguard was not an innovation of the Edwardian government adopted by King Robert. There are examples of castleguard payments in the exchequer rolls from the administration of the guardians.[20] Castleguard payments do not figure regularly in the chamberlain's accounts generally, and it is perhaps possible that they were normally the responsibility of another part of the administration of Scottish kings. Given that in 1328 the chamberlain, Robert de Peebles, took Castleguard payments from the bishopric of St. Andrews[21] and in 1329 from the sheriffdom of Edinburgh,[22] and that in 1359 the sheriff of Lanark collected £13 for castleguard and declared it to the chamberlain[23] we can see that the chamberlain could account for such money, but it is hardly established that he generally, or even normally, did so. The sum collected in 1359 came from ten Lanarkshire baronies at a rate of 20s each and one at 40s,[24] however not all of the Lanarkshire baronies paid castleguard. One of the baronies, Hartshead, in Lanarkshire, paid nothing because it was in ward and two were in the hands of Thomas de Moray, who appears to have been excused castleguard through an arrangement with the late King Robert I.

It would seem unlikely that Lanarkshire barons were alone among the Scottish nobility in having to make castleguard payments and the extent of David II's administration in 1359 surely precludes any possibility that Lothian landholders avoided those payments because they were outwith his rule. If Lanarkshire landholders were paying castleguard we can safely assume that their counterparts in Lothian had to do the same. Certainly castleguard had been deemed collectable in Lothian as recently as May

1329 when Robert I had granted an annual of 20 merks to the Grey Friars of Dundee from castleguard income due from Edinburgh,[25] and it would be unreasonable to assume that his successor, David, did not continue to collect that income. There are instances of castleguard from other communities during Robert I's reign, but none as heavy as that demanded from the Lothian constabularies. The chamberlain's accounts for 1329[26] include £4 10s from Stirling, £7 5s from Dumfries, £14 13s 4d from Berwick and £20 2d from Roxburgh. In 1330 the Castleguard of Edinburgh amounted to only £16.[27] It would seem unlikely that these payments were unique, rather they were either not recorded at all, which seems improbable, or they were recorded elsewhere, or the relevant record simply has not survived. Assuming, as Professor Duncan does,[28] that castleguard was normally administered by the sheriff, this would hardly be surprising given the scarcity of shrieval records generally, although one must wonder why there are isolated examples of castleguard being accounted to the chamberlain. On the other hand the sheriff presumably had to account for his collection, and presumably his disbursement, of these funds to a responsible officer in the king's government.

A relationship between tenure by knight service and castleguard responsibilities and its continuity from one generation to another is supported by a charter[29] of Alexander II to the laird of Hadden, Roxburghshire which required the recipient to pay 20s annually for his castleguard due to Roxburgh Castle 'for what pertains to a knight's fief'. The evidence for the existence of this charter derives from its confirmation by Robert I in favour of Bernard de Hadden confirming the commutation for a cash settlement of his castleguard duties. This charter clearly states that Bernard was obliged to pay 20s annually for castleguard at Roxburgh, or, if required, to serve there for forty days in lieu of that payment as the service that pertains to the 'service of one knight'. It would be rash to assume that castleguard service was only required from knights (Bernard is not described as 'miles' in the charter) or that the stipulated forty days or 20s payment was the sum total of responsibility. Bernard's charter makes it quite clear that further garrison duty at Roxburgh would be required in an emergency; however, if Bernard served in the king's army either north of the Forth or south of the border he would be excused service or payment for that year.[30] Evidently the provision that Bernard should serve at Roxburgh in the event of an emergency still held regardless of his army service elsewhere; what is not so clear is whether the type of service performed had a bearing on castleguard exemption. Like anyone else, Bernard owed service in the king's army as a general obligation to the state, but if his knight service for landholding was a separate obligation it is surely possible that he might have to discharge that service without affecting his castleguard duties.

That castleguard obligation on Bernard and his heirs was specifically apportioned to Roxburgh suggests a system designed to provide garrisons for the king's castles in a manner that would allow for a rotation of troops from the vicinity; men who would be likely to know one another, or at least share common regional interests. This does not mean that the entirety of a garrison was necessarily provided by castleguard obligations, and we may be on safer ground if we assume that the intention was to supplement a permanent complement. In 1366[31] Simon Reid, custodian of Edinburgh Castle, received £26 13s 4d, or 40 merks, for sentries and expenses and similar arrangements can be found for other castles. Forty merks was a considerable sum, but the 'roundness' of the sum rather suggests a customary payment or agreed fee as opposed to an exact accounting of actual costs, a possibility supported by the £20 paid to Malcolm Fleming for his role at Dumbarton Castle recorded in the same document. It might be reasonable to assume that these payments were intended to cover, or at least contribute toward, the running costs of the garrison additional to the castleguard income.

Even a very tiny permanent garrison structure has implications for army service more generally, particularly with regard to training and articulation. The evolutions and drill standards required of medieval soldiers might not have been terribly sophisticated, but some degree of practice among even a very small cadre would be essential if Scottish troops were to be made effective in the rather short periods for which large forces were raised. The controlled deployment and engagement of bodies of men – in scores, let alone hundreds or thousands – requires a degree of articulation that cannot be easily achieved without an element of structured training.[32] The organisation of the army for most administrative purposes might be adequately discharged by local or customary leadership in the sense of personal followings, but in the event of such a leader becoming a casualty or simply not being present at a given place and moment, there would need to be another means of exerting control if the commanders' orders were to be carried out. A rotation of men serving in garrisons would have been a good opportunity to provide a cadre of at least partially trained men without calling upon 'Scottish' or 'common army' service which would have – potentially – a very positive effect on the competence of a large force when one was required. If the men of the army were reasonably competent personally very little would be required in the way of subordinate leadership, but it would be almost impossible to achieve any sort of continuity of command without some means of ensuring that orders were executed in the absence of specific individuals. This is conjecture of course, but there must have been some means of achieving and maintaining operational and administrative control over the army, over and above aristocratic leadership liabilities. Since we are aware that particular individuals could have leadership responsibilities in particular arms of service (two men killed in action at Perth are described as 'commanders of the Scottish archers,[33] we must accept that the articulation of medieval Scottish forces allowed for division by arm of service within the army. If the rank and file of Scottish archers served under what historians[34] have agreed to be the normal conditions of military service to the Scottish crown, they could expect to be in the field for forty days (at their own expense) before being 'rotated' with other men. The fiscal advantage to the crown of such a system is obvious, but the practical difficulties are just as clear. Without a well-established and clearly understood hierarchy and tactical and administrative practices the forces raised would be extremely inefficient since each new draft of 'forty day' men would have to be brought to a state of combat readiness from a very low base indeed.

The theoretical means of providing castles with garrisons, castleguard, also required a sophisticated approach to accounting if the service and/ or money owed were to be collected effectively. The sums demanded for castleguard were not large. The rate of commuted payment works out at 6d per day, but we should not necessarily assume that 6d a day was in any sense the 'going rate' for army service generally. Presumably men performing castleguard served 'all found', i.e. the administration of the castle provided the men of the garrison with rations rather than the men having to arrange their own food supply. The onus on Paisley Abbey to find five chalders of oatmeal for Dumbarton Castle[35] in exchange for exemption from various royal obligations surely supports this – but in any case the castleguard commutation rate had been set as much as one hundred years before Bernard de Hadden received his charter and was probably no longer genuinely economic due to the increasingly monetised Scottish economy of the twelfth and thirteenth centuries.[36] Certainly it would not compare favourably with the rates of pay offered by Edwardian administrations between 1296 and the middle of the fourteenth century. However those rates were of recent origin and perhaps reflect the necessity to attract men to military service. We cannot be sure that we are comparing like with like. The 2s per day offered for knightly men-at-arms serving the Edwardian government in Scottish garrisons in the fourteenth century[37] is a reflection of a rather more 'active', and therefore potentially more dangerous form of service and also the requirement for men undertaking that service to provide themselves with an expensive charger as well as an inducement for those men to serve away from home, or, in the case of Scots in Edwardian garrisons, perhaps to induce men to serve in a less than popular cause. Edwardian government may have been stable at different times, but that does not mean that it was welcome.

More significantly, paid garrison service under the Plantagenets was a contractual arrangement of a 'stand alone' nature, independent of landholding, whereas castleguard was part of a more complex structure, traditionally assumed to be connected to knight service and land tenure. The two forms of service were not mutually exclusive in the sense that they were performed by different personnel. There is no reason to assume that men who were granted Scottish estates by the Plantagenets or by Edward Balliol as a reward for service were excused the existing castleguard obligations attached to those estates, though there is the possibility that men who were in service all the year round might be excused their obligation or pay a fee in lieu of their service – they were, after all, receiving wages from the crown.

When we read of men in Edwardian garrisons serving 'for their lands in Scotland'[38] they might, theoretically, just as easily be men fulfilling their obligations as Scottish landholders in the 'peace' of English kings or men who had gained Scottish properties through service to those kings and they might be discharging castleguard or 'normal' military service commitments. In each case their unpaid service may be additional to salaried professional soldiering but since they are not named we have no way of identifying either the nature of their commitment or their nationality. It would seem likely that most of them were men in the following of English lords who had received extensive property in Scotland from Edward I. Given that Sir John de St. John's retinue alone was short of forty men-at-arms in the summer of 1302 when the planned strength of the Scottish garrisons was only 507 this would seem to have been a policy of limited value.[39]

Army service for Scots seems to have been divided into two separate forms of responsibility – a duty to serve north of the Forth or south of the Forth. Bernard's service (if required) north of the Forth or south of the border – is clearly defined, but no mention is made of service between the Forth and the border. It may therefore be reasonable to assume that such service was covered by the universal obligation for a man to serve for forty days at his own expense and that such service did not need to be defined since it was an obligation on all of the king's subjects. On the basis of the early thirteenth-century charter (or rather King Robert's confirmation of that charter) to the lairds of Hadden, Professor Duncan has suggested that castleguard 'represents that army service that did not cross the bounds of Lothian; it is the defence of the province which is found in both Northumbria and Scotia as forinsec service or its equivalent'.[40] This may be a valid interpretation, but the case is not securely made. Since all men had an obligation to perform military service we must accept at least the possibility that since castle-guard was a defined duty it was an additional burden.

Income designed to support the king's castles was not necessarily either financial or physical. As we have seen, an undated act of Robert I [41] freed Paisley Abbey from an annual burden of five chalders of oatmeal for the garrison of Dumbarton Castle and in 1339[42] Robert the Steward relieved the Priory of St. Andrews from the responsibility for payments toward the support of the Loch Leven garrison that the priory had undertaken on behalf of the 'community' of Fife. Whether this was a normal burden on that community or an extraordinary demand occasioned by the demands of the war is unclear, but there can be no doubt that communities could be responsible for such support at least in times of crisis.

The precise theoretical nature of castleguard as a burden is not absolutely clear and the operational nature of that service is no more so, inasmuch as we cannot be sure that documents that define castleguard responsibilities of an individual are typical of such arrangements or if the clear definition of duties implies that the stated obligations were atypical, hence the need to make a formal statement of those duties. Furthermore it is unclear whether it was related only to the needs of the king or whether it extended to the relationship between nobles and their tenants. Nobles had to garrison their castles somehow and in the absence of references to hired soldiers it would seem fair to assume that the tenants of barons contributed in some way to the manpower requirements of their superiors. In 1335–36 Dunbar Castle was receiving castleguard payments – mostly of 10s – from properties in the vicinity, but it is not clear if these payments were a normal part of the earl's income or if they were extraordinary payments allowed to him as an adherent of Edward III for the upgrading of the castle. However since similar sums were still being collected[43] more than 100 years later (when the value of currency had dwindled considerably) we might be entitled to assume that they *were* normal practice for the Earls of Dunbar. Earl Patrick in turn owed £30[44] per annum castleguard to Berwick castle while it was in the hands of Edward III, but it is not clear whether this was the normal practice under the kings of Scots; the evidence we have for this payment in the accounts of the Edwardian sheriff of Berwick 1336–37 refers to the period after the Earl's defection to the Scots and may not be a valid reflection of normal practice but an innovation of Edward III's government of the territories.

What we might call – for want of a better term – national, or perhaps kingly, war was a much more regular event in the first half of the fourteenth century than it had been in the thirteenth, but what landholder was going to be able to defy a king's army at the gate? The landholder might have the men to defend his walls, but only for a certain number of days, and the men on whom the landholder depended had their own concerns. While they were undoubtedly due service to their lord they were also due both service and obedience to the king. As long as there was competition between rivals for the crown the position of minor landholders was very vulnerable to changes in higher authority. If they chose to support their immediate superior they might find themselves on the wrong side of whichever crown claimant was currently in control of the area; if they chose not to support their immediate landlord they might well find themselves dispossessed should the changing fortunes of war start to favour the other side. In 1296 Patrick, Earl of Dunbar was granted[45] by Edward I the forfeitures of those of his tenants who had not yet come to the king's peace, complete with the services of all relevant subtenants. Patrick was not the only recipient of this bounty. Writs were issued to several sheriffs in favour of ten other magnates at the same time. Edward III was not so generous (or trusting?). In March 1334 he gave instructions to sheriffs to allow Patrick to occupy the property of forfeited tenants, but only for a fixed period[46] and also allowed him to retain the £30 per annum of castleguard due to Berwick from his properties until a total of 100 merks had been retained for upgrading Dunbar Castle; a privilege no doubt much resented when the castle was under siege by the English in 1338 assuming that the funds had actually been spent on re-fortification.[47]

Castleguard evidence is thin and scattered and the threads of information are quite varied. The obligation on Paisley Abbey to supply oatmeal for Dumbarton, the undertaking of St. Andrews Priory of responsibility for payment to the Loch Leven garrison on behalf of the community, the sums collected by Edwardian and Bruce administrations: all suggest a structured system of financial, produce and personal service contributions to a network of royal garrisons supported by a wider segment of the society than just landholders with knight service obligations.

INCENTIVES, COERCION, LEADERSHIP AND COMMAND

Traditionally it has been assumed that only English kings and their lieutenants could mobilise the resources to pay soldier's wages, but this is making an assumption based on a lack of evidence rather than a deduction based on knowledge. There are no Scottish magnate financial accounts showing wage rates for employed troops, but there is very little in the way of Scottish financial records for the transactions of the crown let alone of the aristocracy. David II, when faced with the prospect of a major aristocratic revolt, drew £600[48] from his treasury to pay soldiers. It has been generally assumed that this money would have been expended on men-at-arms.[49] At a rate of a shilling a day[50] he could have procured the services of 1200 men-at-arms for ten days, but such a force would have been of very limited value without the archers and spearmen necessary to conduct a combined arms battle, and in any case, those of sufficient standing to equip themselves as men-at-arms were exactly the people with most to lose from changes in the government through conquest or revolution. If they did not turn out to support the king they might well find themselves disinherited by a new regime which would inevitably have supporters who would need to be rewarded – and the same people were also most at risk from retribution should the crown survive an attempted revolution without their help. They did after all owe army service to the king, even if they did not hold land from him directly. In any case, 1200 men-at-arms was a substantial, but not huge force even by the standards of the mid-fourteenth century, and the quality of Scottish men-at-arms (and their horses) was not necessarily of the highest calibre. A combination of two or three powerful magnates might well aspire to raise such a force.

According to Fordun, in the winter of 1335, when much of southern Scotland was under Plantagenet control, Sir William Douglas of Liddesdale, the Earl of Dunbar and Sir Andrew Murray were able to raise a considerable force, from the counties below the Forth and lead it to Culblean.[51] If on the other hand David was paying wages to more humble types of soldier his money could go a long way to procuring an army beyond the capacities of any group of nobles. At a rate of threepence a day – which would be reasonable wages by the standards of the mid-fourteenth century – he would be able to maintain 4800 infantry for the same ten-day period. An infantry army was very vulnerable to sudden attack, particularly on the march, but David was due knight service and perhaps the earlier, less prestigious 'riding service'[52] from landholders in sufficient quantity that he should have had no great difficulty in raising an appropriate cavalry arm whose loyalty was dependent not on daily wages but on their continuing ownership of land.

The composition of David's army in 1363 is not the issue, however. The point is that this is a clear example of a Scottish army in receipt of wages. That this is the earliest example of waged Scottish soldiers (other than knights in household service) does not mean that Scottish soldiers had not been paid on previous occasions. Robert I was able to keep his armies in England from despoiling those areas that paid their ransoms; the army besieging Stirling in 1299 was in action for several months; the troops besieging Perth in 1339[53] were maintained by a cash subsidy from the Abbey of Arbroath (although it should be noted that the Steward, acting as guardian was clear that this was not to be regarded as a precedent). The garrison of Loch Leven Castle in the same year[54] was supported by a financial levy on the community of Fife, administered by the prior of St. Andrews, and presumably had been supported in previous years through the same or similar arrangements. It would seem unreasonable to assume that the men who performed military service, particularly in situations where little or nothing could be expected in the way of ransoms[55] or plunder, were rewarded with nothing more than their keep for their efforts. Naturally men who had been forfeited by one side would likely appear on the other in the hope of regaining their heritages. Such men could be relied upon to fight for the sake of their keep, but there would not have been a great many of them. Whilst accepting that numerical strength is only one factor among many, and that although it is always significant it is very seldom the *most* significant factor in achieving victory, it is clear that the eventual successes of the Bruce party were dependent on their ability to draw men away from Plantagenet lordship in greater quantity than the Plantagenets could induce acceptance of their rule.

In any conflict, examining the relationship of the size of the force to the extent of the area of operational responsibility is a crucial part of gaining an understanding of the progress and outcome of the operations that comprise that conflict. Neither looking at the map nor counting heads on wage rolls can enhance such an understanding unless it is done with an eye to the nature of terrain applied rather more closely than maps will allow and with a thought to both the objectives of operations conducted and the demands and conditions – economic, military and political – that the force in place must also address. We may be aware that the garrison of a particular castle consisted of a specified number of men, and even the distribution of those men between men-at-arms, archers (perhaps divided between longbowmen and crossbowmen) and other infantry, but that does not give us any information about how many men the garrison commander could afford to commit to a field operation. The men of the garrison would have a number of duties to fulfil: enforcing general law-and-order; collecting rents and taxes; pro-tecting convoys; gathering intelligence; disrupting the operations of the enemy; maintaining a visible military (and therefore political) presence in front of the local populace and, of course, the defence of the castle or burgh where the garrison was based.

The forfeiture of Lothian landowners in the years before Bannockburn[56] clearly shows that the Bruce party was not without sup-port in the Lothian area. Some of this support was undoubtedly because the landowners concerned had extensive property elsewhere in Scotland, which they feared losing if King Robert was successful, and which they did not think they would regain through the actions of King Edward.

Some of these Lothian landholders may have been motivated by a strong sense of what, as Professor Barrow says, 'older historians were content to call the national cause',[57] but we should not ignore the possibility that increasing desertion of the Edwardian cause in the period 1307–1314, demonstrated by a handful of forfeitures in 1312[58] was a product of the operational situation, brought on by the inability of the administration to keep the Bruce party out of Lothian or by the general military success of King Robert's forces.

The extensive restorations that can be identified after the Battle of Dunbar are a strong indication that some form of 'blanket' forfeiture may have been enacted against all those who served King John in the 1296 campaign. It is not impossible that such an act may even have preceded hostilities in the hope, perhaps successful, that some people might be deterred from serving at all. The forfeiture of minor landholders seems to have been a sentence that could be rescinded on acceptance into the Plantagenet peace at the discretion of the sheriff or by a writ from the King to the sheriff. In the summer and autumn of 1296 restorations were ordered for at least thirty-five mesne tenants and forty-three tenants-in-chief in twenty-eight different counties in Scotland[59] and a further fifty-eight, mostly free tenants from Lothian, Berwick, Roxburgh, Lanark and Stirling were restored on 3 September 1296,[60] perhaps as a result of formally giving their allegiance to Edward since virtually all of them were Ragman Roll homagers on or before 28 August 1296.

Forfeiture was the 'last resort' sanction against rebellious landholders because although it could be reversed, and in the period after the Battle of Dunbar there are many examples of this, repeated restoration and forfeiture undermined the value of it as a threat to the recalcitrant and thereby damaged the prestige of the king. Although forfeiture was evidently not a successful policy, insofar as it was not effective in deterring defection to the Balliol or Bruce causes, it would be wrong to assume that it was a failed policy kept in place through inertia. The application of forfeiture was by no means the same in 1312 for example as it was in 1335.[61] In any event, we should not assume that the lands forfeited were necessarily in the control of the Edwardian administration, though some certainly were since revenue was being raised from them. In one case the return was actually greater than the normal peacetime valuation,[62] an indication perhaps of the difference between the rental of the property and the actual return to the landholder. The landholder could be declared forfeit even though the administration was not in a position to enforce its will. Nor should we assume that an area outwith the control of English administration was inevitably under the control of the Scots. The inability of local garrisons to collect rents and taxes, even the development of 'no-go' areas, is not sufficient indication that the opposition have actually gained that territory for themselves. Whether or not that denial of territory is the product of the actions of the enemy is of course of secondary importance to the overall situation to the 'occupying' power – the fact is they have lost control of that area and inevitably the public perception of the ability of that power to maintain law and order would be damaged. Even with a very powerful and mobile force, maintaining effective civil order in the face of armed opposition would be a considerable challenge due to the nature of the terrain if nothing else.

Although Lothian has, by Scottish standards, a good deal of high-quality arable land there is also a great deal of broken country. An English writer complained in the winter of 1299[63] that as little as eight miles from Edinburgh an enemy force – in this case Hugh de Penicuik and his followers – could operate from a range of hills (the Pentlands) not easily penetrated by a large force. The arable areas of Lothian are hardly great rolling plains. The landscape is riven with deep river gorges separating low hill formations affording an unusually high incidence of covered approaches and withdrawals to the insurgent and is an exceptionally difficult terrain for reconnaissance by garrisons. There are of course many hilltops throughout Lothian from which one can see a great swathe of territory, but such 'vistas' are very misleading in almost any terrain. Regardless of the nature of the country it is very seldom that anything less than sixty per cent of the area bounded by a horizon is 'dead ground'.[64] Given the fact that even the largest medieval armies were little more than a mere speck on the landscape it should be clear that small raiding forces would have been exceedingly difficult to detect and therefore almost impossible to intercept. Even if the insurgents could be identified as a target in time to deploy a force to pursue them, the nature of the countryside favours escape through concealment, and if the insurgents found it impossible to 'shake' their pursuers in daylight, they would almost inevitably do so with ease at nightfall. Line-of-sight considerations may seem a little laboured when applied to medieval conflict, but in fact topography is the defining non-human factor in any tactical problem.

Even with the active intelligence-gathering support of a large part of the population, counter-insurgency operations are notoriously difficult; without such support they are virtually impossible. The imposition of authority by military means, or the disruption of that authority are more dependent on a regular and convincing appearance of strength than on combat; both sides seek to further their interests essentially by intimidation of the population (and of course one another) rather than fighting. This is a two-edged weapon however, particularly for an administration that is seen as an imposition. If the visible presence of the garrison forces is not extensive, the local populace may feel increasingly vulnerable to the insurgents; equally if it is too intrusive, it might become a focus for resentment.

Forcing battle would in itself have been a tactically challenging proposition for the garrison forces. In addition to the terrain problems, the garrisons were not generally strong enough to afford a large field force to chase the Scots. Even if the Scots were heavily outnumbered at any point in terms of men on active service throughout the theatre generally, the Edwardian administrations had far greater commitments. Achieving local superiority in numbers was probably no great problem for the Scots, therefore Edwardian forces could not afford to precipitately pursue and attack Scottish forces. It is, after all, difficult to tell when you are pursuing a fleeing enemy and when you are entering an ambush. The challenge of responding to such a situation can be seen in the structure of the Battle of Roslin. Although the numbers involved were probably quite small – a few hundred Scots rather than the several thousand described by Bower and Fordun – the English forces were unable to concentrate in time to apply their superior numbers, partly, perhaps, due to their inability to find billets for the troops within easy supporting distance of one another.

Naturally, it is the objective of any rebel organisation – and Edward did describe his Scottish opponents as rebels – to replace the existing administration, which in the fourteenth century meant the eventual acquisition of the various centres of military and economic significance throughout the region, just as it would in any comparable insurgent conflict. Some modern thinkers[65] have believed that 'urban' (in the very loosest sense of the word) areas must inevitably fall to insurgents that have secured the rural hinterlands on which those centres depend. This is not necessarily valid in a medieval context. The great castles of Lothian, such as Edinburgh or Dirleton, could be securely held by remarkably small garrisons[66] so long as they were not called upon to conduct extensive field operations, nor do they seem to have been under threat from the burgh community at Edinburgh other than those occasions when a force from outside Lothian (as in 1338 and 1341) could intervene. As long as Edwardian governments were prepared to bear the expense of supporting their Lothian garrisons – if necessary from resources beyond the income that could be raised locally – those garrisons could severely compromise the establishment of a Bruce administration.

At some point in a conflict, if the insurgents enjoy enough success, the roles of insurgent and administration start to become reversed; in a sense, the garrisons become insurgents. The 'favourable terrain' to which they would withdraw after operations would be castles rather than camps in the hills, but their tactical and strategic condition would be based on the disruption of the Scots rather than the domination of the territory. Even if the Scots were to hold a town but not the castle within it (as might have been the case at Stirling before the fall of the castle in 1299 or Edinburgh in 1314 and 1341), they would not necessarily be able adequately or consistently to contain the garrison militarily and its visible presence (compared to a band of fighters in the woods) would undermine the authority and prestige of King Robert's government. If the castle was a symbol of regal authority as well as a centre of government, the fact that it was in the possession of the enemy would not be beneficial to the public perception of the king, which may offer a political explanation for King Robert's destruction of castles to complement the accepted military rationale – that he was not in a position to garrison castles securely and that their recovery by the Edwardian administration would threaten the security of his rule.

As the general political situation developed, people adjusted their individual positions; someone who had been steadfast in support of King John was not necessarily going to transfer their loyalty to King Robert, who was really no less an usurper than Edward I and a sacrilegious murderer to boot, and the vast majority of those landholders had already given their allegiance to Edward in 1296.[67] Even if an individual was strongly motivated in favour of King Robert or by a 'national consciousness' or other motive, they might find themselves in the 'peace' or even service of the Edwards for simple practical reasons like stability and cash wages. The subject of Scots in Plantagenet service has already been addressed, but the presence of Edwardian garrisons would hardly be an incentive for Lothian men to turn out for the other side and the attractions of (supposedly) regular pay or the belief that the Bruce party were not going to win – and in 1307–1308 at the very least that would not have been an unrealistic assumption – would surely discourage defection.

Those strongly opposed to the Bruces had a clear incentive to support the Edwardian government. However, they too were affected by the wider situation. Immediately after Bannockburn any Edwardian administration as had survived the fall of Edinburgh Castle seems to have disappeared overnight. Those who had been in Edward's peace but wished to retain their Lothian properties would obviously have had to seek an accommodation with King Robert. Some, but by no means all, of these people would make their peace with Edward III after Halidon Hill for the same reasons. It would seem that constancy was not a highly developed part of the psyche of Lothian landowners in the first half of the fourteenth century, and many historians have been at pains to point this out.[68] Even so, we should avoid being judgmental about complex social situations where there are so many obvious factors, – and likely many more of which we can have no knowledge – or where our understanding is particularly limited. Leadership, both local and national, must have had bearing on military and political affairs. No clear pattern of long-term leadership groups has emerged in this study at either regional or local level. That should not be taken as evidence that such leadership did not exist; merely that it cannot be incontrovertibly demonstrated by example. If it were possible to chart all of the familial, social, economic, legal and geographic relationships of all the members of the political community of Lothian through the period from 1296 to the 1350s it might well be possible to identify groups with the same, or similar membership entering or leaving the peace of contending authorities, but that would not automatically make clear to us the basis of membership in that group nor that the people concerned really constitute a 'group' at all. Their official admission to Edward's peace on the same day is not evidence that they were necessarily acting in concert, merely that they were included in the same instrument such as the writ of 3 September 1296 instructing the sheriff of Edinburgh to restore the property of Walter de Drylawe and John le Blund among others.[69]

On the occasions that we can genuinely identify a group changing sides[70] we might assume that there is a 'common interest' factor involved, but the nature of that relationship is not immediately apparent. Several individuals might come to the peace of Edward I, in the company of this or that prominent person,[71] but the nature of the relationship is elusive. The members of the group might be connected by familial relationships, tradition or geographical proximity, but that relationship may not be clear to us. Family connections might be too tenuous to be identified at a distance of 700 years, but sufficiently well-known in the four-teenth century to require no comment. Traditions of political alignment between family groups might have no real currency, just the product of a friendship/mutual interest in a previous generation; geographical relationships could be obscured by the titles used by specific individuals. Equally, an identified group may represent a political structure of sorts. A great lord might derive the preponderance of his wealth and power from one region, but he would be very likely to have property in other areas and it is not impossible that the men admitted to the peace of a king in the company of an earl represent the senior tenants of the lordships comprising the property of that earl throughout the country.

Additionally, where we do find a group of people coming to the peace of a king in the company of a great lord it may be the case that they are not particularly aligned with that person in a long-term sense, merely that they have found a means of taking advantage of that lord's prestige to effect a change of sides in a relatively painless manner. The lord in question – as long as he was not going to be held responsible for the future conduct of the members of the group – would have his own prestige enhanced by the fact that people were seeking his lordship, perhaps particularly so if those people were not long-term adherents or dependants. When the Earl of Fife came to the peace of Edward Balliol after the Battle of Dupplin Muir he brought with him men who were, if not his tenants, certainly his neighbours[72] and it is fair to assume that his local prominence was a major factor in their submission. The relation-ship between the Earl of Strathearn and the five men who had their lands restored in September 1296[73] having come to the peace of Edward I in his company is not so clear – William Byset a 'county' Ragman Roll homager may have been a dependant of the Earl – through famil-ial relationship, family tradition or on the strength of land tenure. The Earl's interests were not limited to Strathearn; he granted land in the Barony of Balnacreiff in the constabulary of Linlithgow (easily con-fused with Balencrefe in Haddington constabulary) to John Murray of

Drumsergard[74] but the relationship is not readily apparent now, though it may have been abundantly so at the time. William's commitment to the Edwardian cause was sufficient to take him into action at the Battle of Falkirk where he had a horse – a hackney valued at eight merks[75] – killed in the fighting. William's service to King Edward may have been the product of the earl's lordship or leadership, but the extent of lordly control can in any case be exaggerated. In 1304 King Edward found it necessary to order the Earl to prevent his men from supplying the Scottish garrison at Stirling.[76] This was hardly a point where the patriotic star was in the ascendant and the Earl was most certainly in Edward's peace at the time.

While the entire scope of an individual's motivation to fight for either side, or for that matter to avoid involvement, can hardly be ascertained at a distance of seven centuries, we should have no doubt that personal considerations of a non-political nature could be a significant, even paramount factor in deciding alignment. A love match might be enough to carry a person away from the traditional loyalties of their family or region and into the affinity of the other side.[77] Personal career interests might do the same, a factor demonstrated by the inheritance dispute that arose between the supporters of Edward Balliol in 1334. John Moubray had been killed in action at Annan in 1332 when the Bruce party had surprised Balliol's rather meagre following. Unlike other prominent members of the disinherited, the Moubrays had lost their estates in Scotland, not through war, despite their adherence to the Plantagenet cause before 1314, but through their involvement in the de Soulis conspiracy of 1320, an attempt to place Edward Balliol on the throne. Evidently the Balliol party was happy to accept defectors from the Bruce party and the Moubrays were prepared to support Edward Balliol but not to the extent of surrendering their individual ambitions for territorial expansion. The Moubrays sought shelter in England and were forfeited by Robert I of a wide range of property, much of which was granted to the Stewarts. In August 1334, under the kingship of Edward Balliol, Sir Alexander Moubray claimed John Moubrays estates as the nearest male relative but this was contested by Richard Talbot, Henry Beaumont and David de Strathbogie. According to Bower, these three sought the exclusion of Alexander in favour of the daughters of his late brother, John. Those members of the disinherited who had been pursuing their lost heritages for rather longer than the Moubrays may have resented Balliol's decision to support their claims, however since the Moubrays had lost their lands in the 1320 attempt to restore the Balliol monarchy (no other credible candidate existed) Edward could hardly avoid offering whatever help he could if he was to be seen as a source of 'good lordship'.

These three men that he offended were prominent Balliol supporters. Edward would almost certainly have been unable to mount his invasion of Scotland in the summer of 1332 without their manpower, money and influence.[78] Maintaining even the semblance of Scottish kingship without their active military participation would have been quite impossible since they represented such a large portion of his power base. Despite this – and with the obvious aim of keeping the Moubrays on his side – Edward decided in favour of Sir Alexander. The dissent sown among the three counter-claimants was short-lived because Sir Alexander soon made his own accommodation with the Scots, but the damage to Edward's prestige among his own supporters was probably complemented by damage to his relationship with Edward III. If Edward Balliol could not exert his kingship among his closest associates how successful was he going to be at attracting, and, more importantly, retaining support from the Bruce cause? Edward III may have envisaged a client king, but a client king who could not deliver a stable Scottish administration, or at least containment of the Bruce party, was of very limited value. The defection of Sir Alexander was an indication that the Bruce party was far from being contained. On the contrary, Moubray had joined them despite the fact that Edward Balliol had taken his part against three men, Beaumont, Strathbogie and Talbot whose support was crucial to the fortunes of the Balliol cause. Edward Balliol's authority was severely undermined because Moubray's defection demonstrated a lack of faith in Edward's ability to form a permanent administration.

Defections were not always the product of land disputes. An important consideration in several instances was the most personal ambition of all – namely keeping one's head attached to one's neck. David de Strathbogie, generally a stalwart supporter of the Balliol cause, defected to the Bruce party in September 1334 when confronted with the prospect of capture and very possibly death. He was entrusted with the administration of the north by the Earl of Moray, King David's lieutenant.[79] This begs the question as to why Moray should have been so accommodating. Did he feel that Strathbogie could be trusted to adhere to his new allegiance? Did he feel that confident that he could afford to take a gamble on that allegiance or was he simply not strong enough to exe-cute Strathbogie out of hand for fear of alienating support in the north? Strathbogie returned to the Balliol party in August 1335. His defection, however temporary, must have been detrimental to the authority of the Plantagenet party, but the reality of his situation must have been clear to Edward Balliol and to Edward III, neither of whom hesitated to accept Strathbogie into their peace. Naturally, not all defections were by such exalted persons, nor is the documentary evidence sufficiently intact to date all such changes of heart. However the restorations and forfeitures that do survive can give us some picture of the regularity with which they occurred. Geoffrey de Fressingleye, a 'county' Ragman Roll hom-ager, would seem to have remained in the peace of the Plantagenets until 1308 but was not forfeited of his property of half the 'vill' of Wester Duddingston until February 1312, when he was declared to have been an enemy 'for four years'.[80] His heir – presumably his son – William, having apparently been in the peace of Edward III was forfeited of the entire 'vill' of Duddingston before July 1336.[81] Not only is this an indication of defection, it suggests – at least in the reign of Edward II – a certain reluctance to forfeit people for rebellion. The titles by which people are known to us may well obscure important aspects of their life because our attention is not drawn to those factors. Sir Thomas Randolph can serve as an example of this. As the Earl of Moray it is no surprise to us that he had extensive interests in the north, but his properties elsewhere were hardly insignificant.[82] Each of these landholdings involved Randolph or his representative in the political life of that particular vicinity. These involvements were not discrete; the value of being able to draw resources from one area to provide armed strength in another can be seen in the force of southern Scots led to Culblean by Sir Andrew Moray. The action was obviously a function of war and politics in the north,[83] but the men on either side were largely 'recruited' from other areas – southern Scots on one side and the retinues of English Lords on the other. This is, in a sense, the direct contradiction of Barron's proposition that the Wars of Independence were conducted by the men of what he saw as 'Celtic' Scotland; he went so far as to state that the 'men of Lothian had neither lot nor part' in the 'nationalist' cause, presumably unaware that Culblean was won by a Scottish army which contained a large body recruited from south of the river Forth.[84]

If political leadership groups are, to say the least, shadowy, what can we say about local military leadership, and can it really be separated from political leadership? Again, although it would seem that such leadership was crucial to the Scottish recoveries after major reversals on the battle-field, the nature of that leadership is just as elusive as political leadership. Certainly there were more and less powerful and influential people in any region we care to examine, but how was that leadership obtained and retained?

The basis for local power might spring from the crown in the form of grants of land or positions of authority in a particular vicinity, but the preservation, development and application of that power would depend, at least in part, on the ability of the lord in question to maintain his prestige and credibility through what would in due course be termed 'good lordship'. In the volatile arena of fourteenth-century political life this would almost inevitably involve military activity from time to time and there is no question but that success in the field could enhance the prestige of great lords and kings, and this was surely reflected at a regional level in the actions of local magnates. Within the Lothian community it is clear that men who would not normally have been of any great conse-quence on the national political scene could acquire a following, initially through their local network of relatives, friends and neighbours and develop that through their own leadership abilities. In the 1330s William Douglas of Lothian, a minor baron, rose to prominence through suc-cessful leadership in war, amply reported by Fordun[85] and Bower,[86] not because of his status in the national political community. A magnate pat-tern of leadership in Lothian at the same period may not be discernible, but that does not mean it did not exist. Inevitably the political choices of a local potentate must have had some impact, not only on the tenants of those magnates but also on their neighbours. We might reasonably assume, for instance, that the defection of Patrick Earl of Dunbar to the peace of Edward III after Halidon Hill resulted in a similar change of allegiance among his tenants and neighbours, but the fact that Patrick was specifically granted[87] the properties of any of his tenants that were forfeited by Edward III surely indicates that local leadership was not universally effective in enforcing lordship, or at least that local potentates could be defied. The reversion of Earl Patrick to the Bruce cause might, for all we know, have given him a second opportunity to dispose of tenants, this time those who were unwilling to return to the allegiance

of David II. The right to the removal and the forfeitures of free tenants might be construed as no more than an opportunity for the lord
concerned to dispose of difficult tenants and reward faithful service or
to provide an income for less fortunate dependants through re-granting
the forfeited properties. However it may indicate a need to make some
examples to ensure the future loyalty of the surviving tenants. Whether
the Earl of Dunbar was able to benefit from his grant of the forfeitures of
his tenants is unclear; his own defection to the Bruce party must surely
have effectively prevented him from prosecuting any of his tenants who
had joined the Bruces at an earlier date.

Local leadership did not have to be limited to tenants however.
Neighbouring landowners, regardless from whom they held their estate
would be likely to be influenced by the actions of the most powerful
person in their vicinity, particularly in periods of crown weakness. By
the 1330s and 1340s the concentration of local authority in the hands of a
small number of trusted lieutenants that had taken place under Robert I
had engendered a small class of warlord magnates with enormous power
in those localities if only they could effectively exert lordship. That lordship was, in many cases, threatened by the claims of the disinherited lords
who had lost their lands through their opposition to Robert I and who
hoped to regain their lands through their support of Edward Balliol.[88]
The competition for authority between the members of these groups
was certainly expressed in armed conflict, but it would be short-sighted
to assume that they did not actively seek the support of the local political
community by less belligerent means, like remissions of rents and casualties, grants of land, office or privilege. In short, they had to offer 'good
lordship' if they were to make themselves secure in their possession of
territory. Sir Thomas Grey was of the opinion that Edward III lost his
conquest lands in Scotland primarily through a lack of 'good lordship'.[89]
Sir Thomas did not give any specific examples of this failure, nor did he
offer an explanation for its occurrence, but since he was actively involved
in both the civil and military aspects of Edward's government we should
perhaps accept his opinion.

Several prominent lords were forfeited by the Edwardian administration. If these lords were to recover their inheritances they would have to
fight, and if they were to fight successfully they must inevitably mobilise
troops. These troops might not be raised from the contested areas, but it
is difficult to see how a lord could recover his position without a degree

of local support, or how they would retain that position without making their authority acceptable to the local community. In the short term that might be effected through force of arms, but to do so indefinitely would be an unacceptable burden on tenants drawn from other regions and, in the long term, might well alienate the very people that the lord was endeavouring to bring under his control. Again, Patrick Earl of Dunbar can provide an example of practice. When he decided to join the Bruce party, one of the factors that induced his defection was the tendency of troops in Edwardian garrisons, and Berwick in particular,[90] to conduct foraging operations against the local population regardless of which side they were on. Patrick was quite prepared to take this issue to Edward III, but Edward was unable, or perhaps unwilling, to do anything very positive about the problem. Edward's failure to support Earl Patrick undermined his position as a local magnate insofar as he could not deliver the physical protection of his clients that was part of the responsibility of lordship. The strength of Edward II's garrisons was not great enough to enforce his lordship or protect his clients, but it was sufficient to undermine his only really important ally in the south-east.

As the war increasingly favoured the Scots, Earl Patrick's tenants would have been subjected to their demands as well as those of the garrison. If Patrick could not protect his tenants and dependants from the operations of either side he would eventually lose those tenants to a lord who would give them that protection. Patrick's reversion to the Bruce party was not simply a renouncing of allegiance to Edward III (who, since the ceding to him of 2000 librates of southern Scotland by Edward Balliol[91] had been Patrick's liege lord) but an effort to prevent encroachment on his lordship by Scottish lords in the Bruce camp hopeful of extending their influence in the south-east. One could perhaps argue that Patrick had come to the conclusion that he was being damaged more by his absence from the Scottish political community than he was being protected by his presence in the Edwardian political community, which, in a rather grand sense admittedly, is not far removed from the position of the political community of Lothian throughout the period of competition for regal authority. As long as the Edwardian administration could wield enough strength to prevent extensive Scottish operations in Lothian, most of the community was prepared to accept it, though what choice they had in the absence of effective Scottish military intervention is hard to say. When the Edwardian administrations were too weak to prevent that intervention most of the community accepted the Bruce administration – with what degree of enthusiasm it is impossible to say, though Professor Barrow has expressed strong views on the subject.[92] The presence of Lothian men in the ranks of Bruce armies certainly demonstrates that not everyone in Lothian was at ease with the Edwardian government, but is hardly proof of widespread opposition to it in the communities between the Avon and Cockburnspath.

KNIGHTS AND MEN-AT-ARMS

The most prestigious form of military obligation was knight service.[93] How exactly knight service was accounted as a financial burden cannot be precisely evaluated. The cost of equipping a first-rate man-at-arms rose dramatically in the latter part of the thirteenth century[94] and must have become an almost intolerable burden for smaller landholders whose estates would hardly be sufficient to support the man-at-arms and his horse let alone discharge the debt incurred if the man were captured and had to find a ransom.

The cost of knight service was not, however, a fixed universal sum. A suitable mount might easily cost as much as £30[95] but even a cursory glance at the horse valuation rolls in *CDS* indicates that for the vast majority of men-at-arms a beast with a value of £5–10 was the norm.[96] The same applies to the equipment. Suits of chainmail referred to in contemporary documents are valued at anything from 20 shillings to 100 shillings.[97] Obviously this is a reflection of the value of the individual hauberk. At the lower end of the price spectrum the hauberk would consist of relatively large links, perhaps a centimetre or more in diameter and the gauge of the metal itself only one millimetre thick. The protective value of such a hauberk would have been very limited compared to one with links of only five or six millimetres diameter.[98]

The cost of a hauberk was not simply dependent on the size and density of the links, but was also, obviously, a reflection of the extent of the protection. A coat of mail that extended to the knee and with long sleeves terminating in chainmail mittens would inevitably be a more costly item than one of similar quality that only reached to the waist and elbows. Self-evidently, assuming a similar quality of link, the latter would comprise many more links than the former; possibly the difference between

15–20,000 links and 30–40,000 links.[99] The single most important cost factor was whether the mail links were butted or riveted. In butted mail the individual links are passed through one another and the ends of each link simply meet or slightly overlap rather like a modern washer. The more expensive variety – riveted mail – was a much more labour intensive product. Each link is firmly closed by one or sometimes two tiny rivets.[100] Chainmail is still being hand-made in India today for the film and re-enactment market, and the price relationship between the two forms (for the same size of hauberk) is approximately 2.5:1 in favour of riveted mail. Given that the method of assembly has not changed in the intervening seven hundred years it would seem unreasonable, failing specific evidence to the contrary, to assume that that relationship was radically different in the fourteenth century, although the 'real price' in relation to incomes was far greater than it is today due to the lower price of the metal itself and the availability of suitable wire to cut into links.

The protective power of chainmail by itself was quite limited. As a guard against an edged weapon mail was quite effective, indeed mail gloves are still sometimes used by butchers, but mail offered little protection against the impact of a blow, thus, to protect the wearer from broken bones the mail hauberk was worn with a thickly padded garment (jack or gambeson) to diffuse impact. Non-metal protection had the advantage of being relatively cheap; it could be made locally by men and women without developing a high level of skills and from materials that were to be found easily in any community – linen, wool and leather.

Some proportion of the munitions used in Scotland (and in England too) was imported from the Low Countries,[101] possibly the majority of it, but this cannot be adequately demonstrated. Certainly some came either directly from England or indirectly as re-exported goods from England via Ireland if we are to accept the repeated demands of English kings[102] that their subjects refrain from trading arms to the Scots as evidence that such legislation was necessary. Whether these imports constituted the mainstay of Scottish armies is a different matter. Any type of medieval weaponry *could* be manufactured locally. As early as William the Lion's reign a man held property in Perth in exchange for two iron helmets and one Perth tradesman (possibly the same man) was specifically described as a *galeator*: a helmet-maker.[103] If helmet-making could be a full-time, or at least primary, occupation, it would seem reasonable to assume that Perth tradesmen could provide any personal military equipment that the local community might require, and that the same would apply in Edinburgh, Stirling or any other sizeable burgh. Since a helmet is as hard, or harder, to produce than any other piece of armour it follows that all the necessary appurtenances of knightly combat were available in a town like Perth.[104] Whether the local producers could meet the demands of entire armies is another matter. It seems reasonable to conclude that the Scots imported arms, not because they could not be produced locally, but because they could not be produced in sufficient quantity, or, after a particularly heavy defeat such as Falkirk, because lost equipment could not be replaced quickly.

Before the close of the thirteenth century the sword had ceased to be the primary weapon of battle even for dismounted men-at-arms. A body of men equipped with spears could face cavalry with some degree of confidence compared to a similar body bearing only swords. The sword of course was much more practical for individual combat than the spear, but the development of better quality armour, and in particular the growing practice of adding protective plates on top of and eventually in place of mail reduced its effectiveness in fighting between men at arms. The net result was the increasing popularity of pole-arms and mace, hammer and axe type weapons which could reasonably be expected to break or penetrate even the strongest plates if the wielder could achieve a clean blow on his enemy, or at least to cause internal injuries – including broken bones – with a less than perfect strike. The sword was retained because of its convenience as a side arm for personal defence outwith operational conditions – criminal assaults and disorder – and because of its social significance as the weapon of gentlemen.

THE HORSE

No man-at-arms could serve properly without a suitable horse; so much so that records of garrison complements mention not only the lack of horses but sometimes that a particular animal was 'insufficient'.[105] Dr. Ayton has demonstrated that most mounts in Scotland were valued at substantially more than the 100s ($£5$)[106] which was generally the minimum value of horse acceptable for restauro assessment. It is almost axiomatic that Scottish medieval armies were almost devoid of cavalry due to the difficulty of maintaining suitable mounts through the winter. However the very extensive level of man-at-arms service performed by Lothian men for Plantagenet governments would indicate that such animals were reasonably readily available and that there were men competent to serve on horseback suggests that the availability of horses was not a product of the campaign of 1296. The evolutions of medieval armies were extremely basic, but the quality of horsemanship necessary for the individual to function competently on the battlefield would have been very high indeed, a level of skill that would be impossible to achieve without the appropriate mount.

The limited amount of archaeological[107] evidence relating to the horse in Scotland – skeletal remains and horse furniture – would seem to indicate that short, thickset animals of 12 to 14 hands were the norm. However virtually all of the data comes from urban excavations. Since only a very small portion (perhaps 10 per cent at most) of medieval Scots lived in urban areas we should be very careful in our application of the material gathered. There should be no doubt that the majority of animals across the country were short enough that today they would be described as ponies rather than horses, but the number of Scottish men who performed mounted military service in Edwardian garrisons surely suggests that there was a high enough incidence of ownership of horses fit for such duties for the society to be able to furnish competent cavalry soldiers in sufficient numbers to justify the effort of administering the necessary records of service. A number of these men[108] were given the use of one of the king's horses to carry out their duties, but that is not a particularly good indicator that such horses were not readily available to Scots.[109] It could just as easily be the case that these individuals could not afford to buy – or just as importantly maintain – a horse of that calibre, or simply that they had already lost their own horse and had the use of one from the king as a temporary measure pending the Wardrobe paying out for a replacement, or that they have been provided with a horse 'by gift of the king'.[110] This might be on account of good service in the past or perhaps for personal reasons with no particular relevance to historians, but no doubt it was chiefly to ensure that the king's army was not deprived of the service of an adequate man-at-arms.

The height of a horse did not determine its usefulness for war. Recent research[111] suggests that the great war horses of the early fourteenth century – when body armour for the battlefield was at its heaviest – were rather shorter than traditionally believed, perhaps closer to fifteen hands than seventeen, and that the advantage of these horses over other breeds lay more in their greater endurance than in superior speed or stature. Mounted combat in great engagements – although still the preferred arena for deeds of chivalry – was extremely rare.[112] In the more mundane forms of activity that were more typical of campaigning – reconnaissance, raiding, counter-raiding, convoy, and what we might call operations in support of the civil power – the chief function of the horse was to move troops from A to B and back again. For both sides this would often mean traversing difficult terrain. Scots operating an insurgent strategy from inaccessible strongholds would have to cross such terrain in order to reach objectives, and the Edwardian garrison troops would have to negotiate it if they were to attack the Scots in their camps or pursue them after incursions. To conduct these operations both sides would have had to make use of cheap, sturdy horses that would not be a huge loss if they were lost – they needed animals that could be replaced readily and locally; more mounted infantry nags rather than knightly chargers. Nonetheless, there was still a place for the great horse. There are a number of instances of what we might think of as 'classic' knightly fighting; actions like Dunbar, Roslin and Methven where the *schwerpunkt*[113] of the engagement was the meeting of mounted men-at-arms. These fights, and the tournaments that took place in the later phases of the wars, were the arena in which the 'destrier' horses were a necessary part of a gentleman's equipment. The Scots enjoyed a number of successes in mounted combat and in tournaments, and it is therefore hard to accept the traditional view that the Scots did not have access to heavy cavalry horses.[114] Certainly it is true that the Scots could not raise such large forces of men-at-arms as the English or the French, but then, Scotland was a rather smaller country, and the maintenance of a heavy war horse would be likely to have been a rather greater burden simply because of the relative poverty of the Scottish nobility and gentry. There are enough instances of mounted Scottish men-at-arms in action throughout the entire period of the Wars of Independence to demonstrate that they were a crucial part of the Scottish approach to war generally, and since it would seem that at least one in three of the men selected for this study served as men-at-arms, it is impossible to avoid the conclusion that heavy cavalry service was a normal practice for Lothian gentlemen.

The extent to which Scottish chargers were armoured is open to question. However there is no evidence to suggest that Scottish men-at-arms were equipped to a lower standard than their English counterparts. In 1299 the Balliol party, under the leadership of John Comyn and Robert Bruce, stationed a force under Sir Robert Keith and Sir Ingram d'Umfraville, in Ettrick Forest to harass the English. In addition to the local men the force consisted of 1500 infantry and one hundred men-at-arms with covered (barbed, barded or armoured) horses.[115] It would be very unlikely that the Scots would commit a very substantial part of their armoured cavalry to operations in a forest, or that they would select that force primarily from the men with covered horses or indeed to commit them to operations that did not involve the higher commanders. As we have already seen (Chapter 4), receipt of full man-at-arms wages in English armies and garrisons was dependent on possession of adequate horse armour. If it was normal for Scots on unarmoured horses to fight garrison members on armoured ones it would be likely that patriotic Scottish chroniclers would have made the point repeatedly to underline the military achievements of their countrymen.

A comparison of the valuations of the horses of Scottish men-at-arms in Edwardian garrisons with those of their English counterparts would seem to suggest that they might, in the main, have owned somewhat cheaper animals, but this is hardly conclusive since so large a proportion of the men named in valuations cannot be adequately identified as Scots or English. Even if we could demonstrate that a 'typical' Scottish man-at-arms (and how would we decide what was typical?) serving in a particular garrison was less expensively mounted than an English man-at-arms, we would not have proven that this was a universal, or even commonplace condition. The valuations are not in themselves a good guide to the quality of horseflesh available to Scottish men-at-arms; only a record of the animals they took on active service. Superficially it might seem that a man-at-arms would inevitably choose to take a powerful, perhaps prestigious animal on campaign. Englishmen coming to serve in Scotland would presumably take their expensive charger in the expectation of taking part in a conventional chivalrous fight – and that is obviously going to be the animal they have valued, lest it be lost in action. Scotsmen, with a clearer picture of local conditions (and perhaps able to send home for a different mount should they need it) may have elected not to expose their more valuable animals to the hazards of daily military service or to risk the animal's health by keeping it in a crowded stable.

OPERATIONAL PRACTICE

Although tactical analysis with such limited data is of questionable validity at the best of times it is worth giving some consideration to the composition of the armies from what we know of combat. The dependence on men-at-arms as the striking force of Edwardian garrisons is evident from the muster rolls – generally half or more of the entire combatant strength. Where the balance of the garrison includes archers, particularly cross-bowmen, it is reasonable to assume that their usual function would be to maintain the security of the establishment, not to march across the country. Equally, it is reasonable to assume that the main function of retaining a large force of men-at-arms at Linlithgow or Edinburgh was to carry the war to the enemy. The strategic value of cavalry lay primarily in their ability to conduct operations at a greater distance from their base and return without too much risk of interception by a more balanced force and the strong likelihood of being able to escape from such an interception should it occur. The tactical advantage lay in the ability to deploy directly to combat from line-of-march. At its simplest, the Scots needed to be able to achieve local superiority in men-at-arms over the parties that could be committed by the garrison forces. The key consideration is local superiority. It would not be necessary for the Scots to maintain a larger force of men-at-arms than the total English deployment. They would require only as many as would be needed to deter the English force in a particular vicinity at a particular time and to do so on enough occasions to achieve local tactical dominance, at which point the garrison would no longer be able to fulfil its administrative functions for the government and probably start to be seriously at risk of capture by the Scots due to the difficulties of maintaining a fortress in enemy territory.

The majority of the infantry in garrison service were archers or crossbowmen usually receiving 3d or 4d[116] per day and presumably not engaged in offensive operations to any great degree. This may not have been the case in the Edinburgh garrison of 1340 when half of the complement consisted of men-at-arms and the remainder mounted archers. It is possible that these particular 'mounted archers' were in fact foot archers receiving a preferential rate of pay for service in a very exposed stronghold or that the garrison establishment had been changed to conform to developments in English military thinking in the 1330s.[117] The trend toward forces consisting mostly, if not entirely, of men-at-arms and mounted archers has been thoroughly examined by Dr. Ayton and Col. Rogers[118] and a lengthy discussion of that trend here is neither necessary nor desirable, suffice to say that it is widely recognised. There is no reason to assume that Scotland was a military backwater in the 1330s; the rationale that lay behind the adoption of a force that was completely mounted but retaining some of the advantages of dismounted troops – primarily the 'firepower' aspect – was as viable in Scotland as it was in France. One muster roll document is a very slender basis for analysis of a garrison that existed for some years. It may have been the case that archers in previous years had been provided with horses, but that the documents recording those animals, assuming that they were documented at all, have failed to survive. It is also possible that the weak position of the Plantagenet cause in Lothian in 1340 had prompted the government to pay for or even provide a horse for every man in the event of the garrison having to make a hasty withdrawal.

Dr. Powicke was firmly convinced that there was no articulated system of knight service in Scotland,[119] Professor Barrow is equally convinced that there was,[120] though neither has been particularly clear about what exactly they mean by an 'articulated system'. Certainly the incidence of knight service obligations for land under Robert I would hardly have produced a cavalry force of more than a few hundred from the whole of Scotland, but we should bear in mind that the majority of records which tell us anything at all about combat in the fourteenth century refer repeatedly to the service of Scottish men-at-arms; we read of them in English garrisons, we read of them fighting at Dunbar, Roslin, Edinburgh Castle, Culblean and Crichtondene.

At Dunbar it is clear that only heavy cavalry elements were engaged on either side. It is often assumed that the entirety of the Scottish cavalry were present; however there is no evidence to suggest that this is the case, but there is evidence that a considerable party of Scottish men-at-arms were in the garrison of Dunbar Castle. Whilst recognising that the Scottish leadership was inexperienced in war, it would be unreasonable to assume that the whole of the Scottish cavalry, the striking arm of the army, would be constituted as a single formation for any purpose other than as part of a general engagement let alone detached from the army as a raiding force. Even if we assume that men might choose to join an operation without the sanction, or even against the direct orders of their superiors, we can hardly assume that all of the men-at-arms in the army were either disobedient or so very keen to come to blows with the enemy. All the same, the defeat at Dunbar and the subsequent surrender of the castle was a blow sufficient to deter the Scots from any earnest resistance for the rest of the summer and the balance of King John's army disintegrated. By 1300 the Scottish military effort had recovered itself sufficiently that Edward I thought it worthwhile fortifying Berwick and the man-at-arms element had recovered to the extent that Sir Thomas Grey could write of 'great passages of arms between the marches and notably in Teviotdale, before Roxburgh Castle.'[121]

The fight at Roslin was unquestionably an encounter between men-at-arms. The Scots approached from Biggar, surprised the main body of the enemy in a night attack and regrouped in time to attack and defeat another part of the force. Grey tells us that the English expedition was made in 'great strength', but fails to make clear what he means by that. There are two distinct possibilities. Grey may mean that the English force comprised a large body of men-at-arms; the numbers involved would be unlikely to be very large; hundreds perhaps rather than thousands, but the significance of their defeat would be considerable since they would be regarded as an elite formation as well as the more direct military significance of a demonstration that the English could not rely on Lothian as a secure area nor on the ability of their men-at-arms to dominate their Scottish equivalents in battle. Alternatively, if Segrave led a more conventional force of horse and foot, it would suggest that in the absence of the man-at-arms element, already defeated by the Scots, the balance of the army would not be safe in open country and should be obliged to withdraw for fear of further defeat. Sir Thomas describes two other fights of men-at-arms during the same period at Cupar, when his father was the constable of the castle there, an indication that such activity was not limited to Lothian, but the normal practice of war in Scotland. The English expedition of 1322, which penetrated as far as Edinburgh, was seriously hampered by the activity of the Scottish cavalry. Although Grey does not describe any actions in Lothian he makes it clear that the hobelars of the English army were prevented from foraging. The implication is that the Scots could counter English cavalry forces adequately and that the English therefore had lost the reconnaissance battle to a degree that prevented any worthwhile degree of operational activity. Grey tells us that the English army was consistently harassed by the Scots during the retreat to Newcastle, a further indication that the Scots could deploy fast and powerful columns which could disengage easily if threatened by a concentration of the enemy. It is difficult to imagine what kind of force could have fulfilled such a role other than one with a high proportion of men-at-arms. Incidental comments from Grey give us further pointers to the existence of a chivalrous or armigerous class. The participation of Scottish magnates in jousts is unremarkable but the description of a Scottish lord as a 'banneret'[122] is a strong indication that the structures of the Scottish armigerous classes were broadly similar to those in England.

The social niceties of fourteenth-century warfare were practised in Lothian as they might be anywhere else, which is to say intermittently, and with due regard to political realities. The Earl of Moray pursued a force under the Count of Namur from Burghmuir to the ruins of Edinburgh Castle, a distance of at least two miles, in 1335. Contemporary accounts[123] indicate a fight primarily, if not exclusively, between men-at-arms. Bower particularly draws attention to a combat which resulted in the two combatants (one of them female) simultaneously spearing one another. While this is further evidence of the importance of men-at-arms generally, the outcome of the fight demonstrates a willingness to make the sort of grand chivalrous gesture that could enhance a man's reputation as a noble warrior. Moray elected to release the Count of Namur free of ransom on condition that he would never bear arms against David II. Escorting his prisoner to English-held territory, Moray had the misfortune to be captured himself and spent some years as a prisoner of war.[124] Moray could afford to make that generous gesture Namur was not really a militarily or politically significant figure, though he was probably famous enough that his capture and release would be noted. Moray on the other hand was a military leader of some talent and a major figure in the Bruce party. The presence or otherwise of the count of Namur and his hundred men-at-arms in the English army would have made very little difference to Scots militarily. Their release would have helped to establish or maintain the status of the Scots as members of a pan-European chivalrous class, whereas the removal of Moray was a severe material blow. However chivalrous Moray's gesture may have been, it was also a political device, though one that backfired.

The literature of the day is not, of course, an infallible guide to the general nature of the war, only to the parts of the conflict in which the writers were interested. This is particularly true of Grey and Barbour. Each was predominantly concerned with the actions of men-at-arms.

Even where Barbour refers to courageous acts by common men like Thom Dicson or William Bunnock, we might consider the possibility that Barbour uses their stories as a device to encourage the chivalric confidence of his audience by implying that the Scottish commons were braver and more independent than most, and therefore needed particularly fine lords and knights to lead them. These 'middling men' seem to seldom act on their own initiative, but they could be motivated by their leaders, not only to join the action themselves, but to encourage others, thus Thomas Dicson in Book 5 of The Bruce –

> 'Sa wrocht he throu sutelte
> That all the lele men of that land
> That with his fadyr were dwelland
> This gud man gert cum ane and ane
> And mak him manrent everilkane'[125]

Barbour and Grey concentrate on the men-at-arms, not only because of their own social status, but because the bulk of the operational activity was in fact conducted by rather modest formations consisting largely, if not exclusively, of heavy cavalry. This can be assumed for the action at Crichtondene as described by John of Fordun.[126] A force was mustered in the north of England to raise the Scots siege of Edinburgh Castle. The operation was successful in intent in that the siege was raised, but the Scots elected to confront the relief column, meeting them between Clerkington and Crichton. The relief column may not have included a strong contingent of men-at-arms, but it would have been a very unusual structure for an English raiding party if it did not. Equally the Scottish force may not have had a force of men-at-arms, but it would be very unlikely for a force without a strong cavalry element to attempt to intercept and out-manoeuvre an enemy that they would at least expect to have a plentiful supply of men-at-arms. The Scots won the day and then threatened to move on into England, obliging the English force to remain under arms south of the Tweed for two days until the Scots moved away. Again, though we are not told of the nature of the force, it would be very unusual for any raiding party not to include a significant proportion of men-at-arms.

In addition to the literary and administrative records relating to the service of men-at-arms there are many examples of men receiving

prisoner of war allowances appropriate for that status or of being forfeited for their service to the Bruce cause. In a sample of fewer than
300 Lothian men more than 100 can be unquestionably identified as
giving man-at-arms service. Given the scarcity of documents we can
be confident that the real figure would be somewhat greater. Whether
this is proof of an articulated system of knight service is not the issue,
the question is whether or not the Scots were able to field and maintain
a force of heavy cavalry adequate to their needs. Undoubtedly on the
few occasions that large field armies met the English cavalry force was
invariably the stronger, hardly surprising given the disparity in size and
economic conditions between the two countries.[127] Large actions certainly could determine the immediate progress of the war and tend to
receive a disproportionate amount of attention, but they were very few
and far between. Stirling, Falkirk, Bannockburn, Myton, Dupplin Muir,
Halidon Hill and Neville's Cross were all very significant events, but
the several recoveries of the Bruce cause were to a considerable extent
achieved in lengthy campaigns of small actions and it would be difficult
to argue that the brunt of the fighting was not borne by men-at-arms.

Before leaving this topic some observations must be made about general military service as envisaged by Robert I's legislation of 1318.[128] The
obligations on the individual are quite clearly defined: men whose possessions were equal in value to a cow were obliged to find themselves
a spear or a bow with arrows, men with goods to the value of £10
a rather more comprehensive list of equipment. Professor Duncan has
made the point that simply to value the cow – about 10s – hides the
fact that poorer men saw money so rarely that they would have assessed
their goods in terms of cattle-values.[129] One has to question the validity of this, certainly in relation to Lothian, which was already a highly
monetarised society by the close of the thirteenth century. However the
relative scarcity of specie in other parts of the country may have made
cattle-values an effective 'common denominator' of wealth. Obviously
this part of the legislation was not aimed at providing the king with a
force of trained, competent men that he could lead in an offensive campaign, but at raising large forces when required to meet invaders. The
threshold of goods to the value of half a cow was very low indeed, and
while we should recognise that there was undoubtedly a class of people
too poor to own even that much, we should also recognise that the bulk
of the adult male population probably did have goods exceeding that

sum. However conscripting large numbers of these men for any length of time would have economic implications – who would tend the fields if these men were on campaign?

The position of the man with goods to the value of £10 is, if anything, less clear than that of his poorer neighbour. His £10 of goods obliged him to acquire a bacinet, an aketon, armoured gloves, sword and lance.[130] Failing the aketon, he was to have a haubergel with a 'good iron for his body'. The legislation does not make clear what is meant by the terms aketon and haubergel; obviously there was an intention to differentiate between two different forms of protection. Haubergel is a diminutive form of the word 'hauberk' (a chainmail shirt), generally perceived as leather or cloth armour, a perception supported by the phrase 'with a good iron'. The 'good iron' may refer to a small round cap but it may be a description of an early form of what would later be called a brigand-ine; the practice of attaching iron plates to cloth and leather armour was hardly a novelty in 1318. Unfortunately the term aketon is very often used to describe much the same thing. There are two distinct possibili-ties here. Either aketon was used to denote an alternative type of armour – which could hardly be anything other than chainmail – or that aketon and haubergel were generally understood as term for different forms of essentially the same sort of product. Though there is no obvious reason why medieval legislators should have thought the distinction desirable or necessary, they evidently did think it necessary, and presumably with good cause, so perhaps we should assume that the aketon and bacinet was seen as the more desirable choice, but that a haubergel with 'a good iron' was considered an adequate substitute. With the addition of his 'cyrote-cas de guerra' (gloves of war), the £10 man was equipped to the sort of standard to be expected of line of battle infantry in France or England, but the legislation is unclear about what exactly constituted a £10 man, nor do we know if King Robert's law was in the nature of a definition of customary practice or an attempt to broaden the range of men liable to provide service at a certain standard.

Are we to assume that those who owned less than £10 of goods had no more obligation than those with one cow's worth? This would seem to be unusually lenient to men with £9 a year and it surely cannot mean that men with £100 a year were no more heavily burdened than those with a tenth of that income. The division into two groups for mili-tary purposes might suggest that the only equipment scales of medieval

Scots were those of the impoverished peasant archer/spearmen or of the heavy infantry with aketon and bacinet, yet we can easily identify large amounts of man-at-arms service being discharged in virtually every year from 1296 at Dunbar until Neville's Cross in 1346. Should we therefore assume that knight and man-at-arms service was not affected by the 1318 law? Certainly anyone performing man-at-arms service would have to have rather better equipment than that envisaged in the legislation, though if the 'aketon' of the act implies a chainmail shirt the additional equipment required for man-at-arms service might not have been a very heavy investment. The legislation makes no reference to a shield or to leg protection or to a horse, but most men of property would already own an adequate horse and a perfectly adequate shield could be manufactured by any half way competent carpenter. Given that a chainmail shirt could be had for any thing from twenty to one hundred shillings it would be reasonable to estimate leggings at two to twenty-five shillings a pair depending on size, quality and degree of 'tailoring'. A significant sum to a man with goods worth £10 perhaps, but not a very heavy one. If, as seems reasonable to assume, the category extended up to £10, rather than from £10 upward, the cost of 'upgrading' equipment and the upkeep or acquisition of a suitable horse would of course represent a very significant investment for men at the lower end of the wealth scale. For men at the top of that scale acquiring the extra equipment (and skills) might actually have been a means of improving one's status in the community. If a man were equipped to serve with the men-at-arms he would undoubtedly be welcome to do so both in Scottish armies where men-at-arms must have been at a premium and in English garrisons where there were frequently recruiting problems and where there must surely have been a desire to have as many members of the local community as possible to encourage commitment to Plantagenet lordship. Serving with the men-at-arms would bring a man into more contact with men who could offer him patronage and advancement than serving with the infantry.

The act must surely have been concerned with the provision of a large army to conduct or resist invasion, a relatively rare event generally, and particularly so in Lothian. Given that year on year the bulk of the fighting would seem to have been done by men-at-arms, the significance of the legislation may have been rather limited. To the best of our knowledge Scottish men-at-arms served for land tenure obligations.

The precise extent of their armament was not defined, but they, and their superior, were aware of what was required of them. The equipment required would not have been cheap, but it need not have been terribly expensive either. An aketon or haubergel could be made domestically, a spear might cost 3d to 6d, and Edward II (in 1302–3, when he was still Prince of Wales) spent 20s on three bacinets and 10s on a pair of plate gloves.[131] Presumably the bacinets were for members of his retinue, and therefore probably were of a good quality and high price. Edward would hardly be likely to buy the cheapest items available, so it is a safe assumption that these things could be purchased for rather less than the sums he paid. It is likely that in the early fourteenth century the Scottish '£10 man' could equip himself for less than £2, and possibly even less than £1 bearing in mind that Edward's plate gloves would have been very much more costly than a pair of leather mittens with chainmail, or even just very thick, rigid leather attached to the backs which might be worn by the rank and file.

If £10 represented the upper limit of income scale relative to equipment scale we would have to ask why that figure should be selected and what are the implications for our perception of military service among men of greater financial standing? It may be more realistic to regard the requirements of the 1318 legislation as a means of setting a standard for all the men whose goods had a value that lay between 'a cow' and £10. In that case the cost of equipment would have been a real burden on the man whose goods were valued at one or two pounds, but not an impossible one.

Landholder status was apparently not a factor and there is no way of knowing what sort of income could be expected from any particular property on the basis of the rental paid. However the military obligations implicit in William the Lion's grant to his sister – one hundred librates of land in the baronies of Ratho and Bathgate infeft with twenty knights – would suggest that man-at-arms service could be expected from men with tenure of land worth £5 per annum in the early thirteenth century.[132] Obligations may have changed, but the conservative nature of medieval societies would militate against this. The financial obligations of heritable tenants remained static, there is no reason to think that military ones altered in principle, though the regularity with which due services were demanded was presumably much greater in the fourteenth century. Of the properties forfeited by Bruce partisans in Lothian in 1335–36, over seventy were valued at £5 or more, with a high incidence of rentals at £5 (more usually described as 100s) in the Bathgate and Ratho area; possibly revealing the structure of the estates granted by William the Lion to his sister Ada. We might reasonably suppose that the majority of these forfeitures were the result of performing army service for the Bruce cause.

Most of the men with more than £10 of goods would have had defined military obligations attached to land tenure, but by the close of the thirteenth century there was already a well-established mercantile class in Scottish towns and they were – vicissitudes of war excepted – increasingly wealthy. Although no known Edinburgh burgess can be positively identified performing man-at-arms service before John Wyggemore we should not assume that wealthy burgh residents, only a small proportion of whom were actually burgesses, did not perform that service by long standing tradition. If foreign merchants could be obliged to acquire arms and armour and give service at Berwick,[133] it is hard to see how local men of similar standing could avoid doing the same. Burgh men were of course obliged to serve in the defence of their town should the need arise. However the defence of a town with no walls was hardly worth attempting in the face of a field army. Since neither Edinburgh, Haddington nor Linlithgow had town walls the actual discharge of that obligation must have been rare to say the least, but burgh men were called out to serve in the field like anyone else.

To what extent army service could be drawn from Lothian obviously depended to a great degree on who was demanding the service and who held the reins of government and how firmly. Professor Barrow has demonstrated clearly that a sizeable proportion of the tenants of Coldinghamshire were forfeited by Edward I for fighting for the Balliol cause at Falkirk,[134] and we should not doubt that Lothian men also served there, though whether Wallace was able to raise the level of manpower actually due from Lothian is very doubtful. The garrison at Edinburgh and the alignment of the Earl of Dunbar with Edward I must have discouraged some and many must have doubted both the potential of Wallace to defeat the English and the validity of his cause. John's abdication may have been forced, but it was not necessarily invalid from a legal perspective since he had sworn allegiance to Edward I in 1291–92. Additionally, a number of Lothian barons and free tenants were either in Edward's peace or his prisons. In the absence of several men who would normally have had recruitment and/or leadership responsibilities it would surely have proved difficult to call upon the 'service that every man owes for his head'[135] very effectively since there would inevitably be doubts about who was responsible for ensuring enlistment from their baronies and properties and about the validity of their authority.

It is of course quite impossible to make any detailed assessment of the size of the army of Lothian had it been available to Wallace in its entirety. Professor Duncan has drawn attention to a sixteenth-century wappinschaw at which the 'army of Annandale' numbered rather more than 1,000 men and makes the case that the fourteenth-century equivalent would have been of much the same size,[136] and indeed Edward I would seem to have expected that 1,000 men could be raised by the Earl of Carrick in 1297.[137] We can hardly think that the 'army of Lothian' would be any smaller, in fact almost certainly rather larger given the presence of one of the largest towns on the country, Edinburgh, and several smaller towns and nucleated villages large enough to support markets; not a notable feature of medieval Carrick. Men with Lothian connections were certainly recruited for the campaign that resulted in Neville's Cross,[138] but probably not in the numbers we might expect for a general obligation like a wappinschaw. In the event of a general call-out the labouring men of the community – those with goods worth a cow or more anyway – were required to serve, but an expeditionary force would be more likely to include a larger proportion of men selected for service, men who had, or at least were expected to have, adequate arms and armour.

Formulary E, no. 59, contains an instruction for raising troops from the burgh of 'A' – possibly Ayr. The order requires one hundred and twenty men 'armed for fighting' and six men 'sufficiently armed' (perhaps 'appropriately' or 'properly' armed) to be their leaders.[139] The document is from a formulary and cannot be assumed to be typical of the reality of enlistments, also it refers to Ayrshire not Lothian, all the same it is probably fair to assume that an enlistment of the order of 120 with arms men and six men with 'sufficient' armour would not have been an unrealistic expectation for the town. The fact that there is a provision for leadership, like the archers from Bowden and their 'armed man' or the two men said by Bower[140] to be 'leaders of the archers', is a further indication that there was some understanding of the need for people who could fill 'junior leader' roles to aid the articulation[141] of the army. It is also clear from two documents that the crown identified two different levels of obligation on men of the same community: those who had, or could be provided with, weapons, and those required to provide themselves with 'sufficient' armour in Formulary 'E'; then the men with goods to the value of a cow and men with goods to the value of £10 in the 1318 legislation. Neither document defines the service of men with military tenure presumably because each of those tenures was a specific contract between tenant and superior. Men holding land for defined military service still had the universal burden of army service for the state, but would be expected to present themselves for service in the same role as that envisaged in their land grant, which, for most of them at least, would be that of a man–at–arms.

CONCLUSIONS

In a broad sense, the political community of Lothian would seem to have carried much the same range of responsibilities and privileges as their counterparts in England, with similar obligations of court and military service. The local political community formed part of the administrative fabric of the country as jurors, as military leaders, as specialist combatants and, in some cases, as barons with judicial responsibilities additional to their duties to the sheriff court.[1] To retain the family property, and the privileges attendant on landholding, each member of the political community had to achieve and maintain a positive relationship with whichever party was in a position to exert lordship in the sheriffdom. During most of the period between 1296 and 1314 it is very clear that the Plantagenet administration was effective in Lothian, and the very small number of Lothian landholders forfeited in 1306[2] and 1312[3] suggests that the overwhelming majority of the Lothian political community were prepared to accept Plantagenet lordship.

Traditionally that acceptance has been seen by both English and Scottish historians as evidence that the nobility were, by and large anyway, less than enthusiastic about Scottish independence and Scottish kingship and far more interested in retaining their family properties, including, of course, lands in England.[4] Since the maintenance (or improvement) of the status of one's family and the protection of their rights was the primary duty of any landholder it is hardly surprising that they should have accepted Plantagenet lordship when the alternative would have been going to war in support of a kingship that had failed to maintain the independence of the kingdom (the Balliol cause in 1296–1304) or of one that had yet to establish itself as a credible source of authority (the Bruce cause in 1306–1314). Service was inevitable, but not wholly undesirable. The military service performed by Lothian men, both as garrison men-at-arms and for landholding, contributed to the security of the administration, providing some degree of social, political and economic stability through the sheriffdom. This was not simply a matter of combat strength or effectiveness in the field. Even after Robert I had gained the military ascendancy and control of most of Scotland he was unable to penetrate Lothian to any great extent, though he was able to draw blackmail in exchange for truces.[5] Had the Lothian administration not had the military power to resist him, Robert would have had no need to offer truces, and it is extremely unlikely that the administration could have fielded an adequate force of men-at-arms[6] to offer any realistic level of resistance to the Bruce party if it had not been able to call upon the service of Lothian landholders.

The discharge of military obligation to the government was inevitable if landholders were going to retain their positions, but is not really a good guide to their political inclinations. Certainly it is a good indicator of the current and overt allegiance of an individual, but that should not be construed as evidence of political belief any more than paying income tax today is an indicator of support for the party in government. So long as the Plantagenets could offer good lordship Lothian men had good cause to fulfil their obligations and keep on the right side of the government of the day, thus helping to keep the war out of Lothian. That level of acceptance was not universal in Lothian. A number of Lothian men gave their allegiance to Robert in 1306 and were duly forfeited, as were a handful more in 1312. The majority of the political community surely continued to give their service to the administrations of Edward I and Edward II, or the lists of forfeitures would have been much longer, as would be the case in 1335–37.

By 1314 the Plantagenet administration had held power in Lothian for the better part of twenty years and would seem to have been quite firmly established; sufficiently so that despite the fall of Linlithgow and Edinburgh to the Scots, a number of Lothian men served Edward II at Bannockburn.[7] This indicates some level of confidence in the Plantagenet cause, though of what nature and to what extent is open to question. The men concerned may have believed the Bruce cause to be unreasonable in itself or just unrealisable in the face of concerted English opposition. They may have considered it inevitable that the English would win a major battle and restore their power in Scotland and that they should therefore continue in Plantagenet peace as the better prospect in the long run.

Any strong popular support for the Plantagenets would not seem to have endured after Bannockburn, and Robert I seems to have had no difficulty in exerting lordship in Lothian thereafter. This does not mean that he was in any sense king through popular acclaim there, rather that, like the Plantagenets before him, his power was sufficiently evident to discourage opposition. The Bruce party had become the government of the day, and, like the Plantagenets, so long as they could afford good lordship to the community, particularly in regard to keeping war out of Lothian, they could reasonably expect to retain power.

It might be argued that the Bruce party, like the Plantagenets, were acceptable to the community as they provided good government, and that the political community of Lothian were content to accept their lordship until after Halidon Hill (Edward Balliol's brief reign in 1332 does not seem to have had any real significance in Lothian) at which point they were content to accept Plantagenet lordship as they or their predecessors had a generation before. The situations were not the same however. The high incidence of forfeiture that occurred by 1335–36[8] has no counterpart in the reigns of Edward II, and though the large number of restorations made by Edward I in 1296-97[9] might suggest that there had been a spate of wholesale forfeitures in the period immediately after the battle of Dunbar in 1296 it is perhaps more likely that those restorations were the product of 'blanket' forfeitures of men who supported King John and/or men who failed to give service due for lands held in England.

It would seem that Edward III was not able to procure as much service from the Lothian community as his father and grandfather had done. The Bruce party was able to call on the services of 'electi' soldiers (literally 'chosen' men, the numbers involved, the conduct of the engagement and the fact that they were clearly not 'common army' conscripts suggests very strongly that they were men-at-arms) from below the Forth[10] to fight at Culblean in November 1335. It is fair to assume that a portion of those men came from Lothian and that they were not giving army service to the Plantagenet administration. In 1335–36 over one hundred Lothian men and women were recorded as having been forfeited, some at least would surely have been men who had fought at Culblean, but whether they were or not, they were obviously not serving Edward III. The names of men giving service for land (as opposed to men serving for wages) were not recorded for posterity (though sheriffs and other responsible parties must have kept a register of service due and service discharged) so it is impossible to be clear how much service was available, let alone how much of it was performed. Equally, is clear from the accounts of the sheriff of Edinburgh in 1335–36 and 1336–37[11] that a very large proportion of each constabulary was, if not actually under the control of the Scots, destroyed or denied to the administration which must have adversely affected the ability of the administration to draw army service from the community.

Under Edward I and Edward II many Scots served in English garrisons for wages, and this continued to be the case under Edward III, but the pattern of that service was not the same. A large proportion of the identifiable Scots in garrison service in the 1330s would seem to have been drawn from the ranks of the disinherited.[12] As men whose prospects were dependent on the successful establishment of a Balliol/Plantagenet government it is unsurprising that several of them should have joined garrisons, however many of them may have found that garrison service was their only means of livelihood. They might have been theoretically restored to their properties by the Plantagenet administration, but it is open to question how many were ever able to realise their lordship. Those whose property lay outside the areas of Plantagenet–Balliol lordship would still have been unable to collect their rents and casualties. The appearance of men from the west of Scotland in the garrison records of Edinburgh and Berwick perhaps points in that direction.

If Edward III were to pursue his Scottish ambitions successfully (even if those ambitions were essentially limited to an outpost strategy aimed at preventing serious Scottish intervention in a future war with France) he would have needed to support these men in some way, as he did Edward Balliol. They, in turn, could reasonably expect to further their own ambitions more easily if they were resident in Scotland, and, as active supporters of the Plantagenet–Balliol cause could expect to be rewarded in the event of the Bruce party being defeated. For some at least, garrison service was the only valid option other than defection to the Bruce party, a choice which was less than likely to lead to restoration since that would often require the displacement of a Bruce supporter.

Although it is important to be wary of the tendency, encouraged by pro-Bruce chroniclers and historians, to conflate the Bruce cause and support for Scottish independence, it is equally important to recognise that to some extent at least, there was an association of the two from at least the spring of 1307 in the minds of a segment of the population. In May of that year an English officer or sympathiser stationed in Forfar wrote to a senior official that Robert Bruce 'never had the good will of his own followers or of the people at large or even half of them as now' and that if he could escape to Ross he would 'find them all ready at his will more entirely than ever'.[13] The writer may have felt moved to exaggerate the strength of Bruce support in order to encourage Edward II's government to provide more men-at-arms, but he surely perceived the Bruce party as a serious threat. The statement that Bruce would gain the support of the people 'more than ever' would seem curious in an area where the Bruces did not have a particularly well-established tradition of lordship. If Robert could enjoy popular support in Angus there is no reason to suppose that there was no sympathy at all in Lothian for the Bruce cause, only that it was not strong enough to have any great effect on the political stability of the community. Even in the spring–summer of 1306 there was sufficient disturbance in the south and east of Scotland for Edward II's government to spend 60s on the hire of shipping to carry 200 men-at-arms from Berwick to Perth 'on account of enemies between Berwick and the king's army'.[14] Evidently Plantagenet lines of communication through eastern Scotland were not at all secure if a strong company of men-at-arms could not pass along them with impunity. The same document refers to pay for a man who had spent eighteen days ascertaining 'the will and state of the common men of those parts' (the vicinity of Perthshire). If the opinion of the common people was of no significance, or if there was no expectation that they might side with the Bruce party there would have been no point in making such a reconnaissance.

The Bruce cause and independent kingship presumably did become firmly connected in popular consciousness as the mainsprings of Scottish political identity. A growing tradition of anti-English feeling would inevitably have led to support for the most effective opposition to the English, and such a tradition would almost certainly have developed in the two generations of children that grew up in war zones between the close of the thirteenth century and the middle of the fourteenth. No doubt the exploits of Scottish heroes helped to inspire confidence in times of crisis, though it is questionable whether these crises were necessarily quite as dire as chronicle accounts might lead us to believe. The Bruce party may have been reduced to a handful of castles in 1333–34[15] but how significant is that observation, even assuming its accuracy? The extent of damage inflicted by King Robert's policy of slighting castles may not have been enough to raze them to the ground, but it must have been enough to compromise their security. We might question how many viable fortresses would have been available for the Scots to hold even if the manpower had been available. Fordun and Bower had demands on their work beyond the simple relation of events. The more bleak the fortunes of the Scots in 1333–35, the more spectacular their recovery after 1335. Perhaps more significantly, two years after Halidon Hill, Edward's Scottish administration was already under severe pressure, if not actually failing. The Earl of Dunbar, Edward's most important adherent in the south-east, had returned to Bruce allegiance sometime before February 1335[16] and led troops from below the Forth to fight at Culblean. The forfeiture of over one hundred Lothian free tenants by Michaelmas 1336[17] would hardly suggest that the Plantagenet administration there was attracting the support of the local political community at a time when the Bruce party was gaining the military initiative throughout the country as a whole, indeed there was a 'steady trickle' of defections to the Bruce party from early 1335 onward.[18]

The defection of the Earl must be regarded as particularly significant. As an experienced and cautious politician he would surely not have embraced the Bruce cause in 1335 had he not been extremely confident of their eventual victory. Earl Patrick had more to lose than most and the bulk of his property was very vulnerable to English operations; however he was in an excellent position to gauge the strengths and weaknesses of the English administration since he was a part of its command structure. His example may have been instrumental in persuading other members of the political community to follow suit, or even possibly the other way round; Patrick was granted the lands of any of his tenants forfeited for treason, but he might find it difficult, even impossible to enforce those forfeitures if a large enough proportion of his tenants were active Bruce supporters. Any such failure would undermine his prestige and authority and his credibility as a senior political figure. Any of his tenants could also be confident of restoration in the event of Bruce success, which was hardly the case for the Earl. It is always possible that Patrick underwent an ideological conversion, that he was persuaded of the justice of the Bruce cause and defected as a matter of political principle; however it is more probable that his decision was based very strongly on a sober appreciation of the situation and the desire to back a winner. Had the Plantagenet administration been in good condition in 1334–35 it is very unlikely that the Earl would have defected.

The significance of the defection of Patrick, or of Sir Alexander Seton, may lie more in leadership by example than formal power in a command structure. If prominent men with (probably) better sources of intelligence and with greater estates at risk decided that the time had come to join the Bruce party, then others, beyond their tenants and other dependents, might be moved to join them. If the Bruce party was successful it would do no harm to have followed the lead of local men who were likely to be influential in the community once the war was over. Moreover, these same men might well be of some importance on the national political stage in the future and be helpful in procuring preferment for local men who had proved themselves as supportive neighbours. Seton had in fact been granted particular military leadership privileges in Lothian by Robert I, including the 'superiority' of various properties and the 'leadership' of all his men.[19]

The implication must be that the leadership of the men of these properties had previously lain elsewhere, perhaps with the sheriff. Presumably there was a military command significance to these grants, perhaps giving the baron in question the power to raise a retinue of men-at-arms for the general conduct of war and/or a formation of infantry for the (rather rare) mustering of a large field army. Even very small armies require some form of articulation if they are to function adequately. A provision to enable men of proven military experience to raise discrete formations from men to whom they were already familiar as local figures of authority would be a simple means of achieving some degree of articulation. The 'men' of Alexander Seton or Robert Lauder or James Douglas would become 'units' within the army alongside, or perhaps as sub-units of, the 'armies' of sheriffdoms and earldoms. The usual practice of the war did not, however, depend on the deployment of large armies of manoeuvre, but of small mobile parties, and grants of 'superiority' or 'leadership' may have been more significant in that setting. Whatever the precise implications of leadership and superiority in a military context, it would seem most likely that the intention of such grants was to provide authority and convey responsibility for a structured system of 'units' or retinues that could be deployed individually or in concert to specific tasks or operations without recourse to indentures – and financial rewards – for the supply of troops in general, and perhaps men-at-arms in particular.[20]

Although it is apparent that the majority of operational service was conducted by men-at-arms drawn from the political community, it would be rash to assume that these men, even in the most intense periods of conflict, were continually, even regularly, committed to engagements. In campaigns conducted by small parties of relatively specialised soldiers individual casualties make more impression on the strength, and more significantly the morale, of the forces involved. In a war of small mobile parties a successful contact with the enemy would comprise engaging, achieving an objective and disengaging without serious loss, preferably driving the enemy off without incurring any casualties at all. Operations would be a matter of achieving local dominance through demonstration, rather than actual combat. Even when combat did occur the number of fatalities need not have been high. The mobility and armour of the man-at-arms afforded him some degree of protection in combat and some hope of escaping from an unsuccessful encounter. If defeated and unable to escape, there was every chance that a ransom – or defection – could be negotiated. This may in fact have been the practical battlefield significance of heraldry. The likelihood of being able accurately to recognise several thousand devices and know whether the bearer was in the Bruce or Plantagenet party would be very slim beyond, perhaps, the devices of neighbours and great lords.[21] The fact that a man bore a device at all would indicate that he would probably have sufficient resources to be worth holding for ransom.

Not unnaturally, the wars encouraged the development of a tradition of anti-English sentiment in Scotland. Generations that grew up in time of endemic war with what was fast becoming 'the auld enemy' would be inclined toward the most effective opposition to the Plantagenets. From 1296 to 1304 this was the cause of King John. From 1306 onward it was the Bruce party. Between 1333 and 1341 the war may generally have been conducted by small-scale forces, but it brought men to prominence on the basis of their martial conduct. Men like Sir William Douglas of Lothian or Sir Alexander Ramsay of Dalhousie provided examples of heroic and successful leadership and formed the basis of a Scottish military tradition which, all things considered, was remarkably successful throughout the fourteenth century.

Military activity itself was obviously a factor in the extension or contraction of lordship; however, the product of that activity has to be considered. In the period between 1296 and the fall of Edinburgh Castle in March 1314 the Plantagenet administration in Lothian was reasonably secure. Wallace marched on Haddington and withdrew without noticeable opposition, possibly gaining temporary occupation of some non-royal castles in the process and in 1303 the Scots won a fight at Roslin, but neither event seems to have seriously threatened the existence of the administration. Of course it was not the function of the garrisons to engage a large field army, but to prevent a competing source of authority from exerting lordship in the area. King Robert was able to draw blackmail from the community of Lothian before 1314, but while his ability to do so demonstrates his power, it also demonstrates his inability to exert lordship in the face of the Plantagenet government.

If the Lothian community accepted Plantagenet rule in 1296–1314 with apparent equanimity and Bruce rule in 1314–33 without resistance, is it adequate to say that the Lothian political community was simply willing to accept the authority of the de facto government of the day regardless of its political colour? This may have been the case, but that would demand an explanation of the extent of overt Bruce support in Lothian by 1335–36. If a Bruce victory was not perceived as the likely outcome in the long term it would be incomprehensible that so many of the political community would have been willing to risk life and limb for a political ambition that was unlikely to materialise. Some of the hundred or so Lothian freeholders forfeited in 1335–36 may have been motivated by simple nationalism, but surely the majority made a sober assessment of the situation and decided that the Bruce cause was the more attractive for rather more prosaic reasons. Some of these forfeited persons would of course have lost their property to members of the disinherited and would have an obvious incentive to join the Bruce party. Equally, the desire of Edward III and Edward Balliol to build a 'constituency' of support in the political community, and the perennial shortage of men-at-arms that hampered them both,[22] could have led to negotiated settlements that would have kept such men in the Balliol or Plantagenet peace. The forfeiture of one hundred free tenants, surely many more than had benefited from Bruce grants, would have cut a swathe through the political community, and demonstrates a degree of public confidence in the Bruce cause, but, bearing in mind the severity of the defeats at Dupplin and Halidon Hill and the presence of a powerful garrison at Edinburgh after 1335, may not be representative of Bruce–nationalist sympathy in the Lothian political community as a whole. The absence of resistance to Bruce kingship after 1314 and after 1341, in contrast to the very clear evidence of Bruce support (or at least antipathy to the Plantagenets) in Lothian in 1335–36, suggests that the political community of Lothian came to adhere to the Bruce party over the course of the Wars of Independence.

That adherence need not have been born out of the good lordship of Robert I so much as a confidence that a Bruce government would be more effective at excluding war from Lothian than a Plantagenet one. Edward II's administration failed in 1314 and Edward III's by the spring of 1341 but it had obviously been struggling for some years before that. Indeed, Edward III's authority, like that of his father's, was undermined by his inability to control the behaviour of his garrisons, let alone prevent the encroachment of the Scots. Edward did not attempt to restore his administration in Lothian after Neville's Cross in 1346. Admittedly there were no forces available for the purpose, but it would have been very difficult for any new Plantagenet government in Lothian to establish its credibility at the third attempt. Further, while it is clear that Scottish nationalism was a vehicle for the Bruce party, we should not ignore the possibility that the Bruce party was a vehicle for nationalists. Men and women might well support the Bruces simply because they were the only credible source of authority with a genuinely Scottish agenda.

The Plantagenets adopted a policy of granting extensive estates in Lothian to the men they appointed to office there, particularly Sir Robert Hastang under Edward II[23] and Sir John Strivelin[24] under Edward III. This was presumably intended as a means of giving these men local leadership rights over their tenants, and perhaps neighbours, as a means of bolstering their resources and giving them status in the political community. That policy may have been counter-productive to some extent. The political community of Lothian were not accustomed to the leadership of magnates, and though Robert I may have adopted a similar policy in effect by extending the lands and rights of Sir Alexander Seton[25] and Sir Robert Lauder[26] he was promoting the interests of Lothian men rather than imposing new men in positions of authority.

In the absence of an established magnate the Lothian political community would look to the crown for preferment. Other figures would of course have wielded some degree of influence. The Earls of March and Fife were both extensive landholders in Lothian, though not sufficiently so for them to dominate the political community. The Bishop of St. Andrews was also a significant landholder in the county, as the presence of several 'bishop's tenants' on the Ragman Roll demonstrates.[27] His tenants were obviously considered important enough to be ranked in among the free tenants and burgesses, and no doubt the bishop's tenants were briefed on a general policy position, but it would have been very difficult for the Bishop himself to take a very active part in the deliberations of the community given his duties and responsibilities elsewhere.

It might be a reasonable conclusion that the political community in Lothian was less trammelled by layers of authority and influence than that of other counties. Essentially the Lothian landholder had to keep on the right side of the party in power, but did not have to worry too much about other sources of authority, such as an earl or other great lord whose priorities might clash with those of the government and/or the local community. Roxburghshire and Berwickshire lairds, and not just those who were his tenants, would surely have felt some pressure to support the Earl of Dunbar at each of his defections though they might personally have felt more inclined to stay either in Bruce allegiance in 1333 or in Plantagenet allegiance in 1335. Superficially it would seem that Lothian landholders were spared the complications of an intermediate level of authority between themselves and the crown, but local leadership structures will have existed, however transient or informal.[28] It is possible that leadership groups are reflected in a number of records relating to forfeiture and restoration. A group of men are described as 'coming to the king's peace (Edward I) with the Earl of Strathearn'.[29] Another group were forfeited along with Sir Alexander de Moubray[30] when he defected to the Bruce camp in 1334 over an inheritance dispute. All of the latter group were accepted into Edward III's peace and restored shortly thereafter. What is not clear is the nature of the grouping in either instance. The men who joined Edward I' s peace with the Earl of Strathearn may have been his tenants, his relatives, his friends and acquaintances or simply a body of men who took the opportunity to defect in the company of a powerful and influential man who could secure good terms from Edward's government. It is not impossible that they were not in any sense a conscious grouping, merely a body of men whose defection occurred at a given point and that the Earl was no more than the most prominent figure in that group. It is quite conceivable, that the document in question groups these men together as nothing more than an administrative convenience and that the inclusion of some or all of them was not the outcome of a conscious decision by, or on behalf of, a group of men with shared political views, merely a record of men who had defected.

The defection of Moubray, Alexander Craigie and others in 1334[31] could be seen in a slightly different light. Superficially it would seem that they chose to abandon the Plantagenet/Balliol peace at a time when the fortunes of the Bruce party were at a very low ebb. There is some cause to suspect that the position of David II's government was not perhaps quite so precarious as it appears to have been, but it was certainly in a very weak condition. Craigie[32] submitted to Edward III in August 1335,[33] but both his defection from, and return to, Plantagenet peace were the product of dissent and reconciliation within the Plantagenet–Balliol camp rather than of political ideology.

Neither instance is solid evidence for the existence of long-term leadership groups within Lothian, though Lothian men were involved on both occasions. That does not mean that such groups did not exist. It is quite possible that if all the material concerning relationships – familial, social, local, commercial, judicial, political and military – relating to Lothian people could be collated, instances of concerted political activity by apparently distinct groups within the political community could be identified. Even so, whether the patterns emerging represented actual instances of local political leadership or chance agglomerations of people who happened to be connected with one another would still be open to question. Of course, since we cannot be aware of all of the connections between all of the members of the political community or of all their actions, *any* group that comes together in record might conceivably represent a leadership group of some sort. The jurors on the De Pinkney Post Mortem Inquisition in 1296[34] might, for all we know, be a group of men with a specific, recognisable identity that was readily familiar to fourteenth-century Scots. They might have been the jurors of a particular sub-division of the constabulary of Haddington, men of a particular status with a judicial relationship to a specific barony, men who owed their position to the nepotism of a particular family or group of families. Alternatively, and this is obviously the most likely proposition, they might simply be men chosen at random from those members of the political community with suit of court responsibilities. No doubt several of them were related to one another or were neighbours, but their presence on the Inquisition does not imply membership of a stable leadership group other than that of the Lothian political community as a whole.

Is it reasonable to consider the Lothian political community as a leadership group in itself? The apparent ease with which Lothian accepted Plantagenet rule in 1296–1314 and Bruce rule in 1314–33 might suggest that the community could, to some degree, act in concert in the search for good lordship; Lothian did not accept Robert I's kingship until he had achieved a major battlefield success. It is clear that Edward III's government met much more opposition in the 1330s. Whereas Lothian would not accept the authority of King Robert until some months after the fall of Edinburgh Castle in 1314, the community was prepared to accept the authority of Laurence Preston[35] as sheriff in 1338 when the castle was under siege. This may indicate a loss of confidence in the Plantagenet administration and/or a fear of the Bruce party. It surely indicates both to some extent. However there is a possibility that the political community was quite prepared to accept Bruce authority on the condition that the Bruce party intervened physically against the Plantagenet party. Should such intervention be successful, the Lothian political community would be on the 'right' (winning) side. Should it fail, the political community could claim that they had been obliged to submit through force.

The willingness of the community to accept changes in the source of authority could be seen as the operation of one significant leadership group within the community, focused on the crown as the source of preferment and protection. This might explain the apparently uncontested transfer of power from John to Edward I and from Edward II to Robert I in the wake of 'decisive' battles, but would not sit comfortably with the inability of Edward III consistently to impose his rule in Lothian in 1335–36 despite a position of considerable military superiority, or the acceptance of Bruce authority in 1338 or 1341.

Perhaps the most significant factor in determining the allegiance of Lothian men in the years after Halidon Hill was the activity of two barons, William Douglas of Lothian and Alexander Ramsay of Dalhousie. The families of the two men whose influence in Lothian had been most enhanced by King Robert – Sir Alexander Seton and Sir Robert Lauder – failed to provide the Bruce party with effective leadership in Lothian after Halidon Hill and were eclipsed by Douglas and Ramsay. Their rise to prominence in the 1330s lay in their abilities as soldiers, providing effective war leadership to Bruce sympathisers in Lothian. The extent of that sympathy by late 1334 – early 1335 is impossible to judge, but it must have been substantial enough to help persuade him (and another astute politician, the Earl of Dunbar) that commitment to the Bruce party was in his best long-term interests. To the extent that both Douglas and Ramsay were fighting the same enemy under the same flag they were allies, but each was ambitious to retain in peacetime the lands, offices and leadership status that they had attained in the defeat of Edward III's administration.

On his return from France David II could not afford to alienate Douglas and was obliged to accept the extension of his lordship, but endeavoured, unsuccessfully, to curtail Douglas' ambitions by appointing Ramsay sheriff of Teviotdale and constable of Roxburgh in 1342. Douglas promptly murdered Ramsay,[36] confident that he would be able survive the inevitable fury of the King. The price of Douglas support for the Bruces was effective Douglas dominance in the south-east, but Douglas still sought the King's endorsement of his gains. If Edward I, II and III and Robert I all tried to manufacture Lothian magnates in the shape of Hastangs, Seton and Strivelin, it would seem that Douglas succeeded where they failed. According to Bower there were three magnates in Scotland in September 1335: Andrew Murray, the Earl of Dunbar and Sir William Douglas of Lothian.[37]

Naturally, the allegiance of Lothian landholders did not rest entirely with domestic considerations, be they social, military or political. The difficulties and distractions of Edward I, II and III were important contributory factors to the progress of the Wars, and thus in the political lives of Lothian landholders. For a variety of reasons, none of the three was able consistently to concentrate their resources on the conquest of Scotland. They were intermittently hampered by war in Flanders and France, dissent at home, diplomatic constraints and a perennial shortage of money and troops, particularly men-at-arms, for whom service in France was a more attractive proposition financially.

Effective government requires credibility, and by the later 1330s that may have been a consideration for all parties. Edward III's failure to mount a relief of Edinburgh Castle in 1341, or an operation to bring about its recovery, would surely be a strong indication to the Lothian community that he had lost confidence in the ability of his administration to establish itself. Since Edward had already failed to take Dunbar Castle or to relieve Bothwell Castle it would be surprising if the political community had not lost credibility in Edward's capacity to provide good lordship.

Edward's commitment to war with France is often seen as the key to Scottish success in the late 1330s, but it is worth bearing in mind that by the time Edward went to war with France the Bruce party had already staged a remarkable recovery, despite considerable internal divisions and signal defeats on the battlefield. Edward was unable to afford sufficient support to Edward Balliol, to prevent the recovery of the Scots north of the Forth through the mid to late 1330s despite the deployment of a number of substantial armies. Further, due to the acquisition of better equipment, the Scots no longer had to rely on the failure of supply to force the surrender of a garrison. St. Andrews Castle and Bothwell Castle were each battered into submission in a matter of a few weeks.[38] In the period from the 1290s to fall of Berwick to King Robert, the length of time it took for the Scots to force a surrender had meant that there was a reasonable chance that a relief could be mounted and a siege raised. By 1337 the window of opportunity for such operations had evidently become much smaller. More significantly, the value of such operations had been severely compromised. If the Scots could not be brought to battle and if castles and towns captured by major English invasions could be recovered swiftly, what was the point in mounting expensive expeditions? Obviously the Scots won their war of independence, but at what juncture was it clear that they had done so? Further, at what point did the war cease to be a question of Scottish independence? From an operational viewpoint the issue of independence had been settled before the return of David II from exile in France. Edward III continued to refuse recognition of David's kingship, but was unable to prevent the Bruce party from achieving independence as a political reality. David's operations in the north of England were aimed at forcing recognition of his rule, not at freeing his country from the spectre of conquest and subjugation. Even his capture at Neville's Cross in 1346 did not put Scottish independence at serious risk. The diplomatic and political issues remained at the heart of the relationship between England and Scotland, but the military issue had been effectively resolved by the fall of Edinburgh Castle in 1341. The fact that the Scots chose to garrison the castle, rather than destroy it, is a clear indication of their confidence as much as the failure of Edward III to attempt its recovery is an indication of his acceptance that the war could not be won by military means. Diplomatic initiatives might sweeten the pill of military failure, but the pill still had to be swallowed, however reluctantly.

The precise point at which the tide of the conflict turned in favour of the Scots is open to question, as the point at which it changed from being a war of independence to a war between sovereign kingdoms is open to question, but clearly the course and nature of the conflict did change. In the end of the day, the Scots most certainly won their war. What of the fortunes of the political community of Lothian? Regardless of the processes that induced resistance or defection, it is clear that the majority of Lothian landholding families managed to survive each change of government from the appearance of individuals and their heirs under successive governments and the survival of family names into the later fourteenth century.

Of the thirty-six Lothian-based families (the Siwards, Lubauds, and Sir John Strivelin became figures in the Lothian political community through the fortunes of war) whose histories were examined for this book, only two, the Lardners and the Linlithgows disappeared from Lothian entirely. The disappearance of family groups may be more apparent than real. Merely because a family disappears from a particular location during a war is not evidence that their departure was either directly or indirectly a consequence of the conflict, or even that the family had departed at all. The practice of children bearing the name of their father rather than their mother could lead to the disappearance of the family name even though the descent of the property had never been affected by the war.[39] An estate without a legitimate heir at all would escheat to the crown or a financially incompetent landholder could be forced to sell up, again, without the influence of the war. Further, people might have chosen to relocate in an effort to avoid war in the future, or to remove themselves from the scene of a traumatic past or been offered an attractive opportunity elsewhere. For most, however, the overriding priority was the retention of the family property no matter which party was in power. This was partly a matter of tradition and partly a matter of where they were to go and what they were to do for an income if they were forfeited.

Perhaps surprisingly, given the extent of the conflict, relocation does not seem to have been a priority. The retention of the family property does. At least one member of every family profiled for this book was, at some point, in the peace of Edward I, Edward II or Edward III, several families were in the peace of all three, but members of at least twenty- eight of those thirty-six families were able to reach an accommodation with the Scottish crown after the defeat of Edward III's Lothian administration in 1341. Even the Craigie family, who had been, with the exception of a short period, steadfast in the Plantagenet peace and staunch supporters of the Balliol cause, had a member of the family knighted by David II in 1342,[40] despite the fact that Sir Alexander de Craigie, along with his son and his cousin, both named Alexander, were still in the peace of Edward III in 1343.[41] Clearly the majority of Lothian families managed to retain some, if not all, of their heritage, which strongly suggests that the political community of Lothian survived the Wars of Independence remarkably well despite the political and military stresses of nearly half a century of war.

ENDNOTES

INTRODUCTION

1. Devastation was, in itself, an important military activity. Rogers, *Wars,* pp.271–283, has pointed to the economic consequences of disruption of the enemy's economy and therefore his ability to wage war. He also considers the use of destruction to coerce the enemy into offering or accepting battle in unfavourable circumstances. Pursuing political objectives through devastation operations – whether undermining the credibility of the opposing government or directly enforcing obedience from his subjects – was also an important factor. See also E. Fryde *Peasants and Landlords in Medieval England* (Stroud, 1986) pp.221–233; *CIPM,* i, no. 1795 for damage sustained to the manor of Manilawes in Northumberland; *CDS,* iii, pp.327–41 for many examples of devastation in Lothian in 1335–36. See also Allmand, C., 'War and Non-Combatants' in Keen, M., *Medieval Warfare, a History* (Oxford, 2000) pp.259–61.
2. This is not to suggest that there was no sense of a national identity in Scotland before the Wars of Independence, rather, as Dr. Webster suggests in *Medieval Scotland. The Making of an Identity,* (Basingstoke, 1997) p.77 that it was present but not yet 'extensively articulated in a situation where the Scots had a very difficult problem to solve'.
3. Nicholson, *Middle Ages.*
4. A. Grant, *Independence and Nationhood* (London, 1979).
5. The very titles of several works are indicative of this; F. Watson's *Under the Hammer* and N. MacDougall's *An Antidote to the English* (Edinburgh, 2002).
6. E. M. Barron, *Scottish War.* This volume continues to be influential though much of Barron's analysis is of questionable value at best.
7. C. MacNamee, *The Wars of the Bruce.* (East Linton, 1997).
8. M. Penman, *The Scottish Civil War* (Stroud, 2002).
9. M. Brown, *Wars of Scotland* (Edinburgh, 2004).
10. G.W.S Barrow, 'Lothian in the First War of Independence' *SHR* LV (1976).
11. G.W.S. Barrow, 'The Aftermath of War' *TRHS* (1978).
12. A.A.M. Duncan, 'The War of the Scots, 1306-23', *TRHS* (1992).
13. Several books have been published on the battle of Bannockburn, including W.M. McKenzie's *Battle of Bannockburn* (Glasgow, 1913), A. Nusbacher's *Bannockburn 1314*

(Stroud, 2000) and W.W. Scott's *Bannockburn Revealed* (private, 2000). Curiously, there has been no modern, full-length academic study of this battle.

14. S. Waugh points out that after Halidon Hill, 'The Scots rallied and Edward brought armies northward again and again for the next four years to no avail'. *England in the Reign of Edward III* (Cambridge, 1991), p.14.

15. Knight and man-at-arms service was a vital component in the Scottish Wars of Independence to judge by the regularity with which it is recorded. Professor Howard's assertion that armoured cavalry service was an 'elegant anachronism' in the later middle ages is of questionable value in relation to general engagements and does not bear examination at all in relation to the usual practice of war throughout the fourteenth century. M. Howard, *War in European History* (Oxford, 1976), p.16.

16. The current division into independent Local Authority establishments – West Lothian, Midlothian, East Lothian and City of Edinburgh – does not compromise the validity of Lothian as a term. Many of the institutions of local government continue to be 'combined operations', notably the police and fire services. Perhaps more importantly, Scottish people continue to speak of 'Lothian' or even 'The Lothians' confident that what they mean is what the listener hears.

17. *RMS* lists the various instruments of Scottish kings issued under the Great Seal, *RRS* volumes detail the *acta* of those kings and *ER* records their surviving financial records. *Rot. Scot.* is a collection of material gathered by English governments in connection with Scottish affairs. Stevenson's *Documents* and Bain's *CDS* (and the supplementary volume by G. Simpson and J. Galbraith) are general compilations of material from a variety of sources. In the century and more since their publication many faults have been identified in both Bain and Stevenson's work, particularly in relation to the editorial choices made by the compilers, however it is worth bearing in mind the sheer scale of the undertakings. Bain calendared approximately 10,000 documents. Despite their faults Bain and Stevenson's works have proved to be extremely useful tools.

18. Barrow, *Bruce.*

19. M. Prestwich, *Edward I* (London 1980).

20. M. Penman, *David II.*

21. M. Brown, *The Black Douglases* (East Linton, 1998).

22. A. Young, *The Comyns. Robert the Bruce's Rivals* (East Linton, 1997).

23. *CDS,* ii, no. 823.

24. This was a two-way process; Professor MacQueen has observed that the decentralised nature of Scottish government effectively required the king's law officers – the sheriffs and the justiciars – to co-operate with local men. MacQueen, *Common Law* p.253.

25. Ministerial landholdings – tenures that were not heritable.

26. Duncan, *Scotland* pp.370-1, 377.

27. A. Grant, *Independence and Nationhood* (London, 1984), p.25.

28. Despite the conditions of the 'Perpetual Peace' of 1328, Douglas may have been involved in raids in England late in 1330: *CDS,* iii, no. 1029. If so, it did not prevent him from receiving crown patronage in March 1331. *RRS,* vi, p.57.

29. Between 1307 and 1309 there was a great deal of conflict in the north-east and very little in the south-east, a situation reversed in 1337-41.

30. M. Jones has commented on the diversity of experience of war in France during the Hundred Years' War. 'France in the Fourteenth Century' in Rogers *Wars,* pp.343-8. Differences in geography and traditional loyalties across Scotland and in particular the ability or otherwise of English armies to consistently dominate the north and west led to a similar diversity in Scotland.

31. Barron, *Scottish War*, p.8.

32. Barrow, *Neighbours*, p.156.

33. There is no doubt that Scottish administrative material was recorded before 1296. Edward I's receiver for Scotland accepted delivery of the accounts of the sheriffs and crown estates of northern Scotland 'de tempore' the Kings of Scots. Palgrave, *Docs. Hist Scot.*, p. 277.

34. *Chron. Fordun, i,* p. 361.

35. *Rot.Scot.* i, p. 540.

36. *Scotichronicon*, vii, p.139.

37. The financial challenges of maintaining war in Scotland affected all of the subjects of the Plantagenets, not just those in England, Ireland and Wales. Edward II was obliged to demand support from Gascony in 1315-17. *Gascon Rolls, 1307-17,* nos. 1507-9, 1607-11, 1723-27, 1730.

38. TNA, C47/22/6/18 Alexander de Cragy was gifted a consignment of wine in November 1338 by Edward III to compensate him for his losses.

39. *CDS,* iii, no. 1186. The garrison included eight knights, fifty-two other men-at-arms and sixty archers from Yorkshire. The castle was in need of repair before it could serve as a useful establishment. Its established use as an administrative centre is indicated by the description of one of the buildings as the 'counting house'. TNA, E 101/19/21.

40. *Chron. Fordun,* i, p. 354.

41. *Scotichronicon*, vii, p. 127.

42. *CDS,* iii, pp. 327-41.

43. *RRS,* v, p.627. Donaldson, *Documents*, p.63, gives a translation of Robert I's charter to the Burgh of Edinburgh, given in May 1329. Similar charters exist for Aberdeen (1319) and Berwick (1320).

44. Most significantly the Chamberlain, who accepted their terms, and the sheriff, whose criminal jurisdiction was rather greater than the burgh's own court – MacQueen *Common Law* p.57 – and who may have collected the revenues for forwarding to the Chamberlain, see. Duncan, *Scotland,* p. 159.

45. TNA, E39/3/47. This collection of 59 homages, some illegible, contains the declarations of at least forty-one women. Although most of the documents are very brief and virtually identical, some are very lengthy- especially no.4 at four pages. The documents are dated 15/03/1306 x 25/03/1306 and are perhaps a reaction to Robert I's claim to kingship.

46. TNA, C47/22/2/11. Stevenson, *Documents,* ii, pp 92–97.

47. Galleys. Neil Campbell of Lochawe was obliged to provide a galley of forty oars whenever required for the operations of Robert I in exchange for 'the whole land of Lochawe and the land of Ardscodyrthe' in 1315, Donaldson, *Documents,* p.51.

48. T. Thomson, A. MacDonald, C. Innes (eds.), *Registrum Honoris de Morton* (Edinburgh, 1853).

49. Rev. J. Anderson (ed.), *The Laing Charters* (Edinburgh, 1899).

50. G. Tyndall Bruce (ed.), *Liber Cartarum Prioratus Sancti Andree* (Edinburgh, 1841).

51. Rev. C. Rogers, (ed.), *Chartulary of the Cistercian Priory of Coldstream* (London, 1879).

52. C. Innes (ed.), *Registrum Sancte Marie de Neubotle* (Edinburgh, 1849).

53. Lord Francis Egerton (ed.) *Liber Cartarum Sancte Crucis* (Edinburgh, 1840).

54. J. Stevenson, *Documents Illustrative of the History of Scotland* (Edinburgh, 1870), hereafter Stevenson, *Documents.*

55. *The Accounts of the Great Chamberlains of Scotland* (Edinburgh, 1836). Hereafter *The Chamberlain Rolls.*

56. J. Stuart and G. Burnett (eds.), *The Exchequer Rolls of Scotland* hereafter *ER.*

57. J. Bain, *Calendar of Documents Relating to Scotland* (London, 1881–8), hereafter *CDS*.
58. J. MacPherson, *Rotuli Scotiae in Turri Londiniensi in Domo Capitulari Westmonasteriensi Asservati,* hereafter *Rot. Scot.*
59. *Calendar of the Close Rolls.*
60. *Calendar of Inquisitions Post Mortem,* hereafter *CIPM.*
61. *Scalacronica. The Reigns of Edward I, Edward II and Edward III* (Trans) H. Maxwell (Glasgow, 1907), hereafter *Scalacronica* (Maxwell).
62. The validity even of crown charter witness lists is open to question, see B. Webster, *Scotland from the Eleventh Century to 1603* (Cambridge, 1975) p.73–4.
63. *Laing Chrs.,* nos.19, 21, 27.
64. NAS,GD 122/1/140 (charter of Christina de Preston), *RRS,* v, pp 316,322, 324, *Arbroath Liber,* i, no. 287 and many others are witnessed only by magnates close to the King, typically his brother Edward, Sir Thomas Randolph, Sir Robert Keith and one or more bishops and, increasingly after the death of Edward Bruce, Sir James Douglas. The attestation of 'many others' was not unknown in royal charters – David I's charter announcing the establishment of a house for the religious at Jedburgh (1147 x 1151) was witnessed by his son, Henry, four bishops, three abbots, various named laymen 'et multi alii' G.W.S. Barrow, *The Charters of David I* (Woodbridge, 1999) p.139.
65. NAS, GD 40/1/23, GD82/1, *Liber Holyrood* p.75; *Arbroath Liber,* pp. 7, 9.
66. John de Maleville's charter to Newbattle Abbey was witnessed by the bishops of St. Andrews, Glasgow and Brechin, *Newbattle Registrum,* pp.161–3.
67. NAS, GD 40/1/41; RH 6/98; GD84/1/6.
68. NAS, RH 6, 67, 68, 70, 98, 100, 104, 112, 118, 119, 120; GD86/1/7. *Morton Registrum,* Bannatyne Club (Edinburgh 1853) no.5 bears the less common 'et pluribus aliis'.
69. This seems to apply widely to ecclesiastical documents, *Liber St. Andrews* p.376–7, 383, 390,393 and many others complete the witness list with variants of 'multis aliis', similarly the *Newbattle Registrum,* p.95, 98,100, 157, 165, *Cold. Cart.,* p.41; *Liber Holyrood* pp. 65, 70,74,77,93. There are charters that do have what appears to be a complete list of named witnesses, such as NAS, GD 86/1/4.
70. NAS, GD40/1/24, undated but *c.* 1290–98.
71. NAS, GD40/1/29. Bruce MacAndrew has identified a number of Ragman Roll seals that were used by more than one person. 'The Sigillography of the Ragman Roll.' *Proc.Soc.Antiq.Scot.* 129, 1999, p.670.
72. NAS, GD18/1. The other witnesses were the Bishop of St. Andrews, Sir Walter and Sir Alexander de Haliburton, Alexander Cockburn and Robert de Raynton. It is not clear whether David de Penicuik was any relation to Hugh, Nigel and Margaret de Penicuik or whether he took his title from the name of the estate.

CHAPTER 1

1. Despite the Lanercost Chronicler's assertion (*Chron. Lanercost,* p.175) that more than 10,000 Scots were killed for the loss of only one rash (*incauto*) Englishman, there is no recorded description of a general engagement, only of a Scottish cavalry charge which was easily overcome by the Earl of Surrey's cavalry division. Only one noteworthy Scottish fatality, Patrick Graham (Stevenson, *Documents,* ii, p.26) is recorded – an unlikely outcome had there been an 'all arms' battle. Neither the scale of a battle, nor even of the 'butcher's bill' are infallible guides to the political significance of an engagement.
2. Stevenson, *Documents,* ii, pp.25–32.
3. Barron, *Scottish War,* p.413.

4. TNA, C47/22/10/45.

5. *CDS,* ii, no.1132.

6. *Ibid.*, p.191. Lothian was not alone in accepting Edward's rule. Isabella Beaumont sought possession of the barony of Crail in Fife, Stevenson, *Documents,* ii, p. 122. TNA C47/22/2/14 and Adam le Armourer and his wife Gunnora petitioned for peaceful enjoyment of their tenement at Berwick TNA C47/22/2/16; Stevenson, *Documents,* ii, p.156.

7. *CDS,* ii, pp.193–214.

8. Barron, *Scottish War,* p.413.

9. Barrow, *Bruce,* pp.188-9, 325–8.

10. See note 1, above.

11. The sum of Ragman Roll homagers for Lothian and the prisoners of war from Dunbar.

12. This was certainly the case in England. In May 1314 the Abbot of Abingdon offered to pay a fine of 60 marks in lieu of the service due from three knights' fees held by the abbey. TNA, C47/22/10/12. In 1327 the Abbot of Abingdon was ordered to pay £60, the Abbot of Ramsey £80, the Abbess of Wylton £20 and the Abbot of St. Edmund's £120 in fines for army service in Scotland, as were many other religious houses. *Memoranda Rolls 1326-1327,* no.1939.

13. *Scalacronica* (Maxwell), p.16.

14. The active involvement of women in military command or leadership positions can be identified on several occasions during the Wars of Independence, notably the two countesses of Dunbar, Marjorie and Agnes, who resisted the forces of Edward I and Edward III, and the Countess of Atholl who defended Kildrummy against the forces of David II. This was well within the cultural traditions of the late middle ages, see J.A. Truax 'Anglo-Norman Women at War: Valiant Soldiers, Prudent Strategists or Charismatic Leaders?' in (eds.) D. Kagay and L.J.A. Villalon, *The Circle of War in the Middle Ages.* (Woodbridge, 1999) p.111.

15. The prisoners were listed by name and writs issued to pay them appropriate allowances. *CDS,* ii, no. 742. TNA, C47/22/4/2.

16. *APS,* i, p.424.

17. *Rot. Scot.,* i, p.11.

18. Stevenson, *Documents,* ii, pp.204–209.

19. W. Croft Dickinson, G.D. Donaldson, I. Milne (edd) *A Source Book of Scottish History,* i, (Edinburgh, 1958), p.8.

20. Nicholson, *Edward III,* p.92.

21. J. Sumption, *The Hundred Years War. Trial by Battle* (London, 1990), pp.539, 557–60.

22. Even fairly basic equipment for a man-at-arms could easily cost £10 in the late thirteenth century. A horse valued at 10 marks (*CDS,* ii, pp. 413-32 gives several examples) a chainmail hauberk for 20 shillings (*SHS misc.ix* 1990 p. 111) and a sword for four shillings (*ibid,* p. 65) would cost a total of £7 17s 4d.

23. Stevenson, *Documents,* ii, pp.206–7. The summer of 1297 saw widespread challenges to Edward's government. In addition to the actions of Andrew Murray and William Wallace; there was the 'Noble Revolt' of Bruce and the Stewart in the southwest, TNA C/4722/2/23, Stevenson, *Documents,* ii, pp.200–202. The campaign of Andrew Murray in the north-east was preventing communication between Edward I and Plantagenet adherents like Sir Reginald Cheyne, TNA, C47/22/2/30; Stevenson, *Documents,* ii, p.232 and there was also tension with Alexander of the Isles in the West. TNA C47/22/2/20, Stevenson, *Documents,* ii, p.187.

24. Nicholson, *Middle Ages,* p.55.

25. Watson, *Hammer,* p.65.

26. *CDS,* ii, no. 853.

27. *Ibid.,* no. 824; *CIPM,* iii, p. 363.

28. In addition to the irregular ebb and flow of the military situation there were periods of truce, see *Treaty Rolls,* i, pp. 149-151 for the text of the 1302 truce.

29. *CDS,* ii, p.225.

30. *Ibid.,* ii, nos.1039, 1040.

31. *CDS,* ii, no. 1033.

32. *Ibid.,* ii, no. 1034, TNA, C47/22/6/10

33. TNA, C47/22/6/12

34. *CDS,* ii, no. 1132.

35. Watson, *Hammer,* pp.69–70.

36. On 22 November 1298 the garrison included fifty men-at-arms and eight knights. TNA, E101//7/29.

37. Stevenson, *Documents,* ii, p.303. TNA C47/22/2/41.

38. *Ibid.* It is possible that Sir Thomas' capture might not have occurred at Edinburgh, but it would seem an odd piece of information to include if it were not immediately relevant. Interestingly Sir Thomas' family had a connection with Lothian pre-dating the Wars of Independence. In 1270 Thomas d'Arderne (perhaps the father) held a knight's fee in East Lothian from Henry de Pinkney, who in turn held from Sir Roger de Quincy. *CDS,* i, no. 2582.

39. Stevenson, *Documents,* ii, p.303.

40. Stevenson, *Documents,* ii, p.303.

41. *CDS,* ii, nos. 1481, 1594.

42. *Scotichronicon,* vi, pp. 293–4.

43. *Scalacronica* (Maxwell), p. 23.

44. *Ibid.,* p. 24.

45. *CDS,* v, no. 472.

46. He at least managed to avoid capture; Hugh de Flotterston, holder of a house in Berwick, but presumably with some connection to Flotterston, Midlothian, was taken later and released for ransom. TNA, SC8/9/432.

47. *Scotichronicon,* vi, pp. 293–4.

48. Stevenson, *Documents,* i, dlxxv.

49. Nicholson, *Middle Ages,* p.63.

50. *A.P.S.,* i, p.454.

51. Barrow, *Bruce,* p. 129. Edward was not convinced that hostilities were completely over; Wallace was still at large and in March 1305 Edward was encouraging his son to reinforce Sir Alexander Abernethy at the Fords of Drip in the pursuit of the rump of the Balliol party. Stevenson, *Documents,* ii, p.472.

52. Barrow, *Bruce.* pp.325–8.

53. *CDS,* iii, no. 245.

54. *CDS,* ii, no. 857, TNA, C47/22/10/45. He may have regretted his inheritance later. At some point between 1300 and 1307 the castle, apparently having been gifted to Henry by the king, was back in Edward's hands. Henry petitioned for an allowance 'in consideration' of the heavy expense he had incurred in repairing the castle. TNA, SC/8/43/7141. See NAS, RH5 230 for a less detailed inquisition relating to Henry Brade.

55. *CDS,* ii, no. 857.

56. *Chron. Lanercost,* p.214.

57. *Rot. Scot.,* i, p. 111, *Calendar of Inquisitions Miscellaneous,* ii, no. 452 and *CDS,* iii, no. 858 relating to hostages for the ransom of Ripon.

58. *CDS,* iii, no. 330.

59. *Ibid.*, no. 337, TNA, C47/22/10/11.

60. *Rot. Scot.*, i, p.82.

61. *Chron. Lanercost*, p.200.

62 *Rot. Scot.*, i, p.114.

63. Barrow, *Bruce*, p.326.

64. *RRS*, v, p.386.

65. Barbour, *The Bruce*, pp.381–97.

66. Barbour, *The Bruce*, p.456.

67. *CDS*, ii, pp.408–12.

68. In 1319, when an English army was at Roxburgh, a Scottish army slipped past it and moved as far south as Yorkshire, prompting Edward to write to the Sheriff of Yorkshire urging him to ensure the safety of the town and the castle. TNA, E101/22/10/34. Devastation of the countryside was a normal function of war, undermining the credibility of the enemy. In *c.*1313 Edward III was petitioned for protection by men in his peace in Lothian and Roxburghshire. By 1315 x 1320 he was receiving similar petitions from his subjects in the north of England. TNA, C47/22/10/37.

69. TNA, E101/16/11, records the payment of soldiers' wages at Leith.

70. Barbour *The Bruce*, p.678.

71. Whether he spent much time there reinforcing his power in person is difficult to assess. Dr. Webster has pointed out that there is a strong likelihood that routine crown documents could be dated at Edinburgh regardless of where the King was. B. Webster, *Scotland from the Eleventh Century to 1603* (Cambridge, 1975), p.74.

72. There is abundant evidence of the destruction caused by King Robert's troops. *CIPM*, iv, nos.423, 597, v, nos.536, 583, vi, nos.143, 50, 268, 758.

73. Robert I of course put a great deal of effort into securing acceptance of his authority throughout Scotland, see M. Penman's Ph.D. Thesis, 'The Kingship of David II' (St. Andrews 1999), pp.1–45.

74. *CDS*, iii, pp. 327–41. TNA E101/19/24.

75. *Scalacronica* (Maxwell), p. 164.

76. Henry de Greenford was the constable of Yester in November 1296, collecting over £40 from the issues of Yester and the sale of the horse and goods of John Keu, 'a felon'. Stevenson, *Documents*, ii, no. 345 dates this document to November 1295, however, apart from the fact that war had yet to break out, the document clearly states that the compotus started from the 24th year of Edward's reign – 1296.

77. Nicholson, *Edward III*, p. 168.

78. He may also have been influenced by the international interest in Scotland as a threat to England. It is possible that knights from France and Flanders were in Scotland in 1334 to study the prospects for the Scots. M. Penman, *David II*, p.62.

79. *Rot. Scot.,* i, p.401.

80. See R. J. Smoll 'Off quhat nacioun art thou?' in R.A. MacDonald (ed.) *History, Literature and Music in Scotland, 700 –1560* (Toronto, 2002). Identification by nationality could be a hazardous experiences – Geoffrey de Everwyk, a monk of Dunfermline, sought sustenance from Edward I in 1307 since he had been expelled from his house because he was English and for 'uncovering certain Scottish plots against the King' TNA, SC8/46/22/55. Edmund Hastings, as commander of the garrison of Perth asked that no Scotsman should have jurisdiction over the garrison in wartime. TNA C47/22/10/7.

81. *CDS*, iii, no. 337; TNA, C47/22/10/11.

82. *RRS*, v, p.367.

83. The garrison at Berwick faced more problems than the likelihood of a Scottish attack. In March 1316 the constable of Berwick, Sir Ivo de Aldeburgh, was due

arrears for himself, his garrison and for horses lost in the reign of Edward I. TNA, C47/22/10/25.

84. Nicholson, *Middle Ages,* p.102. Nicholson states that the aim of the De Soulis conspiracy was to replace Robert I with Sir William De Soulis, however any claim that De Soulis might have made would have been tenuous in the extreme. The only plausible candidate would have been Edward Balliol, son of King John. See also Barrow, *Bruce,* pp.309–310. Dr. Penman suggests that Bruce propaganda ascribed the conspiracy to De Soulis to undermine the credibility of the Balliol cause and that the kingship of Robert I was 'undeniably strengthened' by his decisive response, 'A fell Coniuracioun agayn King Robert the Doughty King: the De Soulis Conspiracy of 1318–20' *Innes Review,* 50, (1999).

85. Barbour, *The Bruce,* p.700.

86. See N. Reid 'Crown and Community Under Robert I' in Grant & Stringer (edd), *Medieval Scotland. Crown, Lordship and Community* (Edinburgh, 1993), pp.215–6.

87. Lt. Col. Rogers (pers comm.) has suggested that the defeat at Dupplin Muir would have been seen as a mark of God's favourable attitude to the Balliol cause and that the Bruce cause would have been compromised accordingly in the eyes of the Scots, however it would be reasonable to assume that a similar attitude would have developed in English society after the battles of Bannockburn, Myton and Culblean.

88. *CDS,* iii, no.1223.

89. *Rot. Scot.,* i, p.260.

90. Nicholson, *Edward III,* p.152. Edward Balliol's parliament was attended by some Lothian men, though not, apparently, in great numbers despite the recent Bruce defeats at Dupplin Muir and Halidon Hill. Among the '…bishops, prelates, earls, barons and nobles' of the realm there were Patrick Graham, Michael Wemyss, Patrick Curry, Geoffrey Moubray, Robert de Pinkney and the Earl of Dunbar. TNA, E39/15/1.

91. For John de Stirling (Strivelin)'s grants at Ratho and Bathgate see TNA, C47/22/10/53.

92. *CDS,* iii, p.354.

93. *Scotichronicon,* vii, p.131.

94. *Scalacronica* (Maxwell), p.102.

95. J. Sumption, *The Hundred Years War. Trial by Battle (*London, 1990), pp.143–51.

96. *Scotichronicon,* vii, p.147.

97. *Chron. Wyntoun,* vi, p.83.

98. *CDS,* iii, no. 1291.

99. *Scotichronicon,* vii, p.129.

100. *Scotichronicon,* vii, p.129.

101. *Scalacronica* (Maxwell), p.168.

102. *Scotichronicon,* vii, p.129.

103. The failure of the siege had implications for the reputations of the commanders; '…after spending a long time there, they raised the siege and withdrew, to their no small discredit.' G. Martin, (ed.) *Knighton's Chronicle, 1337–1396* (Oxford, 1995), p. 5.

104. *Rot. Scot.,* i, p.139.

105. *CDS,* ii, no. 653. The clerics of Chemay petitioned for the grant of various Scottish churches in July 1319. TNA, SC35/31. Edward was prepared to make such grants – he gave the prebend of Kilbride to William de Cliffe on 19 July 1319 – since they were unlikely to cost him anything so long as Scotland was within his control.

106. The issue of the 'disinherited' had not been resolved by the time of Robert I's death, but the suitors did not simply reach for their arms, they had been in negotiations for years before the Dupplin Muir campaign. TNA, C47/22/10/48.

107. As ever with medieval battles, the strength of the armies is hard to ascertain. Penman gives the Balliol force 2,000–3,000 participants *David II*, p.47, broadly in line with contemporary figures. The Scottish army is estimated at 30,000 (*Chron. Fordun*, i, p.355), but this should be seen as a literary convention indicating a 'vast' force, not as a literal statement. It would be remarkable if the combined Scottish forces amounted to as many as 15,000.

108. Two men-at-arms from the retinue of Sir Adam de Welle were available for the operations of Sir John de Kingstone in late 1302 (*CDS*, v, no. 305). This was not a unique, nor even perhaps an unusual arrangement. Twenty men-at-arms of the 'gents' of Galloway were to be paid wages for service should they be called upon to pursue the enemy, (Palgrave *Docs. Hist. Scot.*, p.297).

109. *Chron. Wyntoun*, p.83.

110. *CDS*, iii, pp. 360-61.

111. The cash for wages was not always easily achieved. Dalmahoy was paid in wool on at least one occasion. This was not an innovation. In 1305–6 Edward I gave Sir Alexander Abernethy (as 'keeper' of Scotland between the Scottish Sea and the mountains) a license to export wool TNA, SC/32/67 and in November 1338 Edward III gave Sir Alexander Craigie three 'tonels' of wine in recognition of his losses in Scotland. TNA, C47/22/6/18.

112. *CDS*, iii, no. 1184.

113. *Ibid.*, pp.360–3.

114. *Ibid.*, no. 1323.

115. M. Brown, *The Black Douglases*, p.169.

116. *CDS*, iii, pp.352–3.

117. *Rot. Scot.*, i, pp.384–5.

118. Nicholson, *Middle Ages*, p.396.

119. The current situation in Iraq is a case in point. The Coalition forces were able to inflict a massive defeat on the army of Iraq, but have not yet been able to impose a settled political or military environment.

120. Dr. Webster's suggestion that '…at no point were Edward Balliol and Edward III allowed to dominate without opposition' perhaps overstates the case slightly. B. Webster 'Scotland without a King', Grant and Stringer (edd), *Medieval Scotland. Crown, Lordship and Community* (Edinburgh 1993) p. 227.

121. The same rationale would apply to the Earl of Dunbar, with the added complication that the rise of men like Douglas and Ramsay might well diminish the influence of the earl in Lothian and therefore throughout the country.

CHAPTER 2

1. G.W.S. Barrow, *The Kingdom of the Scots* (London, 1973), pp.251–6; Duncan, *Scotland*, p141.

2. *RRS*, VI, pp.652–4.

3. Duncan, *Scotland*, pp.588, 597.

4. Edward I had evidently been convinced of the value of the earl's support, issuing a letter to Sir John de St.John in 1301–2 ordering him not to interfere with the earl's decisions concerning those of his tenants whose lands had been forfeited to the king, but again this surely suggests that the earl could not completely control the political inclinations of his tenants. TNA C47/22/3/24.

5. See Chapter 1, p.26.

6. *CDS*, iii, no. 1121.

7. Sir Alexander Seton and Patrick Earl of Dunbar, for example.
8. William Byset *CDS,* ii, no.1471. William Frere, Archdeacon of Lothian *CDS,* ii, no. 1455, TNA, E/39/2/21 did not formally submit until October 1305, possibly prompted by the capture and execution of Wallace in August that year.
9. Michael Wemyss, William Somerville, Alexander Fraser, James Lindsay. Barrow, *Bruce,* p.326.
10. *CDS,* ii, no.245.
11. Men like Thomas de Caribre, king's tenant Edinburgh and Richard de Erthe (Airth?), king's tenant, Peebles, *CDS,* ii, no. 823.
12. Such as Robert de Brunhus, tenant of the Bishop of St, Andrews, *CDS,* ii, no. 823.
13. Professor Barrow 'Lothian in the First War of Independence' *SHR* LV (1976) p. 159, citing *CDS,* ii, no. 1011, states that Thomas was a 'valettus' of Sir Simon Fraser. Neither the original document, NAS, E101/7/5, nor Bain's translation clearly support this. Lillok is described as 'Sir Simon's valettus' and is the entry subsequent to that of Horsburgh, who is described as 'Sir Simon's Knight'. Horsburgh's record is immediately subsequent to that of Sir Simon Fraser. It is not absolutely clear to which of the 'Sir Simons' Lillok was connected.
14. Thomas was a member of the Stirling garrison which surrendered to Edward I in 1304. He was still a prisoner of war in 1307, when Nicholas Ferinbaud, late constable of Bristol castle, claimed £14 2s 6d for Thomas' allowance of 3d/day for 3 years and 38 days. *CDS,* iii, no. 16.
15. Oman, *History of England* (London 1910) pp. 167–8. Despite the efforts of more recent scholars such as Sean McGlynn, 'The Myths of Medieval Warfare' *History Today,* 44 (1994) and www.DeReMilitari.org/resources/articles/McGlynn Oman continues to exert considerable influence; see A. Nusbacher *The Battle of Bannockburn 1314* (Stroud, 2000), particularly in relation to his perception of Scottish armies and his assumptions about the nature of the engagement.
16. Barron, *Scottish War,* pp.9–10.
17. *CDS,* ii, no. 254.
18. This is not a particularly large figure. Matthew Paris believed that Alexander II's army in 1244 included 'a thousand armed men, upon horses sufficiently good' Anderson, A., *Scottish Annals from English Sources* (Stamford, 1991), p.354. A century later Thomas Sampson estimated that the army David II led to Neville's Cross included around 2000 'bannerets, knights and men-at-arms', quoted in Rollason and Prestwich, *The Battle of Neville's Cross 1346* (1998) p.134. In each case it is unlikely that every man liable for man-at-arms service actually took part.
19. G.W.S. Barrow, 'The Army of Alexander III' in Reid, *Alexander III.,* Duncan, *Scotland,* pp.380–1. S. Wood *The Scottish Soldier* (London, 1980), p.8–12. Wood merely repeats the general perception of Scottish armies of the middle ages, though it is clear that the composition of forces varied according to necessity and availability. Major armies were a rare occurrence throughout the wars of the thirteenth and fourteenth centuries. However it is clear that the Scots army in France in the early fifteenth century consisted of men-at-arms and archers. It would be unrealistic to assume that the forces generally committed by either side for minor operations were smaller versions of the large armies raised for specific tasks.
20. The surrender terms proposed by the leaders of the Noble Revolt in July 1297 mention a fear that Edward '…would have seized all the middle people of Scotland' to serve in his army. Stevenson, *Documents,* ii, p.198. Stevenson states that Edward intended to send these men 'beyond the Scottish sea', though the French text he presented just says 'beyond the sea'. Prestwich, *The Three Edwards* (London 1980), p.48, describes the fear of such conscription as 'widespread, and not wholly unjustified'.

21. *CDS,* iii, pp.327–41.TNA, E101/19/24.

22. *RRS,* v, p.515.

23. *CDS,* ii, p.343;TNA, E101/19/24.

24. John de Wyggemore also served Edward III as collector of customs for Edinburgh, gathering £12 2s 6d in 1337–8.TNA, E101/331/23.

25. *CDS,* iii, pp.408–10.

26. *CDS,* iii, pp.361–2.

27. Such as John Naper and Sir John Butler of Cramond,TNA, C47/22/6/18 and Matthew Naper TNA, E/102/19.

28. *Laing Chrs.,* no. 18 for a cavalry obligation without any mention of knight service.

29. *RRS,* v, pp.633–5.

30. Duncan, *Scotland,* p.383; Fractional knight service was not always a product of division of an existing fief. David I granted land in East Lothian for the service of half a knight. G.W.S. Barrow, *The Charters of David I,* (Woodbridge, 1999), pp.148–9. Miniscule knight service obligations were not a purely Scottish phenomenon. In 1304 16 acres of meadow and pasture and a wood around Wappenham, Northamptonshire were held by Henry de Pinkney of Geoffrey de Lucy for 1/24th of a 'moiety' (half) of a knight's fee, *CIPM,* iv, No 218. A charter of James the Stewart dated 9 January 1295 stipulated *forinsec* service of one archer for one day a year at the Stewarts' castle of Renfrew 'if reasonably forewarned', hardly a severe burden and of very limited practical value. R. Oram (ed.), *The Reign of Alexander II* (Brill, 2005), p. 191.

31. *CDS,* ii, no. 1755.

32. *CDS,* ii, p. 472.

33. *Rot. Scot.,* i, p.3.

34. *CDS,* ii, no. 245.

35. *Rot. Scot.,* i, pp. 397-496; *CDS,* iii, pp.327–41; 376–91;TNA E101/331/23.

36. *CDS,* iii, pp.360–3.

37. *Scotichronicon,* viii, 113.

38. *CDS,* iii, pp.327–41.

39. *CDS,* iii, pp.327–41.

40. *CDS,* iii, pp.339–40. For an examination of land measurement in medieval Scotland see G.W.S. Barrow, *Kingship and Unity* (Edinburgh, 2003), p.197.

41. Stevenson, *Documents,* ii, pp.206–7.

42. Dr.Watson has suggested that the prestige of the castle-builder was often the primary concern, that the castle was 'an expression of power, in the first instance, not the means of it.' 'The expression of power in a medieval kingdom: thirteenth-century Scottish Castles.' in (eds.) S. Foster, A .MacInnes, R. MacInnes. *Scottish Power Centres from the Early Middle Ages to the Twentieth Century* (Glasgow, 1998). See also G. Stell, 'The Scottish Medieval Castle: Form, Function and Evolution' in Stringer, *Nobility Essays.*

43. *CDS,* iii, nos. 230, 258.

44. The grants were not of great duration due to the military success of the Scots. Sir Robert was recompensed for his losses in Scotland with a grant of Kingston-upon-Hull sometime between 1311 and 1316.TNA, SC8/51/2504.

45. Barbour, *The Bruce,* pp.409–10.

46. Alexander Seton was not the only defector on 23–24 June 1314. Sir Laurence Abernethy and his *comitiva* arrived late for the battle and promptly joined the Bruce cause. Barbour, *The Bruce,* p.508

47. *CDS,* iii, no. 245.

48. *Scalacronica,*(Maxwell), p.55.

49. *RMS,* i, no. 62.
50. *RMS,* i, no. 68.
51. TNA, C47/22/10/53.
52. *CDS,* iii, no. 1319.
53. *CDS,* iii, nos. 1323, 1383.
54. At least thirty-one Scots served in the Edinburgh garrison as men-at-arms in 1335–36 (*CDS,* iii, pp.360–1), at least forty-two in 1336–37 (*CDS,* iii, pp.362–3) but perhaps as few as fourteen in 1340–41 (TNA, E101/23/1). These figures should be regarded as absolute minimums since it is reasonable to suppose that some, probably most and very possibly all of the unnamed 'scutifers' attached to Scottish knights in the garrison muster rolls would also have been Scots.
55. Edward Keith, Robert Keith, Edmund Keith, William Hay, William Moubray, William Ramsay, John More, William More, William Livingstone, John Preston, William de Vaus, John Sinclair, James Sandilands and Henry Douglas: all men with strong Lothian connections who all served at Neville's Cross. See M. Penman, *The Kingship of David II* unpublished Ph.D. thesis (St. Andrews, 1998) p.210.
56. This action is generally assumed to have occurred on 30 July, (Nicholson, *Edward III*, p.213) however Dr. Watt has pointed out that that was the date of Namur's entry into Scotland, therefore the action must have occurred on a later date, which can hardly have been earlier than 1 or 2 August. *Scotichronicon,* viii, p.222.
57. A.J. MacDonald 'Kings of the Wild Frontier? The Earls of Dunbar or March, *c.*1070–1435' in S. Boardman and A. Ross (eds.), *The Exercise of Power in Medieval Scotland* (Dublin, 2003), p.154.
58. *CDS,* iii, no. 1115. The sums were rather greater than identified by Bain. In 1334 the Earl gave a receipt for £100 of a grant of £600 from Edward III. TNA, E42/269.
59. If Edward III were successfully to establish his rule in Lothian he might find it expedient to restore Lothian men to the properties granted to Sir John, in which case Sir John would have to be compensated accordingly. Robert I had faced by a similar situation twenty years earlier, see H.L. MacQueen, *Common Law* 106–7.
60. *CDS,* ii, 1023; TNA, E101/47/22/10/48.
61. There is no evidence to suggest that Scottish bishoprics or abbeys were obliged to provide knight service, though common army service was required from their tenants. G.W.S. Barrow, *Kingship and Unity* (London, 1981) p.47. This was not the case in England. The abbots of Tavistock and St. Augustine's, Canterbury would seem to have been on active duty in 1305–6, each of them having 'had his service with the king'. *Calendar of Chancery Rolls, Various, 1277–1326,* p.378. The Abbot of Reading had ten men-at-arms on covered horses serving Edward I in England and Scotland in May 1296, *CDS,* v, no. 151. The Abbey had cause to take part in the Scottish war since they were looking for the restoration of the priory of May, from which they had been ejected by the bishop of St. Andrews when he was guardian of Scotland. *CDS,* v, no. 177. Scottish religious foundations were not entirely exempt from military obligations beyond common army; see below p.166.
62. Watt, *Fasti,* p.198.
63. Translation of the term 'dominus' as 'Sir' rather than 'Lord' certainly accounts for some apparent incidences of clerical knights, however in addition to senior ecclesiastics who pursued military careers, such as Antony Bek, Bishop of Durham, there are instances (see p.106) of clerics fulfilling the role of a knight among the men-at-arms of garrisons.
64. There are earlier examples. In 1206 the Melrose Chronicler accorded the title of 'Sir' to Richard de Cave, but not to his successor, Henry, the prior of the house. The entry for 1208 refers to the late Abbot of Dry burgh as Geoffrey, but his successor is

referred to as Sir William, an indication that this was not simply a courtesy to senior clerics. Anderson, A., *Early sources of Scottish History* (Stamford, 1990), pp.368, 371.

65. When Stirling castle surrendered to the Scots at the end of 1299 the complement included one 'Sir Thomas de Bridderhale, chaplain' in the small list of knights. *CDS,* ii, no. 1119.

66. *CDS,* ii, no. 969.

67. *Ibid.,* no. 1238.

68. *CDS,* ii, p.425.

69. Watt, *Fasti,* p.401.

70. *CDS,* ii, no. 1813.

71. *Ibid.,* no. 188.

72. *CDS,* iii, no. 505.

73. *Ibid.,* no. 653.

74. *Scotichronicon,* vii, p.126 'the priest (presbyteri), Sir William Bullock'; *CDS,* iii, no. 1321. Interestingly, Sir William does not appear in Watt, *Fasti,* possibly an indication that he never held a Scottish benefice.

75. *CDS,* iii, p. 363.

76. G.W.S.Barrow, *Kingdom of the Scots* (London, 1973), p.324.

77. *CDS,* iii, no. 24. Each of them had, however, asked Edward to allow them to continue to enjoy the income from their benefices, TNA, SC 8/30/1494.

78. An Edinburgh merchant and alderman of the city in 1335, John served as collector of customs for Edward III and as a man-at-arms in the castle garrison in 1337, *CDS,* iii, no. 1186, pp.346, 363. Various Botelers, Harpers and Napers appear on the Ragman Roll, *CDS,* ii, pp.194–214 and in the garrison pay rolls of Edinburgh, Perth and Stirling castles under Edward I, II and III.

79. *RRS,* v, p. 261. Professor Duncan makes a strong case that the text of this part of Formulary E – no. 59 – refers to Ayr, and that it originated in the spring of 1296.

80. G.W.S. Barrow 'The Army of Alexander III's Scotland' in Reid *Alexander III.*

81. *Chron. Wyntoun,* vi, p.195.

82. *RRS,* v, p.414.

CHAPTER 3

1. A great many English inquisitions have survived from this period, obviously many are to be found in the *CIPM* volumes, but many more very similar processes appear in other collections such as the *Calendar of Fine Rolls,* iii, pp.227–8, 229–230, 283, 413. The process carried out by the de Pinkney jurors does not seem to have differed significantly from those recorded in England. Bain's *Calendar* lists only the Scottish properties of Sir Robert, he also held several properties in Buckingham, Essex and Northamptonshire. *CIPM,* iii, p.366.

2. Barrow, *Neighbours,* p.219.

3. H. MacQueen, *Common Law* pp.1–3, Professor MacQueen clearly demonstrates that Scotland had an extensive body of law long before the Wars of Independence which must surely have taken account of the necessity for a process for deciding heirs and assessing the value of and burdens on property. Given that the writs of Novel Dissaine (pp.137–143) and Mortancestor (pp.168–70) were already well-established processes by this time, it would seem impossible that there could have been no means of deciding the possession and extent of property. The process in hand might in fact give title to the jury as a *visnet, recognition* or, most significantly an *inquest.* (p.50).

4. *CDS,* ii, no. 854.

5. *CDS,* ii, no. 823.

6. His horse was valued in 1296, TNA, E 101/5/23. His property was restored in 1297, suggesting perhaps a brief defection to the Balliol cause. *CDS*, ii, no. 954.

7. Henry was also a landholder in Northamptonshire, TNA, C143/27/10, C143/28/10.

8. The barony of Kings-Cavil (West Lothian) and Calder–Clere (Mid-Calder, Midlothian) cost James Douglas of Lothian £12 5s. 10d and the service of half a knight, but the charter makes no mention of the income that James might expect to receive from it (*RRS*, v, p.341). Westhall of Ratho (Midlothian) was held by 'Patrick called Noble' for 'accustomed service' in October 1316, but there is no definition of what that service might be or of the actual value of the property, a common condition in charter evidence. Patrick received the land as the heir of his grandfather, a Ragman Roll homager in 1296 *RRS*, v, p. 382.

9. *RRS*, v, pp. 342, 374, 450, 568; *RRS*, vi, pp. 86, 339, 358, 462.

10. *RRS*, v, pp. 352, 455, 609; *RRS*, vi, pp. 527-8. *RMS*, i, app. i, no. 45.

11. *RRS*, v, p. 615.

12. *RRS*, vi, pp. 627-8.

13. *RRS*, p. 341.

14. M. Prestwich *War, Politics and Finance Under Edward I* (London, 1972) p.50

15. *Laing Chrs.*, no. 18. In a charter of 1286 x 1300 William Gurlay granted land at Stonehouse for twelve pennies and 'bodily service in the army on horseback at the cost of the lord of the fee'. The recipient was surely obliged to serve as a man-at-arms, but the term 'knight service' is not used.

16. Duncan, *Scotland*, p. 161; G.W.S. Barrow, *The Kingdom of the Scots* p.23.

17. *RRS*, ii, p.476.

18. TNA E101/69/1/2, *CDS*, ii, nos. 1007, 1691; *CDS*, iii, no. 42.

19. *CDS*, ii, 230

20. Lubaud was ordered to hand over his command to Sir Ebulo de Montibus on 22 February 1314, *Calendar of Fine Rolls*, ii, p.189.

21. *RRS*, v, p.367

22. H.L. MacQueen *Common Law*, pp.20–1.

23. *CDS*, iii, pp. 327–41.

24. *CDS*, iii, pp. 327–41.

25. *Ibid.*

26. *Ibid.*

27. *Ibid.*

28. Nicholson, *Middle Ages*, p.180

29. *CDS*, iii, p.333.

30. *CDS*, iii, p.341.

31. *RRS*, v, p.453.

32. *CDS*, iii, nos. 1186, 1383.

33. These included Bolton, Drem, Dirleton, Duncanlaw, Elphinston, Glencorse, Keith, Neuton, Morham, Tranent, Ratho and Pentland, which may have formed one barony with Cousland and Roslin (however Cousland and Roslin may have been baronies in their own right, but customarily held by the same individual) all of which lay in Haddington constabulary. In Linlithgow constabulary there were Abercorn, Auldcathie, Barnbougle, Carriden, Kingscavill and Calder-Clere, Livingston, Loghorward, Ratho and Musselburgh. Edinburgh constabulary included the baronies of Byres, Colinton, Curry, Dalhousie, Dalkeith, Gorton, Neuton, Norton of Ratho and possibly Redhall of Ratho.

34. *RRS*, v, pp. 41–5. Professor Mac Queen's work on baronies relates mostly to the fifteenth and sixteenth centuries.

35. *RRS*, v, pp.41–44.

36. *RRS*, v, pp.221-3.
37. *RRS*, vi, p.480.
38. *RRS*, v, p.294.
39. Duncan, *Scotland*, p.389; *Kelso Liber*, no. 471.
40. *CDS*, iii, pp.383–412.
41. *Ibid.*, pp.412–32.
42. *Ibid*, iii, pp.317–26.
43. *RRS*, vi, pp.527–8.
44. *RRS*, v, p.54.
45. P. Morgan, *War and Society in Medieval Cheshire, 1277–1403* (Manchester, 1977), p.58; Ayton, *Knights*, p.16.
46. The articulation of an army is essentially the ability of discrete portions of the force to operate independently or as a group of formations subtracted from the main body of the army, both in the course of general operations and in the conduct of battlefield manoeuvres. Without some degree of articulation the army deployed for battle cannot initiate movement other than as a single formation nor can it respond to a change in the tactical situation in subdivisions or adequately combine portions of the army to carry out operations away from the battlefield. The daily existence of an army demands articulation for distribution of rations and ammunition, rotation of sentry duties throughout the force and the detailing of training and work parties.
47. *RRS*, v, pp.41–43.
48. *CDS*, iii, p.336.
49. *CDS*, iii, p.378.
50. *CDS*, iii, p.329.
51. *RRS*, v, p.414.
52. Nicholson, *Middle Ages*, p.18.
53. *CDS*, ii, no.733.
54. For a reasoned appraisal of Scottish agricultural practice in the later middle ages see P. Dixon *Puir Labourers and Busy Husbandmen* (Edinburgh, 2003).
55. Duncan, *Scotland*, p.309.
56. K. Jillings *Scotland's Black Death* (Stroud, 2002) p.46.
57. This offer was, however, part of negotiations aimed at acquiring custody of the Forest of Jedburgh for the Abbey. TNA, C47/22/2/36; C47/22/2/37.
58. *RRS*, vi, p.63.
59. Maslin; a mixture of grains – wheat, oats, rye, barley – sown, reaped and milled together. A quantity of maslin (meslin) figured in an extent of King John's manor of Kemeston, Buckinghamshire in October 1298 *CDS*, ii, 1024. The advantage of this practice is unclear, though it may have been a means of making use of old seed corn in the hope that some of it would ripen properly. Maslin was still being milled in the early nineteenth century, see E.Gauldie *The Scottish Country Miller* (Edinburgh, 1999) p.31.
60. *CDS*, iii, no. 337; TNA, C47/22/10/11.
61. *CDS*, iii, pp.331, 378.
62. *Chronique de Jean Le Bel*, i, p.43.
63. The general northern European famine of 1313–1317 was compounded for communities of northern England by the operations of Robert I's armies. C. MacNamee, *The Wars of the Bruces*, pp. 123–157 examines these operations in great detail.
64. A. Grant, *Independence and Nationhood*, pp.75–6. Conflict and the passage of armies looting and wilfully devastating was also a factor, as in Robert I's 'herschip' of Buchan, Barbour, *The Bruce*, pp. 332–5. Bower's assertion that 'the whole lands

of Gowrie, Angus and the Mearns was reduced to almost irreparable devastation (*Scotichronicon,* vii, p.125) and the widespread destruction of southern and eastern Scotland in the 1330s illustrated in the 'compoti' of Plantagenet sheriffs in 1335–7 (*CDS,* iii, pp. 327–41) undoubtedly caused a shortage of produce and dearth if not famine.

65. *CDS,* iii, p. 361, no. 1323.

66. *Ibid,* nos. 1412, 1390.

67. *Chron. Wyntoun,* vi, 195.

68. Capture and ransom was an occupational hazard. For an interesting record of how two English squires of the early fifteenth century viewed the prospect of falling prisoner see C.T. Allmand, *Society and War* (Edinburgh, 1973), pp.32–4.

69. *RMS,* i, app i, 54, 55.

70. M. Brown, 'The Development of Scottish Border Lordship', *Historical research* LXXX. February 1997.

71. *CDS,* iii, p.336.

72. TNA, E101/331/23.

CHAPTER 4

1. In the sense of replacing the existing Scottish political community with Englishmen. David de Strathbogie appears to have adopted such a policy, removing free tenants who resisted the Balliol cause. *Scotichronicon,* viii, p.107.

2. Robert I's 'herschip' of Buchan is an example of just such a policy.

3. *CDS,* ii, 1323

4. Watson, *Hammer,* p.63.

5. *Rot Scot.,* i, p.31

6. *Documents Illustrative of Sir William Wallace, his Life and Times* (Maitland Club, 1839), no. xv.

7. G.W.S. Barrow, 'Lothian in the First War of Independence' *S.H.R.* LV (1976), pp.151–71.

8. Watson, *Hammer,* p.37.

9. Stevenson, *Documents* i, p.253–6.

10. M.Prestwich, *Edward I* (London, 1998).

11. *CDS,* v, p.175.

12. Stevenson, *Documents,* i, pp.240,260,274.

13. Stevenson, *Documents,* i, p.162. Edward I was not alone in expressing support for continuity of practice. In July 1347 Sir John de Strivelin, former Sheriff of Edinburgh, sought possession of the 'town' of Kellawe 'according to the laws and customs of Scotland' *C.Inqu. Misc.* ii, 2028.

14. *CDS,* ii, 1321.

15. *ER,* i, p.497.

16. *CDS,* ii, no. 1321.

17. The crossbow was an important weapon in the medieval arsenal, though in British history it tends to be overshadowed by the longbow, see Keen, M., *Medieval Warfare, a History* (Oxford, 2000), p.204.

18. Names are not a good guide to nationality, and nationality is not a good guide to allegiance and service. When Sir Robert Clifford undertook to serve at Lochmaben with 30 covered horses, he was not contractually required to exclude Scots, but his contract would be cancelled if his company should fall below thirty men-at-arms. TNA C47/22/2/51. Stevenson, *Documents,* ii, pp. 407–8.

19. *CDS.* ii, no. 1324.

20. *CDS*, ii, no. 1733

21. Barbour, *The Bruce*, p.367.

22. *CDS*, ii, no. 1324.

23. *CDS*, ii, no. 1324. Scottish lords in Edward's peace could expect his support as well, Sir John de St. John was specifically ordered no to interfere with the Earl of Dunbar's treatment of any of his tenants adhering to the Scots. TNA C47/22/3/24.

24. *CDS*, ii, no. 1324.

25. *Ibid.*, no. 1457.

26. *CDS*, ii, no. 1132.

27. *CDS*, v, no. 305.

28. *CDS*, ii, no. 159.

29. *CDS*, iii, pp. 408–11.

30. Ayton, *Knights*, p.89 *n.* 31.

31. The discrepancy is equivalent to 1,552 paid days.

32. Naturally this is a 'basic' rate of pay. In TNA, E101/12/28 the crossbowmen of Linlithgow garrison appear to have consisted of two groups, one of twenty and one of nineteen. Two of the names are marked 'officiarii', indicating an administrative or leadership role within each group and a better rate of pay accordingly. This is also clear evidence of a system of articulation.

33. *CDS*, ii, p.289.

34. Ayton, *Knights*, p.102

35. *CDS*, ii, no. 1446.

36. T. Herbert & G.E. Jones, *Edward I and Wales* (Cardiff, 1988) p.73–82.

37. *CDS*, ii, no. 1324.

38. Barrow, *Neighbours*, Chapter 11, 'Popular Courts' p.219. Professor Barrow has also pointed out the strong likelihood of 'a broad identity between English and Scottish law' *The Anglo-Norman Era in Scottish History* (Oxford, 1980), p.119. This does not imply a universal adoption of English legal practice nor a rejection of existing processes and procedures. Professor MacQueen has drawn attention to a 'blending of older customs with newer rules' thus avoiding the 'cleavage of native and Anglo-French laws characteristic of later medieval Ireland and Wales'. R. Oram (ed.) *The Reign of Alexander II* (Brill, 2005), p.228.

39. Sergeanties seem to have been something of an anachronism by the close of the thirteenth century;. References are few and several of them relate to the same office, the sergeanty of Linlithgow. Of those references, two relate to the failure of the heir of the late sergeant to claim the position. Sergeanty stems from a military and law and order role in the community; a sergeant being a heavy cavalry man, though not a knight, in twelfth or thirteenth century Lothian and an officer of the crown in thirteenth century Galloway, from whose depredations, particularly an exaction called 'surdit de sergeant', the locals sought relief from Alexander III; Duncan, *Scotland*, pp.531–2.

40. *CDS*, ii, no. 1321.

41. *CDS*, ii, p.317.

42. TNA, E101/68/1/20. Indenture for service of Sir Archibald Livingstone.

43. *CDS*, v, no. 220; G.O. Sayles 'The Guardians of Scotland and a Parliament at Rutherglen in 1300' *SHR*, xxiv, pp.245–50.

44. *CDS*, ii, no. 245.

45. Barrow, *Bruce* p.194.

46. G.W.S.Barrow, 'Lothian in the First War of Independence' *SHR* LV, 1976, pp.151–71.

47. Barbour, *The Bruce*, pp.136–8.

48. Watson, *Hammer*, p.186

49. TNA,C47/22/10 /11
50. *CDS*, ii, p.194–211.
51. *CDS*, iii, p.329.
52. Stevenson, *Documents*, i, p.240.
53. *RRS*, vi, p.367.
54. *CDS*, iii, pp.315, 329.
55. Nicholson, *Edward III*, p.100.
56. *Rot. Scot.*, i, p.260.
57. *Rot Scot.*, i, p.261.
58. TNA, E39/7.
59. *Chron. Fordun*, i, p.357
60. Nicholson, *Edward III*, p.191.
61. *Ibid*, p.205.
62. *Scalacronica* (Maxwell), p. 99.
63. *Ibid*, p.100.
64. *Chron. Lanercost*, p.282.
65. Nicholson, *Edward III*, p.213.
66. *Scotichronicon*, viii, p.113–5.
67. *Ibid*.
68. *CDS*, iii, no. 1186.
69. *Ibid*.
70. *CDS*, iii, no. 1176.
71. *Ibid*, p.329.
72. *RRS*, v, p.367.
73. *CDS*, iii, p.360.
74. *CDS*, iii, pp. 327-9, 379–82.
75. *CDS*, iii, pp. 379-82.
76. TNA, E101/22/10/53.
77. *CDS*, iii, pp. 383-9.
78. *Scalacronica* (Maxwell), p.102.
79. D. Rollason & M.Prestwich *The Battle of Neville's Cross* (Stamford, 1998), p.34.
80. *CDS*, iii, no. 1383.
81. TNA, E101/32/1.
82. *CDS*, iii, no. 1323.
83. Blackness was still an important supply point in the period immediately following the Strathord armistice. Edward I called for food supplies to be sent there with all possible haste at the end of March 1304. TNA, C49/22/9/109.
84. In 1300 the garrison of Dirleton was supplied with stockfish, salt, oats and beans, TNA, E101/531/7.
85. The quantities of foodstuffs involved were staggering. See for example Stevenson, *Documents,* ii, p.347, TNA, C47/2/22/45. TNA, C47/22/2/46. Stevenson, *Documents,* ii, p.346 shows an interesting assortment of the incidental stores that a garrison might require at a given point in addition to the grain, flour, malt, meat, beans, fish, wine and hay that were required every week of the year. Clearly, since this document is a receipt, not a requisition, it was possible to procure a wide variety of stores without too much difficulty. In addition the garrisons had to be provided with considerable quantities of arms and thousands of arrows and quarrels. TNA, C47/2/22/57. Stevenson, *Documents,* ii, p.438.
86. *CDS*, iii, p.327.
87. See for example TNA, E101/7/9 and E101/1/17, mostly consisting of correspondence relating to stores for the garrison of Edinburgh under Sir John de

Kingston. Not all of the requisitions are entirely clear – two documents refer simply to 'frumentum' (grain).

88. TNA, SC35/3. The requirements of garrisons were not always adequately fulfilled. When, in 1315, the logistic demand was less heavy due to the fall of Edinburgh, Linlithgow, Jedburgh, Selkirk and Roxburgh, Sir John Weston's force at Berwick was still evidently very short of provisions.

89. *CDS*, v, no. 305.

90. *Ibid*.

91. TNA, E101/531/7.

92. TNA, E39/100/138.

93. TNA, C47/22/2/5, Stevenson, *Documents*, ii, p.79.

94. *CDS*, v, no. 213.

95. *Scotichronicon*, vii, p.135

96. *CDS*, iii, no. 210; *CDS*, iv, p.462; *CDS*, v, nos. 453, 492.

97. TNA, E101/531/7.

98. Or, in the case of Alexander Seton, planned to do so, but chose to defect to the Bruce party

CHAPTER 5

1. G.W.S. Barrow 'The Army of Alexander III's Scotland', Reid, *Alexander III*, p.133; Duncan, *Scotland*, pp.380-81.

2. *RMS*, i, no. 3.

3. *RRS*, v, p. 367.

4. *RMS*, i, no, 6.

5. *RMS*, i, no. 14.

6. *RMS*, i, app. i, no. 14; *RRS*, v, pp.465–6.

7. *CDS*, ii, no. 832.

8. Stevenson, *Documents*, ii, p.140.

9. *Ibid.*, p,166.

10. There is no record of an attempt to demand common army service in Lothian.

11. *Rot Scot.*, i, p.44; *CDS*, ii, nos. 889, 892, 940, 942.

12. Stevenson, *Documents*, i, p.470.

13. *Rot Scot.*, i, p.292.

14. Watson, *Hammer*, pp. 65–66.

15. G.W.S.Barrow 'The Army of Alexander III's Scotland' in Reid, *Alexander III*, p.135.

16. Duncan, *Scotland*, p.383.

17. *RMS*, i, app. i, no. 55.

18. *ER*, i, p.112.

19. *CDS*, iii, p.329.

20. *ER*, i, p. 45. The Castleguard due from Berwickshire amounted to £75 6s 8d for 1288.

21. *Ibid.*, p.112.

22. *Ibid.*, i, p.205.

23. *Ibid.*, i. p.582

24. *Ibid*.

25. *RRS*, v, p.627.

26. *ER, i*, p.205.

27. *Ibid.*, p.283.

28. Duncan, *Scotland*, p.383–6.

29. *RMS*, i, app. i, no. 55.

30. *Ibid*, '… if war or emergency should arise through which they have to do their ward in our said castle, and they remain there for forty days, they are to be quit for that year of the said 20s…[if] an emergency occurs, they are to enter our said castle to defend it or pass to the army should need arise.' Translation from Donaldson, *Documents*, p. 54.

31. *The Chamberlain Rolls*, i, p.459

32. Beyond noting the prohibition of football, golf and other games in favour of archery, training has received little attention from historians. C.T. Allmand *Society at War. The Experience of France and England During the Hundred Years War* pp. 97–100, notes only two pieces of evidence relating to training, both of which allude to the desirability of military training rather than the practice.

33. *Scotichronicon*, vii, p. 142–3. Alan Boyd and John Stirling are described as 'rectores architenencium'. The term 'architenencium' may indicate crossbow archers. One of the advantages of the crossbow, particularly in siege situations, was that it could be held in a 'loaded' condition and was therefore particularly useful against fleeting targets of opportunity and more practical for a 'sniping' role than a longbow.

34. G.W.S. Barrow, 'The Army of Alexander III's Scotland' Reid, *Alexander III*, p.135; Nicholson, *Middle Ages*, p.49.

35. *RRS*, v, p.679.

36. Duncan, *Scotland*. pp. 395–6.

37. *CDS*, ii, no. 1321.

38. *Ibid*., no. 1324.

39. *CDS*, ii, no. 1324. The shortfall form this retinue alone represents nearly 1/10th of the required complement.

40. Duncan, *Scotland*, p.385.

41. *RRS*, v, p.679.

42. *RRS*, vi, p. 63.

43. Duncan, *Scotland*, p.384.

44. *CDS*, iii, p.368.

45. *CDS*, ii, no. 853.

46. *CDS*, iii, no. 1115.

47. *Ibid*., no. 1121. Patrick also received some direct financial support . In 1334 he issued a receipt for £100 of £600 granted by Edward III. TNA, E42/269

48. Nicholson, *Middle Ages*, p.168.

49. M. Penman 'The Kingship of David II' Ph.D. thesis (St. Andrews, 1988) p.140.

50. Ayton, *Knights*, pp.108–120.

51. *Scotichronicon*, vii, p.117. Bower's term is 'electi' – picked men.

52. G.W.S. Barrow 'Northern English Society' in Barrow, *Neighbours*.

53. *RRS*, vi, p.63.

54. *Ibid*., pp.63–4.

55. There was always the possibility of being taken prisoner oneself. Sir Andrew Harcla struggled to raise the money needed for his ransom in the autumn of 1316, TNA, C47/22/10/27. A hostage need not be a prisoner of war in the sense of having been captured on the battlefield. Hostages were given as security for the ransoms of communities. Robert Goldwyn served as a hostage for Bamburgh in 1316. *CIPM*, viii, no. 141.

56. *CDS*, iii, no. 245.

57. Barrow, *Neighbours*, p.156.

58. *CDS*, ii, no. 245.

59. *Ibid*., no. 853.

60. *Ibid*., no. 832.

61. See chapter 2, Rights and Responsibilities.
62. *CDS*, iii, p.327.
63. Stevenson, *Documents*, ii, p.538.
64. 'Dead ground' - areas obscured from view by the nature of the terrain.
65. Most famously Mao Zedong, *The Art of War* (El Paso Norte, 2005) and Che Guevara. *Guerrilla Warfare* (University of Nebraska, 1998).This is also the general thrust of General Wesley Clark's *Winning Modern Wars* (New York, 2003), Chapter 2, 'Decisive Operations'.
66. Nicholson, *Edward III*, pp.245–52.
67. Chiefly by appending their seals to the Ragman Roll, *CDS*, ii, no. 823, but a considerable number had already committed themselves to Edward I throughout the spring and summer of 1296.
68. Barrow, *Neighbours*, p.155–6.
69. *CDS*, ii, no. 832.
70. *Ibid.*, no. 853.
71. Such as Malise Earl of Strathearn or Patrick, Earl of Dunbar.
72. Nicholson, *Edward III*, p.93n.
73. *CDS*, iii, no. 853.
74. NAS, GD 24/5
75. TNA, E 101/7/5.
76. *CDS*, ii, no. 1489.
77. *Scalacronica* (Maxwell), p.14.
78. Nicholson, *Edward III*, pp. 77–8. Henry Beaumont, David de Strathbogie and Gilbert d' Umfraville all raised money in the summer of 1332 by granting or leasing their English estates. Sir Thomas Wake granted a Norfolk property to Sir Thomas Roscelyn in liferent. Roscelyn took an active part in Edward III's Scottish campaign, serving as sheriff of Edinburgh in the autumn of 1335. *CDS*, iii, no. 1186.
79. Nicholson, *Edward III*, p.172; *Scotichronicon*, vii, p.107.
80. *CDS*, ii, no. 258.
81. *CDS*, iii, pp. 341, 346.
82. His property of Stichill, Roxburgh for example.
83. Nicholson, *Edward III*, pp.229–30.
84. *Chron. Fordun*, i, p.360.
85. *Chron. Fordun*, i, pp.351-3, 355, 357.
86. Scotichronicon, vii, 107, 109, 113, 115,125, 135, 139.
87. *CDS*, iii, no. 1121.This grant was clearly a mark of favour, and a lever to bind Patrick to Edward III. Edward might have granted these properties to another person, but that would have undermined Patrick's authority within the earldom.
88. Nicholson, *Edward III*, pp.126–7
89. *Scalacronica* (Maxwell), p.102
90. *Ibid* pp. 190–91.
91. *Rot. Scot.* i, pp.261–3.
92. Barrow, *Neighbours*, pp. 155–6.
93. Several authors have pointed out similarities in the role of the armoured cavalryman and the Main Battle Tank, however the differences substantially outweigh those similarities. J.F.C. Fuller's observations on this topic are compromised by his concentration on general engagements to the exclusion of a wider operational view of medieval campaigning. *Armaments and History* (London, 1946) p.23. The changing application of the tank since WW2 has made the analogy even less appropriate.
94. G.W.S.Barrow 'The Army of Alexander III's Scotland' in Reid, *Alexander III* p.136.
95. *CDS*, iii, p.413.

96. *Ibid.*, pp.413–22.

97. *SHS Miscellany,* xi, C.J. Neville 'A Plea Roll of Edward I's Army in Scotland' p.111.

98. The smaller the links, the better the protection afforded to the wearer, see G.C.Stone *Glossary of the Construction and Decoration of Arms and Armour in all Countries and in all Times* (NewYork, 1961) pp.424–9.

99. *Ibid.*

100. *Ibid.*

101. Numerous Flemish and French ships were seized by the English leading to diplomatic interventions to procure their release, TNA, SC33/37, SC33/184.

102. Edward did not limit such pleas to his own subjects; on 27 October 1309 he asked Robert count of Artois to prevent Scottish and 'Estland' merchants from being received in his territories. Edward III faced the same difficulties. *CIPM,* ii, nos. 397, 940, 1577.

103. Duncan, *Scotland,* p.489.

104. A sword purchased at Perth was the subject of a court case in 1296. *SHS miscellany,* xi, C. Neville 'A Plea Roll of Edward I's Army in Scotland' p.87.

105. *CDS,* ii, no. 1321.

106. Ayton *Knights,* p.229.

107. C. Smith, 'Cats, Dogs and Horses' in *Proc. Soc. Antiq. Scot.* 128 (1998), p.870–72.

108. E101/7/5.

109. Matthew Paris noted that in 1244 the men-at-arms (armed men) of Alexander II's army were mounted 'upon horses sufficiently good, although not Spanish or Italian'. Anderson, A. *Scottish Annals from English Chronicles* (Stamford, 1991), p.354.

110. Sir Richard Siward, *CDS,* ii, no. 1011.

111. Ayton *Knights,* pp. 23–24.

112. See A. King 'A Helm with a Crest of Gold' in (ed.), N. Saul, *Fourteenth Century England.* (Woodbridge, 2000) also A. MacDonald 'Profit, Politics and Personality: War and the Later Medieval Scottish Nobility' in (edd) D. Ditchburn T. Brotherstone *Freedom and Authority* (East Linton, 2000) pp.121, 127.

113. *Schwerpunkt;* not necessarily the largest or most intense sector of the battlefield, but the most crucial location, the focus of the engagement.

114. Scots were certainly prepared to spend money on armour specifically designed for the lists rather than the battlefield. See *The Bannatyne Miscellany* ii, p.106. The will of William Douglas stipulated the recipient of his 'bacinet, hauberk, gauntlets and other armours for tournaments' (hastiludio).

115. *Scotichronicon,* vii p.293–7.

116. *CDS,* ii, no. 1978.

117. M. Prestwich *Armies and Warfare in the Middle Ages. The English Experience.* (New Haven, 1996) p.126.

118. Ayton *Knights,* pp.15–17.

119. M. Powicke *England in the Thirteenth Century* (Oxford 1953), p. 576.

120. Barrow, *Bruce,* First Edition (London, 1965), p.23. This statement does not appear in the Third Edition (Edinburgh, 1988), though the rationale that supports the statement does – 'most of the more fertile land was held by knight service and organised into baronies and knights' fees.' Barrow, *Bruce,* p.16.

121. *Scalacronica* (Maxwell), p.23.

122. *Scalacronica* (Maxwell), p.82. It is of course possible that the term 'banneret' was not used in Scotland at this period and that Grey simply used the appropriate English term, nonetheless, it is clear that the function and status of the senior knight was similar enough in both countries for Grey to use the word to describe Scots.

123. *Scotichronicon,* vii, pp.113, 115; *Chron. Fordun,* i, pp. 350–51; *Scalacronica* (Maxwell), p. 100

124. Nicholson, *Edward III*, p.131.
125. Barbour, *The Bruce,* pp.204–6.
126. *Chron. Fordun* i, p.362.
127. The strength of medieval armies is a thorny issue, either in terms of sheer numbers or of relative strengths. Estimates of the Scottish and English armies at Bannockburn stem, largely, from questionable interpretations of numbers offered in contemporary accounts – essentially dividing Barbour's figure of 100,000 English by four to achieve a 'credible' figure of 25,000 and his estimate of 30,000 Scots by the same factor to achieve a 'credible' figure of 7,500. Barbour's figures were not intended to be taken literally in the first place, therefore an extrapolation based on his estimates is of questionable value. Similarly, it is extremely unlikely that the Scottish force engaged at Dupplin Muir comprised 20,000 men – see. Rogers, *Wars,* p.270 – and even more so bearing in mind that another Scottish force was in the vicinity. In the seventeenth century the Scottish government endeavoured to raise an army of about 20,000 for service in England, but could not keep it up to strength. E. Furgol *Regimental History of the Covenanting Armies* (Edinburgh, 1990) pp.5–6.
128. *RRS,* v, p.414.
129. *Ibid* p.54.
130. The lance was the primary offensive arm of cavalry, as the spear or polearm was for infantry. S. Morillo's suggestion that the sword was 'the real killing weapon' in 'The age of Cavalry Revisited' in *The Circle of War in the Middle Ages* (Woodbridge, 1999) p.55 is not supported by contemporary descriptions of battles. By the early fourteenth century armour had reached a stage of development that made it very difficult to penetrate with a sword. Most of the individual combats recorded in contemporary accounts concern the lance or spear.
131. *CDS,* ii, no. 1413
132. Duncan, *Scotland,* p.377.
133. Duncan, *Scotland,* p.515.
134. Barrow, *Neighbours,* p.192.
135. *Melrose Liber,* no. 351.
136. Duncan, *Scotland.* p.391.
137. TNA, C47/22/2/18; Stevenson, *Documents,* ii, p.178.
138. The Earl of Dunbar and Sir William Douglas of Lothian among others.
139. *RRS,* v, p.261.
140. *Scotichronicon* vii, p.141
141. Appointment to such positions was not necessarily popular. In November 1336 Humphrey de Bohun requested that a 'bachelor of his company' who had been selected as an infantry officer should be excused duty so that he could continue to serve in de Bohun's retinue. TNA, SC1/39/19.

CONCLUSIONS

1. RRS, v, pp.41–44
2. Barrow, Bruce pp. 325–8, including the tenants of Henry Pinkney at Ballencreiff, Michael Wemyss, William Somerville, Alexander Fraser, Alexander Lindsay, James Lindsay, John Fenton and probably William, his father, who had been a Ragman Roll homager in 1296 CDS, ii, pp.194–211, but whose property is not listed. It is more than likely that other men forfeited at the same time also had interests in Lothian, as well as the areas with which they are associated in this document since the instrument in question is essentially a list of properties sought by Edward I's followers

rather that a catalogue of the properties held by the forfeited men.

3. CDS, iii, no. 245, comprising Sir Robert Keith, Sir Thomas de Hay, Peter de Pontekin, Edmund de Ramsay, Godfrey Broun, Edward de Fressingleye and Aymer de Hauden.

4. In 1296 several Lothian landholders held property in England and no doubt some people eventually gave up on their Scottish inheritances and emigrated to England; however, the majority seem to have held no property whatsoever in England, and the properties of those who did were not extensive enough to make the men in question significant members of the political community in England. None of the Lothian men selected for this book – and virtually no other Scots – appear in Moor's Knights of Edward I (London, 1900).

5. C. MacNamee, The Wars of the Bruces (East Linton, 1997), p.130; CDS, iii, no. 337.

6. There is no evidence to indicate that the Plantagenet administrations made any effort whatsoever to call on the common army service of Lothian men, either in 1296–1314 or 1333–41.

7. Laurence de Abernethy apparently led a company of eighty men-at-arms to serve Edward II at Bannockburn. As Barbour puts it 'he was inglis man yheit then' (He was still English then) The Bruce, p.509.

8. CDS, iii, pp. 327–41.

9. CDS, ii, nos. 832, 853.

10. Chron. Fordun i, p.360. Bower refers to this force as 'picked men from Lothian and the borders.' Scotichronicon, vii, p.117.

11. CDS, iii, pp. 347–59.

12. Sir Alexander Cragy, Roger Dalmahoy, John Duncan and Richard Naper all served in Edinburgh garrisons.

13. CDS, iii, no. 1926.

14. CDS, v, no. 492.

15. Chron. Lanercost p.276 lists these as Dumbarton, Kildrummy, Urquhart, Loch Leven and Loch Doon.

16. Chron. Lanercost, p.278.

17. CDS, iii, pp. 327–41.

18. B. Webster 'Scotland without a King' in A. Grant and K. Stringer (edd), Medieval Scotland. Crown, Lordship and Community (Edinburgh, 1993), p.233.

19. RRS, v, p.459.

20. See the indenture between Sir Aymer de Valence and Sir Thomas de Berkely, July 1298, for an example of the sort of terms and conditions which were applied to military service indentures. TNA E101/68/1/1.

21. Duplication of armorial devices was an inevitable consequence of the lack of a universal register which could prevent disputes. See A. Ayton 'Knights, Esquires and Military Service: The Evidence of the Armorial Cases before the Court of Chivalry', A. Ayton & J. Price (edd), The Medieval Military Revolution (London, 1995), pp.84–6.

22. Dr. Ayton has drawn attention to the difficulties of recruiting men-at-arms for service on the continent in 1338–40. Not only was it necessary to employ large numbers of foreign mercenaries, but English men-at-arms were offered double wages. 'English Armies in the Fourteenth Century' in Rogers, Wars, p.310.

23. CDS, iii, nos. 71, 230.

24. Ibid., no. 1209; TNA, E101/22/10/53. Interestingly both Sir Robert Hastang and Sir John de Strivelin were both granted lands in Bathgate and Ratho. William the Lion granted lands in Bathgate and Ratho to the extent of one hundred librates infeft with twenty knights and Alexander III granted lands there to his Queen, Margaret;

Duncan, Scotland, pp.377, 592.

25. RRS, v, pp. 424,425,450,451,453,459,515 and 680 are all grants of land or rights in Lothian to Sir Alexander. He also received two royal confirmations of grants from other nobles – John de Vaus and Patrick Earl of Dunbar (RRS, v, p. 670) – and a grant of land in the burgh of Aberdeen (RRS v, p.519)

26. Ibid., p. 367; RMS, i, nos. 55,62,68,89, all of which refer to lands in Lothian except no. 89 which refers to a property at Larbert.

27. CDS, ii, no. 823.

28. Dr. Ayton has drawn attention to the fluctuating membership of the followings of individual leaders in English armies, suggesting that the close adherents of the leader provided 'a nucleus around which the less stable, more transitory elements in a magnate's war comitiva could be assembled.' 'English Armies in the Fourteenth Century' in Rogers, *Wars*, p.312.

29. CDS, ii, no. 853.

30. CDS, iii, no. 1137.

31. CDS, ii, no. 1184.

32. Sir Alexander remained in Edward III's service after the fall of Edinburgh Castle in 1341, receiving an annuity of £40 as compensation for his lost lands from May 1342 CDS, iii, no. 1388.

33. *Rot. Scot.* i p.381.

34. CDS, ii, no. 857; TNA, C47/22/10/45.

35. *Scotichronicon*, vii, p.117.

36. *Scotichronicon*, vii, p. 153.

37. Ibid., p.139.

38. Nicholson, *Middle Ages*, p.130.

39. The Moubray family, forfeited in the wake of the De Soulis conspiracy, is a case in point. The male members of the Moubray family, and therefore the name, disappeared from Lothian, but Philippa, daughter of John, was granted – with her husband, Bartholomew de Loen – the barony of Barnbougle in May 1342. RRS, vi, pp.136–7.

40. *Scotichronicon*, vii, p.151.

41. CDS, iii, nos. 1404, 1412.

ABBREVIATIONS

The standard abbreviations listed in the October 1963 supplement to the Scottish Historical Review have been used in the footnotes. The following list details a small number of additions to the standard usage.

Ayton, *Knights*
Ayton, A., *Knights and Warhorses* (Woodbridge, 1994).Barbour, *The Bruce.*
The Bruce, J. Barbour (ed.) A.A.M. Duncan (Edinburgh, 1997).
Barron, *Scottish War.*
E.M. Barron, *The Scottish War of Independence* (Inverness, 1934).
Barrow, *Bruce*
G.W.S. Barrow, *Robert the Bruce and the Community of the Realm of Scotland* (Edinburgh, 1988).
Barrow, *Neighbours.*
G.W.S. Barrow, *Scotland and its Neighbours in the Middle Ages* (London, 1982).
CIPM
Calendar of Inquisitions Post Mortem (London 1900-1912).
Duncan, *Scotland*
A.A.M. Duncan *Scotland. The Making of the Kingdom* (Edinburgh, 1975).
Donaldson, *Documents*
G. Donaldson *Scottish Historical Documents* (Edinburgh, 1974).
Nicholson, *Edward III*
R. Nicholson *Edward III and the Scots. The Formative Years of a Military Career, 1327 to 1335.* (Oxford, 1965).
Nicholson, *Middle Ages*
R. Nicholson *Scotland. The Later Middle Ages* (Edinburgh, 1974).
MacQueen, *Common Law*
H. MacQueen *Common Law and Feudal Society in Medieval Scotland* (Edinburgh, 1993).
Penman, *David II*
M. Penman, *David II* (East Linton, 2004).
Reid, *Alexander III.*
N. Reid (ed.), *Scotland in the Reign of Alexander III* (Edinburgh 1990).
Rogers, *Wars*

Colonel C. Rogers (ed), *The Wars of Edward III. Sources and Interpretations* (Woodbridge, 1999).

Scotichronicon

Scotichronicon of Walter Bower, vols. i–ix, (ed). D.E.R. Watt (Aberdeen, 1996).

Stringer, *Nobility Essays*

Essays on the Nobility of medieval Scotland, ed. K. Stringer (Edinburgh, 1985).

Watson, *Hammer*

F. Watson *Under the Hammer. Edward I and Scotland, 1286-1307* (East Linton 1998).

Watt, *Fasti*

D.E.R. Watt *Fasti Ecclesiae Scoticanae Medii Aevi ad annum 1638* (Edinburgh, 1969).

BIBLIOGRAPHY

PRIMARY SOURCE MATERIAL

THE NATIONAL ARCHIVES, KEW:

E/39/2/21	C47/22/2/33
E101/7/5	C143/27/10
E101/7/1	SC13/A57
E101/531/7	SC8/46/2255
E101/531/8	SC13/A102
E39/99/19	SC13/S746
E39/99/18	C47/22/3/24
E101/7/24	C47/22/4/2
E/39/15/3	C47/22/5/57
E101/7/9	C47/22/9/59
E101/7/17	E101/11/9
E101/7/28	E101/12/38
E101/10/5	E101/428/20
E101/11/14	E135/10/1
E101/12/11	E101/16/11
E101/531/13	E39/3/47
E101/13/37	E42/269
E101/17/29	C47/22/2/12
E101/19/24	C47/22/10/53
E101/22/20	E39/100/138
E101/23/1	E39/102/19
E101/68/1/2	C47/3/32/25
E101/68/1/3	C47/22/9/109
E101/331/5	C47/22/6/18
E101/331/23	SC13/S150
E39/102/16	SC13/A88
E101/19/21	SC1/39/19

236

SC1/39/154	SC35/3
SC1/42/202	C47/22/9/65
SC8/9/432	E101/12/12
SC32/67	E101/11/14

NATIONAL ARCHIVES OF SCOTLAND:

The RH5 series consists of documents transferred to the Scottish Records Office form the Public Records Office in London, most of which also have TNA code references. RH6 is a collection of charters in the NAS collection. The GD series comprises family collections gifted to, or deposited with, the National Archives of Scotland.

RH5, 39	C47/22/6(43)	RH6, 98
RH5, 20	C47/22/5(1)	RH6, 99
RH5, 22	C47/22/5(3)	RH6, 100
RH5, 31	C47/22/5(16)	RH6, 104
RH5, 32	C47/22/5(15)	RH6, 105
RH5, 41	C47/22/9(2)	RH6, 106
RH5, 53	C47/22/12(5)	RH6, 107
RH5, 56	E93/94/5(1)	RH6, 112
RH5, 66	E39/94/5(11)	RH6, 118
RH5, 86	E39/94/8(1)	RH6, 119
RH5, 90	E39/84/8(5)	RH6, 120
RH5, 98	E39/94/8(14)	GD 12,
RH5, 114	E99/100/146(2)	GD 18
RH5, 115	E39/100/147(1)	GD 26
RH5, 120	E39/100/150(1)	CD 28
RH5, 205	E39/100/188(8)	GD.40
RH5, 220	E39/100/189/5	GD 82
RH5, 227		GD 84
RH5, 230		GD 86
RH6, 67		GD 122
RH6, 68		GD 164
RH6, 70		GD 430
RH6, 80		RH5, 54
RH6, 83		

PRINTED PRIMARY SOURCE MATERIAL

Acts of the Parliaments of Scotland, C. Innes & T. Thomson (London, 1844).
Anglo-Scottish Relations, 1174-1328, Some Selected Documents. E.L.G. Stones (London, 1965).
Calendar of Chancery Rolls Miscellaneous (London, 1916).
Calendar of Close Rolls, HMSO (London, 1892-1907).
Calendar of Documents Relating to Scotland, vol i-iv. J. Bain. (Edinburgh, 1881-88).
Calendar of Documents Relating to Scotland, vol. v. G. Simpson and J. Galbraith. (Edinburgh, 1988).
Calendar of Inquisitions (Miscellaneous) (London, 1916).
Calendar of Inquisitions Post Mortem (London, 1908-10).
Carte Monialum de Northberwic, Bannatyne Club (Edinburgh, 1847).
Chronica Major, ed. H. Luard (London, 1872).
Chronicle of Holyrood, ed. O. Anderson. SHS (Edinburgh, 1938).

Chronicles (of Jean Froissart), ed. G. Brereton. (London, 1968).

Chronicles of the Reigns of Edward I and Edward II, ed. W. Stubbs (London, 1882).

Chronicon de Lanercost, Bannatyne Club. (Edinburgh, 1839).

Chronique de Jean Le Bel, ed. J. Viard & E. Deprez. Societe de l'Histoire de France (Paris, 1904).

Documents and Records Illustrating the History of Scotland, Sir F. Palgrave. (London, 1837).

Documents Illustrative of the History of Scotland, J. Stevenson. (Edinburgh, 1870).

Early Sources of Scottish History, A.O. Anderson (Stamford, 1990).

Edward I and the Throne of Scotland, 1290-96, E.L.G. Stones and G. Simpson. (Oxford, 1978).

Exchequer Rolls of Scotland, vol i, ed. J. Stuart and G. Burnett. (Edinburgh, 1876).

Foedera, Conventiones, Litterae et Cuiuscunque Generis Acta Publica, ed. T. Rymer (London, 1816-69).

Gascon Rolls, 1307-17, ed. Y. Renouard (London, 1962).

Knighton's Chronicle, 1337-1396, ed. G. Martin (Oxford, 1995).

Liber Cartarum Prioratus Sancti Andree in Scotia, Bannatyne Club (Edinburgh, 1841).

Liber de Sancte Marie de Calchou, Bannatyne Club. (Edinburgh, 1846).

Liber Sancte Marie de Melros, Bannatyne Club. (Edinburgh, 1887).

Liner Sancte Thomas de Aberrbrothoc, Bannatyne Club (Edinburgh, 1848-56).

Memoranda Rolls 1326-1327 (London, 1968)

Orygenale Cronykil of Scotland, Andrew Wyntoun, ed. D. Laing (Edinburgh, 1872-9).

Parliamentary Writs and Writs of Military Summons, ed. F. Palgrave (London, 1827-33).

Records of the Wardrobe and Household, ed. F. and C. Beyerley (London, 1985).

Regesta Regum Scottorum, vol. vi, ed. B. Webster (Edinburgh, 1982).

Regesta Regum Scottorum, vol. v, ed. A.A.M. Duncan (Edinburgh, 1988).

Registrum de Sancte Marie de Neubotle, ed. C. Innes (Edinburgh, 1849).

Registrum Honoris de Morton, Bannatyne Club (Edinburgh, 1853).

Registrum Monasterii de Cambuskenneth, ed. W. Fraser, Grampian Club (1872).

Rotuli Scotiae, J. MacPherson, Record Commission (London, 1814-19).

Scalacronica of Sir Thomas Grey (Ed.& Trans) Sir H. Maxwell (Edinburgh, 1907).

Scotichronicon of Walter Bower, ed. D.E.R. Watt (Aberdeen, 1991).

Scotland in 1298: Documents relating to the campaign of Edward I in that year and especially to the battle of Falkirk H. Gough (Paisley, 1888).

Scottish Historical Documents, G. Donaldson (Edinburgh, 1974).

Source book of Scottish History, edd. W. Croft Dickinson, G. Donaldson and I. Milne (Edinburgh, 1952).

The Bannatyne Miscellany (Edinburgh 1836).

The Book of Fayttes of Armes and of Chivalry, ed. A. Byles (Oxford 1932)

The Bruce, J. Barbour, ed. A.A.M. Duncan Canongate (Edinburgh, 1997).

The Charters of David II, ed. G.W.S. Barrow (Woodbridge, 1999).

The Charters of Holyrood, Bannatyne Club (Edinburgh, 1840).

The Chartulary of Newbattle, Bannatyne Club (Edinburgh, 1849).

The Chartulary of Coldstream, ed. C. Rogers. (London, 1879).

The Chronicle of Lanercost, (Trans.) H. Maxwell (Glasgow, 1913).

The Chronicle of Walter of Guisborough, ed. J. Rothwell (Camden, 1957).

The Laing Charters, ed. J. Anderson (Edinburgh, 1899).

The Original Chronicle of Andrew of Wyntoun, ed. J. Amours (Edinburgh, 1903-14).

The Register of the Great Seal of Scotland, ed. J. Thomson (Edinburgh, 1984).

The Roll of Caerlaverock, ed. T. Wright (London, 1864).

Treaty Rolls, ed. P. Chaplais (London, 1955)

The Scottish King's Household, ed. M. Bateson, (Edinburgh, 1904).

Vita Edwardi Secundi, ed. N. Denholm-Young (London, 1957).

SECONDARY MATERIAL

Allmand, C., *Society at War. The Experience of England and France during the Hundred Years War* (Edinburgh, 1973).

Allmand, C., *Power, Culture and Religion in France* (Woodbridge, 1989).

Allmand, C., *The Hundred Years War* (Cambridge, 1998).

Armstrong, O., *Edward Bruce's Invasion of Ireland* (London, 1923).

Anderson, A., *Early Sources of Scottish History* (Stamford, 1990).

Anderson, A., *Scottish Annals from English Chronicles* (Stamford, 1991).

Ayton, A., *Knights and Warhorses* (Woodbridge, 1994).

Ayton, A. & Price, J., *The Medieval Military Revolution* (London, 1995).

Bain, J., *The Edwards in Scotland 1296-1377* (Edinburgh, 1901).

Balfour Paul, Sir John, *The Scots Peerage* (Edinburgh, 1904-14).

Barker, J., *The Tournament in England, 1100-1400* (Stroud, 1986).

Barrell, A., *Medieval Scotland* (Cambridge, 2000).

Barrne, J., *War in Medieval Society* (London, 1974).

Barron, E.M., *The Scottish War of Independence* (Inverness, 1934).

Barrow, G.W.S., *Feudal Britain* (London, 1956).

Barrow, G.W.S., *The Kingdom of the Scots* (London, 1973).

Barrow, G.W.S., *Robert the Bruce and the Community of the Realm of Scotland* (London, 1965)

Barrow, G.W.S., *Scotland and its Neighbours in the Middle Ages* (London, 1992).

Barrow, G.W.S., *Scotland and her Neighbours in the Later Middle Ages* (London, 1992).

Barrow, G.W.S., *The Anglo-Norman Era in Scottish History* (Oxford, 1980).

Beresford M., *The New Towns of the Middle Ages* (London, 1957).

Bingham, C., *The Life and Times of Edward II* (London, 1973).

Black, G., *The Surnames of Scotland* (Edinburgh, 1999).

Blair, C., *European Armour 1066–1700* (New York, 1972).

Boardman, S. & Ross, A. edd. *The Exercise of Power in Medieval Scotland* (Chippenham, 2003).

Bothwell, J., *The Age of Edward III* (Woodbridge, 2001).

Bradbury, J., *The Medieval Siege* (Woodbridge, 1992).

Brotherstone, T, & Ditchburn, D. edd. *Freedom and Authority* (East Lothian, 2000).

Broun, Finlay and Lynch edd. *Image and Identity* (Edinburgh, 1998).

Brown, C., *Robert the Bruce. A Life Chronicled* (Stroud, 2003).

Brown, C., *William Wallace* (Stroud, 2005).

Brown, M., *The Black Douglases* (East Linton, 1998).

Brown, M., *The Wars of Scotland 1214-1371* (East Linton, 2005).

Brown, R.A., Colvin, H.M. & Taylor, A.J. *The History of the King's Works* vol.i (London, 1963).

Burne, A., *The Crecy War* (London, 1956).

Burns, W., *The Scottish War of Independence* (Glasgow, 1874).

Bush, M., *Rich Noble, Poor Noble* (Manchester, 1988).

Clark, J. ed. *The Medieval Horse and its Equipment c.1150-1450* (Woodbridge, 2004).

Clausewitz, C., *On War* (Harmondsworth, 1968).

Contamine, P. (Trans) M. Jones *War in the Middle Ages* (Oxford, 1987).

Coss, P., *Lordship, Knighthood and Locality: A study in English Society* (Cambridge, 1991).

Coss, P., *The Knight in Medieval England* (Stroud, 1993).

Costain, T., *The Three Edwards* (New York, 1958).

Cruden, S., *The Scottish Castle* (Edinburgh, 1981).

Curry, A & Hughes, M. edd. *Arms, Armies and Fortifications in the Hundred Years War* (Woodbridge, 1994).

Davies, R., *The Medieval Warhorse* (London, 1989).

Davies, R., *Conquest, Co-existence and Change; Wales 1063-1415* (Oxford, 1987).

De Vries, K., *Infantry Warfare in the Early Fourteenth Century: Discipline, Tactics and Technology* (Woodbridge, 1996).

De Vries, K., *Medieval Military Technology* (Ontario, 1992).

Dickinson, J., *The Battle of Neville's Cross* (Durham, 1991).

Ditchburn, D., *Scotland and Europe* (East Linton, 2001).

Dixon, P., *Puir Labourers and Busy Husbandmen* (Edinburgh, 2003)

Dodghson, R.A., *Land and Society in Early Scotland* (Oxford, 1981).

Dowden, J., *The Medieval Church in Scotland* (Glasgow, 1910).

Duffy, S., *Robert the Bruce's Irish Wars* (Stroud, 2002).

Duncan A.A.M., *Scotland. The Making of the Kingdom* (Edinburgh, 1975).

Dunne, D. ed. *War and Society in Early Medieval Britain* (Liverpool, 2000).

Dupuy, R.& T., *Numbers Prediction and War* (Indianapolis, 1979)..

Dupuy, T., *Understanding Defeat* (New York, 1990).

Dyer, C., *Standards of Living in the Later Middle Age: Social Change in England c. 1200-1520* (Cambridge, 1989).

Easson, E., *Medieval Religious Houses in Scotland* (London, 1957).

Ewan, E., *Townlife in Fourteenth Century Scotland* (Edinburgh, 1990).

Fergusson. W., *Scotland's Relations with England. A Survey to 1701* (Edinburgh, 1977).

Fergusson, W., *The Identity of the Scottish Nation: An Historic Quest* (Edinburgh, 1998).

Fisher, A., *William Wallace* (Edinburgh, 1986).

Fowler, K., *The Age of Plantagenet and Valois* (London, 1968).

Fowler, K., *The Hundred years War* (London, 1971).

Frame, R., *The Political Development of the British Isles, 1100 – 1500.* (Oxford 1995).

Fryde, E., *Peasants and Landlords in Later Medieval England* (Stroud, 1986).

Fryde, N., *The Tyranny and Fall of Edward II, 1321-26* (Cambridge, 1979).

Gauldie, E., *The Scottish Miller* (Edinburgh, 1999).

Gilbert, J.M., *Hunting and Hunting Reserves in Medieval Scotland* (Edinburgh, 1979).

Gillingham, J & Holt, J. ed. *War and Government in the Middle Ages* (Woodbridge, 1984).

Girouard, M., *Life in the English Country House* (London, 1978).

Grant, A. & Stringer, K. (edd), *Medieval Scotland. Crown, Lordship and Community* (Edinburgh, 1993).

Grant, A., *Independence and Nationhood* (London, 1984).

Grant, I.F., *The Social and Economic Development of Scotland before 1603* (Edinburgh, 1930).

Gravett, C., *Medieval Siege Warfare* (Oxford, 1991).

Haines, R., *King Edward II. Edward of Caernarfon. His Life, His Reign and its Aftermath* (Montreal, 2003).

Hale, J. ed. *Europe in the Late Middle Ages* (London, 1965).

Hall, D., *Burgess, Merchant and Priest. Burgh life in the Scottish Medieval Town* (Edinburgh, 2002).

Hamilton, G., *Piers Gaveston, Earl of Cornwall, 1307-1312* (London, 1988).

Handel, M., *Masters of War. Classical Strategic Thought.* (London, 2004).

Hanawalt, B., *The Ties that Bound; Peasant Families in Medieval England* (Oxford, 1986).

Harding, A., *England in the Thirteenth Century* (Cambridge, 1993).

Hardy, R., *The Longbow, a Social and Military History* (London, 1992).

Harvey, J., *The Plantagenets* (London, 1959).

Herbert, T., and Jones, G.E. *Edward I and Wales* (Cardiff, 1988).

Hewitt, H., *The Black Prince's Expedition 1355-5* (Manchester 1958).

Hilton, R., *The English Peasantry in the Later Middle Ages* (Oxford, 1975).

Howard, M., *War in European History* (Oxford, 1976).

Jones, A., *The Art of War in Western Civilization* (Chicago, 1987).

Jones, M. ed. *Gentry and Lesser Nobility in Later Medieval England* (Gloucester, 1986).

Kaeuper, R., *Chivalry and Violence in Medieval Europe* (Oxford, 2001)

Kagay, D. & Villalon, L., *The Circle of War in the Middle Ages* (Woodbridge, 1999).

Keen, M., *Chivalry* (New Haven, 1984).

Keen, M., *England in the Later Middle Ages* (London, 1973)

Kosminsky, E., *Studies in the Agrarian History of England in the Thirteenth Century* (Oxford, 1956).

Ladurie, E.L., *Montaillou.Cathars and Catholics in a French village 1294-1324* (London, 1978).

Leyser, H., *Medieval Women. A Social History of England 450-1500* (London, 1995).

Lloyd, T., *The English Wool Trade in the Middle Ages* (Cambridge, 1977).

Lomas, R., *North-East England in the Middle Ages* (Edinburgh, 1992)

Lord, E., *The Knights Templar in Britain* (London, 2002).

Lucas, H., *The Low Countries and the Hundred Years War* (Michigan, 1929).

Lynch, M., Spearman, M., & Stell, G. (Eds) *The Scottish Medieval Town* (Edinburgh, 1988)

MacDonald, A., *Border Bloodshed* (East Linton, 2000).

MacDougall, N. ed. *Scotland and War* (Edinburgh, 1991).

MacDougall, N., *An Antidote to the English* (East Lothian, 2001).

MacFarlane, K.B., *The Nobility of Later Medieval England* (Oxford, 1973).

MacKay, J., *William Wallace, Braveheart* (Edinburgh, 1995).

MacQuarrie, A., *Scotland and the Crusades* (Edinburgh, 1997).

MacQueen, H.L., *Common Law and Feudal Society in Medieval Scotland* (Edinburgh, 1993).

MacNamee, C., *The Wars of the Bruces* (East Linton, 1997).

McKenzie, W.M., *The Battle of Bannockburn* (Glasgow, 1913).

McKisack, M., *The Fourteenth Century* (Oxford, 1959).

McLeod, W., *Divided Gaels* (Oxford, 2004).

McNeill, P. and Nicholson, R., *An Atlas of Scottish History to 1707* (Edinburgh, 1996).

McWilliam, C., *The Buildings of Scotland: Lothian* (Harmondsworth, 1978).

Mapstone, S. & Wood. J. ed. *The Rose and the Thistle* (East Lothian 1998).

Mason, R. ed. *Scotland and England, 1286-1817* (Edinburgh, 1987).

Mason, R. & MacDougall, N. edd. *People and Power in Scotland* (Edinburgh, 1992).

Maxtone, A., *The Maxtones of Cultoqhuey* (Perth, 1936).

Mayhew, N and Gemmill, E. *The Changing Value of Money in Medieval Scotland.*(Cambridge, 1996).

Mertes, K., *The English Noble Household 1250-1600* (Oxford, 1988).

Miller, E., *War in the North. The Anglo-Scottish Wars of the Middle Ages* (Hull, 1960).

Miller, E. & Hatcher, J., *Medieval England – Rural Society and Economic Change, 1086-1348* (London, 1978).

Morgan, P., *War and Society in Medieval Cheshire 1277-1403* (Manchester, 1977).

Moor, C., *The Knights of Edward I* (London, 1930).

Morris, J., *The Welsh Wars of Edward I* (London, 1901).

Morris, J., *Bannockburn* (Cambridge, 1914).

Nicholson, R., *Scotland. The Later Middle Ages* (Edinburgh, 1974).

Nicholson, R. *Edward III and the Scots. The Formative Years of a Military career* (Oxford, 1965).

Oakeshott, R. *A Knight and His Horse* (London, 1995).

Oman, Sir Charles. *A History of England* (London, 1910).

Oman, Sir Charles *A History of the Art of War* (London, 1898).

Ormrod, W.M., *The Reign of Edward III. Crown and Political Society in England, 1327–77* (New Haven, 1990).

Parry, M.L. & Slater, T., *The Making of the Scottish Countryside* (London, 1980).

Penman, M., *David II* (East Linton, 2002).

Penman, M., *The Scottish Civil War* (Stroud, 2003).

Pillar, P., *Negotiating Peace: War Termination as a Bargaining Process* (New Jersey, 1983).

Phillips J.R.S., *Aymer de Valence* (Oxford, 1972).

Postan, M., *The Medieval Economy and Society* (Harmondsworth, 1972).

Powicke, F. M., *The Thirteenth Century* (Oxford, 1953).

Powicke, F.M., *Military Obligation in England* (Connecticut, 1975).
Prestwich, M., *Armies and Warfare in the Middle Ages* (New Haven, 1996).
Prestwich, M., *Edward I.* (London, 1988).
Prestwich, M., *The Place of war in English History* (Woodbridge, 2004).
Prestwich, M., *The Three Edwards; War and State in England, 1272-1377* (London, 1980).
Prestwich, M., *War, Politics and Finance Under Edward I* (London, 1972).
Rait, R., *The Parliaments of Scotland* (Glasgow, 1924).
Rayner, M., *English Battlefields* (Stroud, 2004).
RCAHMS Inventory of East Lothian (1926).
RCAHMS Inventory of the City of Edinburgh (1951).
RCAHMS, Midlothian and West Lothian (1929).
Reid, N. ed. *Scotland in the Reign of Alexander III* (Edinburgh, 1990).
Ridpath, P., *Border History of England and Scotland* (Berwick, 1848).
Ritchie, R., *The Normans in Scotland* (Edinburgh, 1954).
Rogers, C., *The Wars of Edward III* (Woodbridge, 1999).
Rogers, C., *War Cruel and Sharp* (Woodbridge, 2000).
Rollason, D. & Prestwich, M edd. *The Battle of Neville's Cross* (Stamford, 1998)..
Saul, N. ed. *Fourteenth Century England; I* (Woodbridge, 2000).
Sadler, J., *Scottish Battles* (Edinburgh, 1996).
Scott, J., *History of Berwick-upon Tweed* (London, 1888).
Simpson G., ed. *Scotland and the Low Countries.*(East Linton, 1996).
Simpson, G., *Scottish Handwriting 1150-1650* (Aberdeen, 1977).
Simpson, G., ed. *The Scottish Soldier Abroad* Edinburgh, 1992).
Simpson, W. Douglas, *The Province of Mar* (Aberdeen, 1943).
Smout, T. C., *A History of the Scottish People* (Glasgow, 1969).
Snell, F., *The Fourteenth Century* (Edinburgh, 1999).
Southern, R., *Western Society and the Church in the Middle Ages* (London, 1970).
Smurthwaite, D., *Battlefields of Britain* (London, 1984).
Stevenson, J. and Wood, M., *Scottish Heraldic Seals* (Glasgow, 1940).
Stenton, D., *English Society in the Early Middle Ages (1066-1307)* (Harmondsworth, 1965).
Strickland, M., *Armies, Chivalry and Warfare in Medieval Britain and France* (Stamford, 1998).
Stringer, K. ed. *Essays on the Scottish Nobility* (Edinburgh, 1985).
Sumption, J., *The Hundred Years War* (London, 1990).
Taylor, J. & Childs, W. ed. *Politics and Crisis in Fourteenth Century England* (Gloucester, 1990).
Tuck, A., *Crown and Nobility, 1272-1461; Political Conflict in Late Medieval England* (London, 1985).
Vale, M., *Edward III and Chivalry* (Woodbridge, 1983).
Vale, M., *War and Chivalry* (London, 1981)
Watson, F., *Under the Hammer* (East Linton, 1998).
Waugh, S., *England in the Reign of Edward III* (Cambridge 1991).
Whittington, G. and Whyte, I. edd. *A Historical geography of Scotland* (London, 1983).
Young, A., *Robert the Bruce's Rivals; The Comyns.* (East Linton, 1997).

UNPUBLISHED THESES AND PAPERS

The Kingship of David II. Michael Penman. St. Andrews University, (1998)
Burgesses and Landed Men in North-east Scotland in the Later Middle Ages. Harold Booton, Aberdeen University. (1987)
Military Service of Northumbrian Knights. A. King. Durham University Medieval Conference. (2001)

Technology and Military Technology in Medieval England. Randall Storey, University of Reading, (2003).

ARTICLES

Ash, M., 'The Diocese of Glasgow Under its 'Norman' Bishops' *SHR* lv (1976).

Barrow, G.W.S., 'Lothian in the First War of Independence.' *SHR* 55 (1976).

Barrow, G.W.S., 'The Aftermath of War.' *TRHS*, 28 (1978).

Bateson, J. and P. Stott, P. 'A Late Fourteenth Coin Hoard from Tranent.' *PSAS*, 120 (1990).

Beyerchen, A., 'Clausewitz, Nonlinearity and the Unpredictability of War' *International Security* 17.3 (1992).

Boardman, S., 'Chronicle Propaganda in Fourteenth Century Scotland.' *SHR* 76 (1977).

Brown, M., 'The Development of Scottish Border Lordship, 1332-58.' *Historical Research* lxxv, no.171. (February 1997).

Brown, M., 'War, Allegiance and Community in the Anglo-Scottish Marches; Teviotdale in the Fourteenth Century.' *Northern History* xli (2004)..

Campbell, C., 'Scottish Arms in the Bellenville Roll' *Scot. Geneal*, xxv.

Dixon, P., 'Excavations at Springwood Park, Kelso.' *PSAS* 115 (1985).

Donelly, J., 'Thomas of Coldingham.' SHR lix, (1980).

Donelly, J., 'In the Territory of Auchencrow: Long Continuity or Late Development in early Scottish Field Systems.' *PSAS* 130 (2000).

Duncan, A.A.M., 'The Community of the Realm of Scotland and Robert Bruce.' *SHR* xlv.

Duncan, A.A.M., 'The War of the Scots, 1306-23.' Prothero Lecture, *TRHS* (1992).

Evans, D., and Thain, S., 'New Light on Old Coin Hoards from the Aberdeen Area' *PSAS* 119 (1989).

Hall, D., and Bowler, D., 'North Berwick, East Lothian; its Archaeology Revisited.' *PSAS* 127 (1997).

Hanham, A., 'A medieval Scots Merchant's Handbook' *SHR* l, 1971.

Holmes, N., 'Excavations South of Bernard Street, Leith, 1980', *PSAS* 115 f. (1985).

McAndrew, B., 'The Sigillography of the Ragman Roll.' *PSAS* 129 (1999).

McGlynn, S., 'The Myths of Medieval Warfare'. *History Today* vol. 44 (1994).

O'Sullivan, J., 'Archaeological Excavations at Cockpen Medieval Parish Church, Midlothian, 1993' *PSAS* 125 (1995).

Penman, D., 'A Fell Coniuracioun again King Robert the Doughty King; the Soules Conspiacy of 1318-20' *Innes Review*, 50 (1999).

Penman, D., 'Christian Days and Knights: the Religious Devotions and Court of David II of Scotland, 1329-71' *BIHR* no. 75 (2002).

Pollock., D., 'The Lunan Valley Project: Medieval Rural Settlement in Angus.' *PSAS* 115 (1985).

Prestwich, M., 'English Armies in the Early Hundred Years War: A Scheme in 1341.', *BIHR* 56-57 (1983-4).

Sayles, G., 'The Guardians of Scotland and a Parliament at Rutherglen in 1300' *SHR* xxiv (1945).

Scott, W., 'The Use of Money in Scotland, 1124-1230.' *SHR* lviii (1979).

Simpson, G., 'Why was John Balliol Called 'Toom Tabard'?' *SHR* xlvii (1968).

Smith, I., 'Sprouston, Roxburghshire; an early Anglian Centre of the Eastern Tweed Basin' *PSAS*, 121 (1991).

Stell, G. 'By Land and Sea in Medieval and Early Modern Scotland.' *Review of Scottish Culture* No, 4 (1988).

Yeoman, P., 'Edinburgh Castle, Iron Age fort to Garrison Fortress.' *Fortress Magazine* 4 (1990).

ACKNOWLEDGMENTS

This book is based closely on my Ph.D. thesis 'We are command of Gentlemen' (St. Andrews, 2006)

I would like to express my gratitude to Professor Roger Mason and Dr. Norman Reid of St. Andrews, who, over a few months in 2005–6, rescued me from years of aimless and ineffective supervision and whose patience and 'raddure' cannot be too highly praised. Supervising me was an extra and unexpected addition to their workload, but one that they undertook with fortitude and patience. Thanks are also due to many other members of the university, including Dr. Hamish Scott, Mr. Alex Woolf, Dr. Colin Martin, Ms. Lorraine Fraser, Ms. Elizabeth Johnson, but most of all to Dr. Bill Knox, without whom, as they say, none of this would have been possible and, of course, Jonathan Reeve of Tempus Publishing.

Several institutions have helped along the way, including the National Archives of Scotland at East Register House, the National Archives at Kew, St. Andrews University Library and the Local Studies Collection at Loanhead Public Library. Historians do not exist in isolation, and there are many scholars whose work has informed my opinions, including Professors Geoffrey Barrow, Ranald Nicholson, A.A.M. Duncan, Gordon Donaldson, Michael Prestwich, Archer Jones and Maurice Keen, also Drs. Fiona Watson, Steven Boardman, Elizabeth Ewan, Alexander Grant, Colm MacNamee, Michael Penman, Andrew Barrell and the late Michael Handel.

On a more personal level I am grateful, as ever, to my wife, Pat, and my children and their partners; Robert, Charis, Alex, Christopher, Mariola, Colin and Juliet and to my parents Peter and Margaret Brown. The list of friends and acquaintances (some of them very fleeting) who have given me encouragement or inspiration at different times cannot be exhaustive, but includes Anne McGregor, Craig Sinclair, Sally Wallis, Jon Cooper, Graham Gabriel, Dr. Matthew Strickland, David and Rosemary Bishop-White, Derek Dick (Fish), Kelvin Boyes-Yates, Rob Maxton Graham, Rod MacKay, Steve Bishop, Gus Boyd, Dougie MacLean, John Ramsay, Craig McMurdo, the late Dr. W. Douglas Simpson, Patty Knox, Cad and Linda Delworth, Loura Brooks, John Treadgold, Ian Colquhoun, Major George Athey, the late Brigadier M.R.J. Hope-Thomson, George Willman, Sam and my grandchildren, Laird and Laila Hewitt.

LIST OF ILLUSTRATIONS

All illustrations are author's collection.

1   Stirling Bridge. A view from the battlefield from the top of the Wallace Monument. The leading elements of the English Army were trapped in a loop of the Forth and were forced onto the area now occupied by the Rugby club whose pitch can be seen in the middle distance of the photograph.

2   The Battle of Stirling Bridge. A view from Stirling Castle, across the battlefield toward the Wallace monument.

3   Torpichen Receptory. In the thirteenth century the headquarters of the knights of St. John in Scotland was at Torpichen in West Lothian. The knight of St. John, like the Templars, had long lost their military role and had become an international commercial concern. One of the few surviving instruments issued during Wallace's government, a grant to Alexander Scrymgeour, was made at Torpichen.

4   Incholm Abbey. Walter Bower wrote his *Scotichronicon* at the island abbey of Incholm on the River Forth in the mid-fifteenth century.

5   The Wallace Monument. Built at great expense, and plenty of controversy, in the nineteenth century, the Wallace Monument overlooks the field of William Wallace's greatest triumph, the Battle of Stirling Bridge.

6   Linlithgow Peel. Edward I commissioned the erection of a large 'Peel' of fortified camp at the Linthglow which incorporated the parish kirk. The peel was the base for a large mobile force of men-at-arms until it fell to the Scots *c.*1313. In addition to the peel at Linlithgow, Edward contruscted a small satellite peel at Livingstone, a larger peel and horse hospital at Selkirk and planned another peel at Dunfermline.

7   Blackness Castle. Blackness was an important depot for the English occupation between 1296 and its recovery by Robert I *c.*1313. Great quantities of grain, ale, wine and beef were delivered here for the supply of strongholds such as Edinburgh and Linlithgow.

8   Edinburgh Castle. Although Wallace was able to mount an operation into Lothian in 1297, he was unable to bring the sheriffdom under his control, due chiefly to the strength of the castles held by English garrisons.

9   Trebuchet. For many decades after the introduction of gunpowder, kinetic weapons – catapults, ballistae and trebuchets, continued to be a major element in siege warfare. Edward I obtained gunpowder for the siege of Stirling Castle in 1304, but as an explosive thrown at the target rather than as the propellant in a firearm.

10   The catapult exhibit at Caverlock Castle.

11   Men-at-arms in combat. Both of these men carry equipment typical of the later thirteenth century. By the time of Bannockburn most, if not all, of the men-at-arms on either side would have acquired plate armour for the arms and legs as well as the lighter bacinet helmet. The figure on the right bears the arms of Sir Aymer de Valence, Earl of Pembroke. Pembroke spent much of his considerable military career in Scotland.

12   Men-at-arms and infantrymen (photo by Lydia Diamond).

13a,b A jack may be worn over chainmail or underneath it.

14   The term spearman should not be taken too literally; since men were generally responsible for providing their own weapons there would inevitably be quite a variety of polearms in use. The experience of re-enactors would seem to suggest that spears and polearms were rather more robust than the slender and elegant weapon shafts of Victorian artworks.

15   Liveried archer. Livery was becoming increasingly common by the mid-fourteenth century.

16   King Robert's encounter with de Bohun by a Victorian artist.

17   Spearmen standing and kneeling to receive cavalry. This is very much the general conception of Scottish tactics during the Wars of Independence, however the Scots were, in the main, offensively-minded, and were inclined to attack rather than stand on the defensive.

18   English troops at Stirling Bridge and Falkirk were confronted by large bodies of spearmen. As long as the integrity of the formation was maintained, these schiltroms were virtually impossible to defeat, however they were extremely vulnerable to archery.

19   Chapel-de-fer, or 'Irn hat'. These were widely used throughout later medieval Europe, and appeared in a variety of styles.

20   Another style of Chapel-de-fer, or what the 1318 legislation of Robert I referred to as a 'good iron', was probably the most expensive article that the rank and file needed to invest in if they were to fulfil their military obligations.

21   Cambuskenneth Abbey. Only one tower remains of what was, in the thirteenth century, an extensive suite of buildings. Close to Stirling Castle, Cambuskenneth would have been a likely venue for the deliberations after the battle of Stirling Bridge in 1297.

22   The first recorded instance of glass windows in a secular building in Scotland is of their purchase for King Robert's manor house at Cardross. This modern reconstruction at Blackness Castle, Midlothian, is probably quite similar in design and construction to those purchased for Cardross.

23   Looking towards Culblean Hill, just to the left behind the tree line.

24   View north from Halidon Hill. The English position was virtually impregnable.

INDEX

TEMPUS – REVEALING HISTORY

William II Rufus, the Red King
EMMA MASON

'A thoroughly new reappraisal of a much maligned king. The dramatic story of his life is told with great pace and insight'
John Gillingham

£25

0 7524 3528 0

William Wallace The True Story of Braveheart
CHRIS BROWN

'A formidable new biography... sieves through masses of medieval records to distinguish the man from the myth' *Magnus Magnusson*

£17.99

0 7524 3432 2

Elizabeth Wydeville: The Slandered Queen
ARLENE OKERLUND

'A penetrating, thorough and wholly convincing vindication of this unlucky queen'
Sarah Gristwood

'A gripping tale of lust, loss and tragedy'
Alison Weir

A *BBC History Magazine* Book of the Year 2005

£9.99   978 07524 3807 8

The Battle of Hastings 1066
M.K. LAWSON

'Blows away many fundamental assumptions about the battle of Hastings... an exciting and indispensable read' *David Bates*

A *BBC History Magazine* Book of the Year 2003

£12.99   978 07524 4177 1

 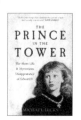

The Welsh Wars of Independence
DAVID MOORE

'Beautifully written, subtle and remarkably perceptive' *John Davies*

£12.99

978 07524 4128 3

Medieval England
From Hastings to Bosworth
EDMUND KING

'The best illustrated history of medieval England' *John Gillingham*

£12.99

0 7524 2827 5

A Companion to Medieval England
NIGEL SAUL

'Wonderful... everything you could wish to know about life in medieval England'
Heritage Today

£19.99

0 7524 2969 8

The Prince In The Tower
MICHAEL HICKS

'The first time in ages that a publisher has sent me a book I actually want to read' *David Starkey*

£9.99

978 07524 4386 7

If you are interested in purchasing other books published by Tempus, or in case you have difficulty finding any Tempus books in your local bookshop, you can also place orders directly through our website:
www.tempus-publishing.com

TEMPUS – REVEALING HISTORY

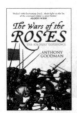   

The Wars of the Roses
The Soldiers' Experience
ANTHONY GOODMAN
'A fascinating book' *TLS*
£12.99
0 7524 3731 3

William the Conqueror
DAVID BATES
'As expertly woven as the Bayeux Tapestry'
BBC History Magazine
£12.99
0 7524 2960 4

The Vikings
MAGNUS MAGNUSSON
'Serious, engaging history'
BBC History Magazine
£9.99
0 7524 2699 0

Agincourt: A New History
ANNE CURRY
'A tour de force' *Alison Weir*
'*The* book on the battle' *Richard Holmes*
  BBC History Magazine BOOK OF THE YEAR 2005
£12.99
0 7524 2828 4

Hereward The Last Englishman
PETER REX
'An enthralling work of historical detection'
Robert Lacey
£17.99
0 7524 3318 0

Richard III
MICHAEL HICKS
'A most important book by the greatest living expert on Richard' *Desmond Seward*
£9.99
0 7524 2589 7

The English Resistance
The Underground War Against the Normans
PETER REX
'An invaluable rehabilitation of an ignored resistance movement' *The Sunday Times*
£12.99
0 7524 3733 X

The Peasants' Revolt
England's Failed Revolution of 1381
ALASTAIR DUNN
'A stunningly good book... totally absorbing'
Melvyn Bragg
£9.99
0 7524 2965 5

If you are interested in purchasing other books published by Tempus, or in case you have difficulty finding any Tempus books in your local bookshop, you can also place orders directly through our website:
www.tempus-publishing.com

TEMPUS REVEALING HISTORY

William Wallace
The True Story of Braveheart
CHRIS BROWN
'The truth about Braveheart'
The Scottish Daily Mail
£17.99
0 7524 3432 2

An Abundance of Witches
The Great Scottish Witch-Hunt
P.G. MAXWELL-STUART
'An amazing account of Scots women in league with the Devil' **The Sunday Post**
£17.99
0 7524 3329 6

The Roman Conquest of Scotland
The Battle of Mons Graupius AD 84
JAMES E. FRASER
'Challenges a long held view'
The Scottish Sunday Express
£17.99
0 7524 3325 3

Scottish Voices from the Great War
DEREK YOUNG
'A treasure trove of personal letters and diaries from the archives' **Trevor Royle**
£17.99
0 7524 3326 1

Culloden
The Last Charge of the Highland Clans
JOHN SADLER
'Drawing extensively on first-hand accounts, paints a vivid picture of the campaign and battle' **Scotland in Trust: The Magazine of the National Trust for Scotland**
£25
0 7524 3955 3

The Scottish Civil War
The Bruces & the Balliols & the War for the Control of Scotland
MICHAEL PENMAN
'A highly informative and engaging account' **Historic Scotland**
£16.99
0 7524 2319 3

The Pictish Conquest
The Battle of Dunnichen 685 & the Birth of Scotland
'A well-researched account... a must'
The Scots Magazine
'Informatively illustrated and well-written'
War in History
JAMES E. FRASER
£12.99

Scottish Voices from the Second World War
DEREK YOUNG
'Poignant memories of a lost generation... heart-rending' **The Sunday Post**
£17.99
0 7524 3710 0

If you are interested in purchasing other books published by Tempus, or in case you have difficulty finding any Tempus books in your local bookshop, you can also place orders directly through our website
www.tempus-publishing.com

TEMPUS REVEALING HISTORY

Scotland
From Prehistory to the Present
FIONA WATSON
The Scotsman Bestseller
£9.99
0 7524 2591 9

1314 Bannockburn
ARYEH NUSBACHER
'Written with good-humoured verve as
befits a rattling "yarn of sex, violence and
terror"'
History Scotland
£9.99
0 7524 2982 5

Flodden
NIALL BARR
'Tells the story brilliantly'
The Sunday Post
£9.99
0 7524 2593 5

Scotland's Black Death
The Foul Death of the English
KAREN JILLINGS
'So incongruously enjoyable a read, and so
attractively presented by the publishers'
The Scotsman
£12.99
978 07524 3732 3

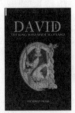   

David I The King Who Made Scotland
RICHARD ORAM
'Enthralling... sets just the right tone as the
launch-volume of an important new series
of royal biographies' **Magnus Magnusson**
£17.99
0 7524 2825 X

The Kings & Queens of Scotland
RICHARD ORAM
'A serious, readable work that sweeps across
a vast historical landscape' **The Daily Mail**
£12.99
0 7524 3814 X

The Second Scottish Wars of Independence 1332–1363
CHRIS BROWN
'Explodes the myth of the invincible Bruces...
lucid and highly readable' **History Scotland**
£12.99
0 7524 3812 3

Robert the Bruce: A Life Chronicled
CHRIS BROWN
'A masterpiece of research'
The Scots Magazine
£30
0 7524 2575 7

If you are interested in purchasing other books published by Tempus, or in case you have difficulty finding any Tempus
books in your local bookshop, you can also place orders directly through our website
www.tempus-publishing.com